I0198811

The First 100 days

(From January 10 to April 19 or 20)

The Evil and Archaic Practice of Human Sacrifices by the Freemasonic Branch of the U.S. Government

And the 2013 Journal of the Great Tribulation: Barak Obama's Global War Against the Saints of the Living God

By

Harry Francois

Published by Topaz Enterprises and Publishing LLC

304 Main Ave # 369

Norwalk, CT 06851

International Standard Book Number: 9780984644698

The writing of this book was completed in December 2013 as volume 5 of the Great Tribulation

Dedication

I dedicate this book to my Mother CELIMENE VALCOURT and to ESTHER, the Haitian born Queen of Persia who, together with her uncle Mordecai, saved the Haitian, the black and the white American Hebrews during the Persian Empire in the **12th year of King Xerxes** from a Jewish conspiracy to shed the blood of the Hebrews for the atonement of the sins of the Jewish people.

Thanks and Acknowledgments

Special acknowledgments to my brother Jude Francois and to my Hebrew friends from Hebron:

Robinson aka Ben, Christophe, Rico, Boubou, Colbert, Brunel, Ti Fritz, Marie-Francoise, Mario and Mariose; to Jehu Pierre, Frantz Lafontant, Ti konbran and to my Hebrew relatives and friends from Miami, formerly Mian Mian of Mexico, the biblical Egypt: Marie Sony François, Fritz Francois and Emmanuel François; to Wilner and Marie Carmel Fleurant, Eustache Fleurant, Yves Gérard, Amos, Mireille "Michou" Pierre; and to my friends from Fontamara and Cite Martissant; Jaques Muller, KIKI, Patrick, Jacques, aka Jacko, and Renald, aka Ti Nano Caprice; Leslie and Fanfan Laguerre, Ti Rene, Harry Turene, Nana, Gerald and Ti Monche Pinchinat ; Ti Gaston, Poupette, Cocotte, Nason ; Blanc, Titi, and Mario Fleurima.

Table of Contents

Table of Contents

Chapter 1

The Great Tribulation

Barak Hussein Obama made a PPACT with Satan through the passing of the Health Care law to provoke civil wars in Haiti and in the United States in order to shed the blood of the innocent Hebrews, the children of Jacob for the atonement of the Jews, the Catholics, the Freemasons and everyone who follows the ways of Satan, in order to satisfy the blood liability of this Sabbath. This is precisely why Bill Clinton took a plane to Haiti the very day after Obama signed the Health Care Law in the twilight of March 23, 2010. The American media refer to the law as ACA, but that is not the full acronym. The acronym is found in the full name of the legislation as follows:

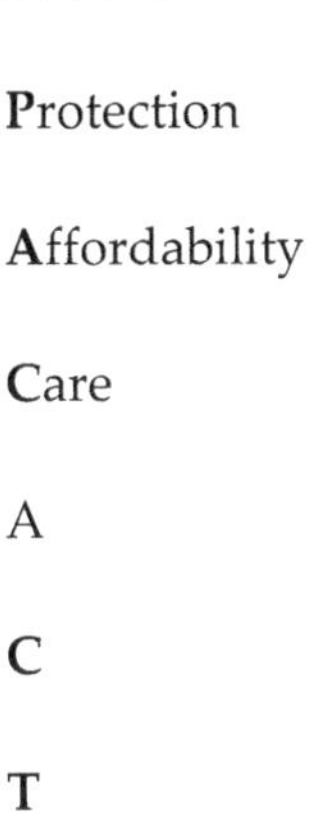

Patients

Protection

Affordability

Care

A

C

T

The 'A' in ACT is silent; hence the word PPACCT is produced as an acronym. However, those who would tend to defend Obama by arguing that the "A" is not meant to be silent and that the word PPACCT is just an accident, he or she needs to consider the following acronyms found in other Obama's legislations titles:

American

Reinvestment

And

Recovery

A

C

T

In this title, two hidden acronyms are found; ARARAT, which is produced with a silent "C" in ACT and Mene, which is produced with the set of the second letters from the first four words. And finally, among others, the acronym TAJAT is produced in the title of the Jobs Act legislation as follows:

The

American

Jobs

A

C

T

Again this acronym is produced by a silent "C" in ACT. It is therefore evident that a number of well defined words with biblical and religious significance have been found hidden in the titles of many of Obama's legislations by keeping at least one letter from the word ACT silent. This science cannot be ignored, especially when Obama has acted consistently according to the sinister acronyms. For example, the word ARARAT which is found as a hidden acronym in the title of Obama's stimulus package, first surfaced in the Bible as the name of the mountain on which Noah's Ark came to rest after the Great Deluge which started on February 17. Yet, Obama signed the stimulus package exactly on February 17, 2009; one could have entertained the fact that the acronym ARARAT was produced by accident, but when coupled with the fact that Obama signed the stimulus package on the same day the deluge started it becomes clear that this cannot be a coincidence. I will discuss these acronyms in greater details in a later chapter.

Barak Obama is the antichrist. He came to kill, to steal and destroy, but he is being severely opposed by the living God and his son Jesus. Barak Obama will not be able to achieve the mission of Satan, which is to shed the blood of the innocents in this Sabbath, there is not going to be a civil war in Haiti or in the United States, period.

Washington is managed by a secret religious sect known as the illuminati. The members of this religious organization include the few overlords who own the American media, as well as other people in the news organizations, not excluding the reporters, the Radio Talk show hosts. It also includes business leaders from every sector; from the banking sector to the retail and the technology sectors; it also includes leaders of major Universities, especially those with secret memberships in underground organizations like the 'Skull and Bones' at Yale University. They are the offsprings of Satan even though they belong to different religious or secular dominations. Many of them are freemasons, Jews, Catholics, Mormons, Moslem and Christians like Pat Robertson whose Christ is Solomon, the original antichrist, as suggested by his Radio Show called the "700 Club", so named to worship the 700 wives of King Solomon, the mulatto Haitian. In addition, Pat Robertson further gave himself away when he adopted the logo found in the design of the Solomon throne, which featured six lions on either side of six steps leading to the throne of Solomon, the same design found in the Lincoln Memorial. Pat Robertson adopted a design with two lions on either shoulder of a king's crown for the 700 Club TV show.

These leaders have conspired to put Barak Obama, the mulatto son of Satan, the antichrist in office by lying about everything in his background. And they have continued to lie to cover up his crimes against humanity, against the Haitian people and against the American people, especially the black and the white Hebrew children of Jacob.

The American media have conspired to remain silent in order to cover up the crimes Barak Obama is committing all over the world. The media have conspired not to report the news from the war in Afghanistan, from drone operations in Yemen, from many other military operations in different parts of Africa where the opposition to Obama is very strong and from places like Egypt, Syria, and Libya among others. Television news organizations like CNN have converted their news crew into talk shows where paid liars are invited to express their opinions about subject matters that have nothing to do with actual news of what is really going on in the world. Fox and MSNBC have done the same; they have all corrupted the concept of news by hiring people to express their own personal opinions while ignoring the real news. The same is found with major newspaper organizations like the New York Times where the line between the news section and the Op-ed section has merged. The New York Times and other news organizations lie by producing phony Poll numbers to mislead people about Obama's approval ratings, they lie to shape public opinions and to promote the candidacy of Hilary Clinton as the 2016 Democratic candidate for president and to promote Christ Christy of New Jersey as the 2016 Republican candidate for president, so Hilary Clinton could have an easy path to the White House. They have kept quiet about the plight of the American homeless, the jobless; they have ignored the high price of gas at the pump, they have kept quiet about the incredibly high unemployment rate among all Americans and they have been careful not to show the long lines of desperate Americans looking for jobs. They have ignored one of the greatest ecological disasters in the history of the world, a disaster that was engineered by Barak Obama and Hilary Clinton in the Gulf of Mexico to promote the first 100-day Jewish voodoo ceremony in which they have allowed the oil to leak from the Gulf of Mexico for precisely 86 days, from April 20, 2010 through July 15, 2010. The American media and the leaders of the American nation, from business to academia have also turned away from reporting the crimes Obama and Hilary Clinton and Bill Clinton have been committing all over the world; from Afghanistan, the biblical Armageddon, a war Obama was selected to fight for the offsprings of Satan, but in reality, Obama is losing decisively in Afghanistan. In his desperation, Obama has decided to use drones to murder women and children indiscriminately in order to inflict mental and psychological anguish on the Taliban so they would stop fighting and resisting, but the Taliban have remained strong and firmly resolved in their desire to repel the NATO invasion and to regain control of their country.

The living God, our Father in Heaven, and Jesus, his Son and his only Christ have activated a great spirit of resistance against Obama everywhere in the world to fulfill what is written in the scriptures about the second coming of Jesus; "There will be wars and rumors of wars, nations will rise against nations and kingdoms will rise against kingdoms and there will be earthquakes and famines in different places." It is clear that these events are being fulfilled to undermine and to destroy the kingdom of Satan. On January 12, 2010, a huge earthquake hit Haiti and killed the entire army of Satan in Haiti where all the UN soldiers died, including the leadership, but in his desperation, Barak Obama responded by reinvading Haiti and by adopting, together with Bill and Hilary Clinton, a policy of poisoning the Haitian waters with Agent Orange to kill the Haitians with a disease they are calling cholera in the hope to take over their land, but they are hoping in vain.

When a group of criminals and lawless band of paid assassins rose against Qaddafi in Libya in early 2011, Obama and Hilary Clinton asked Qaddafi to resign, but in fulfillment of scriptures, Qaddafi rebelled against Washington by refusing to resign and he proceeded to crush the opposition, but in his desperation to remain in control of the kingdom of the earth, Obama invaded Libya on March 19, 2011to subdue the spirit of resistance against him. However, Qaddafi and his black fighters surprised NATO by resisting the NATO powers until late October 2011, long enough to keep Bill Clinton from provoking a Civil War in Haiti through the Conille's nomination for Prime Minister of Haiti. When Hilary Clinton realized that she and her criminal husband, Satan himself had missed the window to shed the blood of the Haitians, she became enraged and she flew to Libya to give the order to kill Qaddafi like a dog in the street, even after she had made an agreement with Vladimir Putin of Russia to allow Qaddafi to go into exile.

The spirit of resistance against Satan has been activated everywhere and Barak Obama has invaded virtually every African nation either directly or indirectly through the United Nations with the conspiring silence of the media. There is war everywhere, yet the American people is largely unaware of the sufferings, the atrocities and all the crimes Barak Obama and his NATO and UN allies are committing in Sudan where war is fiercely waging, in Mali, in Central Africa, notably in Uganda where fierce fightings are going on at this very moment. Obama has sent American troops throughout all the African jungles looking for the children of God who descended from Shem so he could murder them for the benefit of the Jews so that the world could remain a world of half free and half slaves and so that one group can continue to exist at the expense of another like Cain had come to exist at the expense of Abel after he had murdered him. There are wars in the Ivory Coast, in Nigeria, in Somalia, in Rwanda, in Ethiopia, in Congo, in Sudan, in Libya, in Iraq, in Afghanistan, in Yemen, in Syria, in Egypt, yet the American media have attempted to shield Obama from responsibilities for provoking and for his current engagement in these conflicts.

The spirit of resistance is strong in Pakistan and there is war in Pakistan where the CIA forces are fighting against the people of Pakistan; the spirit of resistance is strong in Yemen where Obama and the CIA have been supporting a corrupt government in order to further the oppression of the Yemeni people. The spirit of resistance is strong in Egypt where Obama has been working against the people of Egypt to reverse the revolution that brought Mubarak out of office. The spirit of resistance is strong in Syria where Bashar Al Assad refuses to resign and where Hilary Clinton has personally organized a proxy force by first setting up a Trust Fund for the family of those who would defect from the Syrian army or the Syrian government and for everyone else willing to fight against Al Assad.

Hilary Clinton is personally responsible, jointly with Barak Obama, for all the bloodshed in Syria. She has urged her Middle East allies like Saudi Arabia to send troops to Syria and she has paid criminals to recruit young Moslem throughout Europe, especially in Belgium to go to Syria and to fight against Bashar Al Assad on behalf of the United States. And yet with all these conflicts, the worst is yet to come as Hilary Clinton has put the United States on a collision course with Russia through her emotional policies in

Libya. This political blunder, the unlawful killing of Qaddafi has strained the U.S. relation with Russia vis-à-vis Syria. However, in her frustration, Hilary continues an ill advised policy in Syria where she has once again alienated Russia and advocated that Russia must pay a price for not allowing NATO to invade Syria as they have done in Libya. Hilary has also made it a virtual certainty for Israel to attack Iran over its nuclear program, which will trigger a direct confrontation between the U.S. and Russia. Yet, the Jews in the American media want her to become president in 2017 so she could continue to murder innocent people to further the world of half free and half slaves, but the vision of the criminals will not come to pass.

The Great Tribulation as prophesized by the Bible is here; the antichrist is here in the person of Barak Obama, the false prophet, the homosexual college drop-out, the liar, the deceiver, the murderer; Lucifer is here in the person of Hilary Clinton, the link between the false prophet and Satan personified in Bill Clinton, her husband.

Hilary Clinton is the worse woman murderer in the history of humanity; she has teamed up with Satan, her husband Bill Clinton, to engineer the bombing of the North Tower of the former World Trade Center in 1993, soon after she and her husband took office that year. She quickly followed up with the siege that led to the Waco fire that devoured 86 people on April 19, 1993, including women and children and the unborn, but she was just getting started in her murderous rampage. Hilary Clinton murdered 168 people, including women and children and the unborn in the Oklahoma City Bombing on April 19, 1995. Hilary Clinton engineered the slaughter of 13 young people in her evil practice of 100-day human sacrifices at Columbine High School in Littleton, Colorado on April 20, 1999. Hilary Clinton murdered John Kennedy Jr. on July 16, 1999 to offer him as a human sacrifice during the Feast of Tabernacles so she could find mystical power to become a Senator from New York. Hilary Clinton murdered Vince Foster to cover her tract in the scandal involving the Rose law firm where she was involved in potential criminal activities. Hilary Clinton advised Bill Clinton to invade Haiti in 1994 under the guise of returning Jean Bertrand Haiti to office and she proceeded to murder hundreds of thousands of Haitians. That same year, Hilary Clinton engineered a Civil War in Rwanda where millions died. 1994, the year the black Satan named Nelson Mandela took office in South Africa has been the worst year ever for blacks everywhere. Hilary and Bill Clinton have doubled the rate of incarceration of Americans, especially the blacks from 1993 when the American prison population was only about 1.3 million to well over two million by 2000 when they left office. Hilary Clinton has the blood of millions of innocent people in her hands.

After Hilary Clinton had teamed up with Satan to commit all the crimes that I have underlined above, and then in 2009 she has teamed up with the mulatto antichrist named Barak Obama as his Secretary of State to commit even worst crimes against Americans and against humanity at large, including the engineering of the April 20, 2010 86-day oil leak in the Gulf of Mexico; the reinvasion of Haiti after the January 12, 2010 earthquake killed all the UN soldiers in Haiti; the 2011 invasion of Libya where she murdered hundreds of thousands; she engineered a proxy war in Syria and she has invaded countless African nations like Sudan, Uganda, Congo, Ivory Coast, Mali and many more. Hilary Clinton is the worst murderer along with Bill Clinton and Barak Obama since Hitler provoked the Second World War. In fact, Hilary Clinton is the second coming of Hitler. The names Hilary and Hitler are the same. Hilary is the female version of Hitler; the very same spirit that indwelled Hitler is now in Hilary Clinton just as the spirit of Abraham Lincoln now lives in Bill Clinton. However, Hilary is even worse than Hitler because she has already provoked World War Three; her actions in Syria and Libya will ultimately lead to a direct military conflict between the U.S. and Russia as the U.S. will be forced to intervene in Syria in 2014, Obama and Bill and Hilary Clinton have no choice but to intervene in Syria pursuant to their practices of human sacrifices.

This spirit of resistance has moved the people of the world to engage in political protests against their own governments. These protests are found in Asia, like the protests that have been going on in Thailand to demand changes and the resignation of the Prime Minister. These protests are found in Turkey, in Bangladesh, in Bulgaria, in Slovenia, in Italy, in Spain, in Greece, everywhere in the world. And at the same time, many people have been killed and displaced through earthquakes, tornadoes, tsunamis from the U.S. to the Philippines and everywhere else in the world to fulfill the biblical prophecies. There has never been a time such as these times in the world, even during World War Two the world was not as disturbed as it is today; yet, the worst is yet to come.

The Great Tribulation is here and Barak Obama along with Bill and Hilary Clinton are responsible for the judgment that the living God is about to impose on the world through severe earthquakes, tsunamis, tornadoes, hurricanes, fire from heaven and more. However, the elite and the people in the media have conspired to keep the American people in the dark by giving them a false sense of prosperity. Obama has been printing money to drive up the stock market and to enrich the investor class through their (401K) and other personal investments to deceive them into thinking that everything is well and life is good, while the judgment is fast approaching. The images on American television do not reflect the ugly reality of the brutal conditions that exist throughout the entire world; American, NATO and UN soldiers are dying everywhere, but the news is not been reported to the American people who want to believe that everything is fine when they know in their hearts that the world is not well.

Chapter 2

The Biblical Origin of the Evil Practice of Human Sacrifices in the First 100 days of the Year

In order to fully explain the mysteries behind some of the disturbing news of violence that are being perpetuated by Barak Obama, including the Boston bombing, I find it particularly important to crystallize the biblical guidelines that established the practices of human sacrifices that are committed in the first 100 days of the year by the freemasons from the U.S. Government in Washington D.C. The evil and archaic practice of human sacrifices originated from the de facto Passover covenant the Living God made with the mulatto Cain by putting a "Mark" on his forehead with the blood of Abel whom he had killed. By killing Abel, Cain made a de facto human offering to Satan by shedding the blood of Abel. However, since the living God is the only one who can forgive sins, Satan inspired Cain to make an appeal for his life to the living God and God responded by making a 'Mark' on Cain's forehead—that mark was made with the blood of Abel and through the blood of his own victim, Cain found temporary forgiveness and legitimacy to assume the wealth and the place of Abel on earth; as it is written, **"without the shedding of blood, there is no forgiveness of sins".** If the practice of human sacrifices originated from the murder of Abel by Cain, the practice of the 100-day human sacrifices originated from the war of the living God again Satan in Egypt when God liberated his people in the Great Exodus. This presentation is a course in mysticism; it exposes the secrets of Satan and the practices of human sacrifices in Washington D.C. and all over the United States of America. The pastors have lied; they have conspired with the U.S. government to bury the truth, as written in the bible, to keep the people of the living God in darkness. The first five books of the Bible came to be written in a period when Satan was still in heaven in a coalition government with the Living God, and Moses received guidelines from the Living God and from Satan as well. Moses was not a faithful servant of the living God; he argued with God when God first approached him, making it possible for his brother Aaron (the chosen of Satan) to become involved in leading Israel out of Egypt. The festival calendar of the children of the living God is based on historical facts, while the festival calendar of the offsprings of Satan is based on the position of the moon, so their dates change according to the astrological position of the moon, but they remain very close to the dates the children of God use to celebrate and to worship God. Satan's goal is to become like God and to even surpass God if it were possible, to this end, whenever God speaks, Satan uses that date to make his own declaration in imitation of God. So in this context, the notion of the first 100 days begins when God approached Moses in Mexico, the biblical Egypt and instructed him to choose a lamb on the 10th of January for each Hebrew family. So since God spoke on January 10, that date automatically becomes a power date and Satan would seek to use it for his own evil purpose and vision.

God instructed Moses to select the lamb on January 10, the lamb was to be kept for four (4) days until the night of January 14 when it will be killed for the Passover meal and the blood of the lamb will be put over the doorframe of every family to protect them from the destroyer of the first born who was to come and destroy all the first born of Egypt that very night. These instructions are recorded in the biblical book of Exodus;

"The Lord said to Moses and Aaron in Egypt, 'this month is to be for you the first month, the first month of the year. Tell the whole community of Israel that on the tenth of this month, each man is to take a lamb for his family, one for every household......take care of them until the fourteenth day of the month, when all the members of the community of Israel must slaughter them at twilight. Then they are to take some of the blood and put it on the sides and tops of the doorframes of the houses where they eat the lambs. That same night they are to eat the meat roasted over the fire, along with bitter herbs, and bread without yeast."

(Exodus 12: 1-8NIV)

100 days from January 10 when the lamb is chosen leads exactly to April 20, and April 19 on leap years. So from the time God gave the first instructions to Moses about the selection of the lamb on January 10 to deliver the Hebrew Israelis out of bondage from Mexico, Satan was already planning to destroy them and to stall their deliverance. And the rebellion started 30 days after they left Mexico when they started to complain to Moses about not having water to drink and about how they should have stayed in Mexico where there was plenty of food for them to eat—even though they were in slavery. And about 90 to 100 days after they left Mexico when the Hebrew community reached the Black Hills of South Dakota, the biblical Mount Sinai, they staged a final rebellion against Moses when Aaron led the people in sins against the living God by building a Golden Cow and urged the people to worship it as the god of Israel while Moses was on top of the mountain securing the Ten Commandments for them. The genesis of the Carnival celebration came from that rebellion. Moses became angry when he realized what Aaron and the people had done so he threw the two tablets upon which the Ten Commandments were written at them in disgust, but he returned to the mountain to secure a new set of tablets with the law written on them. Moses' anger was provoked by Satan and Moses should have never destroyed the first two tablets. This has become a satanic doctrine; to confuse God's plan by provoking his servants to anger and thereby introducing his own nefarious policy onto the world.

"The Appointed Festivals

The LORD said to Moses, "Speak to the Israelites and say to them: 'These are my appointed festivals, the appointed festivals of the LORD, which you are to proclaim as sacred assemblies.

The Sabbath

"'There are six days when you may work, but the seventh day is a day of Sabbath rest, a day of sacred assembly. You are not to do any work; wherever you live, it is a Sabbath to the LORD.

The Passover and the Festival of Unleavened Bread

"'These are the LORD's appointed festivals; the sacred assemblies you are to proclaim at their appointed times: The LORD's Passover begins at twilight on the fourteenth day of the first month. On the fifteenth day of that month the LORD's Festival of Unleavened Bread begins; for seven days you must eat bread made without yeast. On the first day hold a sacred assembly and do no regular work. For seven days present a food offering to the LORD. And on the seventh day hold a sacred assembly and do no regular work.'"

Offering the First fruits

The LORD said to Moses, "Speak to the Israelites and say to them: 'When you enter the land I am going to give you and you reap its harvest, bring to the priest a sheaf of the first grain you harvest. He is to wave the sheaf before the LORD so it will be accepted on your behalf; the priest is to wave it on the day after the Sabbath. On the day you wave the sheaf, you must sacrifice as a burnt offering to the LORD a lamb a year old without defect, together with its grain offering of two-tenths of an ephah of the finest flour mixed with olive oil—a food offering presented to the LORD, a pleasing aroma—and its drink offering of a quarter of a hin of wine. You must not eat any bread, or roasted or new grain, until the very day you bring this offering to your God. This is to be a lasting ordinance for the generations to come, wherever you live.

The Festival of Weeks

"'From the day after the Sabbath, the day you brought the sheaf of the wave offering, count off seven full weeks. Count off fifty days up to the day after the seventh Sabbath, and then present an offering of new grain to the LORD. From wherever you live, bring two loaves made of two-tenths of an ephah of the finest flour, baked with yeast, as a wave offering of firstfruits to the LORD. Present with this bread seven male lambs, each a year old and without defect, one young bull and two rams. They will be a burnt offering to the LORD, together with their grain offerings and drink offerings—a food offering, an aroma pleasing to the LORD. Then sacrifice one male goat for a sin offering and two lambs, each a year old, for a fellowship offering. The priest is to wave the two lambs before the LORD as a wave offering, together with the bread of the firstfruits. They are a sacred offering to the LORD for the priest. On that same day you are to proclaim a sacred assembly and do no regular work. This is to be a lasting ordinance for the generations to come, wherever you live.

"'When you reap the harvest of your land, do not reap to the very edges of your field or gather the gleanings of your harvest. Leave them for the poor and for the foreigner residing among you. I am the LORD your God.'"

The Festival of Trumpets

The LORD said to Moses, "Say to the Israelites: 'On the first day of the seventh month you are to have a day of Sabbath rest, a sacred assembly commemorated with trumpet blasts. Do no regular work, but present a food offering to the LORD.'"

The Day of Atonement

The LORD said to Moses, "The tenth day of this seventh month is the Day of Atonement. Hold a sacred assembly and deny yourselves, and present a food offering to the LORD. Do not do any work on that day, because it is the Day of Atonement, when atonement is made for you before the LORD your God. Those who do not deny themselves on that day must be cut off from their people. I will destroy from among their people anyone who does any work on that day. You shall do no work at all. This is to be a lasting ordinance for the generations to come, wherever you live. It is a day of Sabbath rest for you, and you must deny yourselves. From the evening of the ninth day of the month until the following evening you are to observe your Sabbath."

The Festival of Tabernacles

The LORD said to Moses, "Say to the Israelites: 'On the fifteenth day of the seventh month the LORD's Festival of Tabernacles begins, and it lasts for seven days. The first day is a sacred assembly; do no regular work. For seven days' present food offerings to the LORD and on the eighth day hold a sacred assembly and present a food offering to the LORD. It is the closing special assembly; do no regular work.

("'These are the LORD's appointed festivals, which you are to proclaim as sacred assemblies for bringing food offerings to the LORD—the burnt offerings and grain offerings, sacrifices and drink offerings required for each day. These offerings are in addition to those for the LORD's Sabbaths and in addition to your gifts and whatever you have vowed and all the freewill offerings you give to the LORD.)

"'So beginning with the fifteenth day of the seventh month, after you have gathered the crops of the land, celebrate the festival to the LORD for seven days; the first day is a day of Sabbath rest, and the eighth day also is a day of Sabbath rest. On the first day you are to take branches from luxuriant trees—from palms, willows and other leafy trees—and rejoice before the LORD your God for seven days. Celebrate this as a festival to the LORD for seven days each year. This is to be a lasting ordinance for the generations to come; celebrate it in the seventh month. Live in temporary shelters for seven days: All native-born Israelites are to live in such shelters so your descendants will know that I had the Israelites live in temporary shelters when I brought them out of Egypt. I am the LORD your God.'"

So Moses announced to the Israelites the appointed festivals of the LORD."

(Leviticus 23:1-44 NIV)

These represent the entire official holiday calendar for the people of Israel for the entire year. Thus, Washington, in its satanic imitation of the Israeli calendar, divides the year in two sets of 196 days by adding 27 extra days, leading to January 27 of the following year.

Moses received instructions from the living God about the Sabbath, a day of rest, a day of sacred assembly.

As it may be observed, the first holiday of the year is the Passover; this Passover is the covenant of animal sacrifice that was instituted by Moses when the living God freed the Hebrews from slavery in Egypt, the modern nation of Mexico. On the night of the Passover, Moses was told to direct every Hebrew household to kill a lamb for dinner and to eat it with bitter herb and to put the blood of the lamb on their doorpost, this way, when the spirit of destroyer came at midnight, it would see the blood and it would Pass over the house; thus, sparing the occupants from death—so the Hebrews were saved because of the blood of the animal. This holiday begins at the twilight of January 14 through January 15, the day the Haitians, the Jamaicans, the Trinidadians, the Puerto Ricans, the Cubans, the southern black and white American Hebrews left Mexico, the real biblical Egypt to enter the desert of Arizona on their way to the Promised Land: The Southern Confederate states (except Florida) and the Caribbean. The American satanic theocracy celebrates this holiday by pretending to celebrate the birthday of Martin Luther king Jr., but that is a blatant lie. Martin Luther King Jr. is a Hebrew, not a Jew like Barak Obama. The Jews would never really honor a Hebrew, just as the Catholic Church pretends to honor the black Jesus, while referring to their Jesus as a Jew in their Judeo-Christian tradition.

The Passover holiday is a commemorative holiday referred to as the holiday of unleavened bread or bread without yeast to commemorate Moses' last supper in Mexico, this holiday lasts a week from the twilight of January 14, January 15 until January 21. Please notice that the date of birth is spiritually significant: Martin Luther King Jr. was born on January 15, the day the Hebrews left Mexico, the day the exodus began, but I was born on July 17, the day the Arch of Noah came rested on Mount Ararat, I was born to give the Haitians, the Jamaicans, the Cubans, the Puerto Ricans, the Trinidadians, the black and the white Hebrews from the Confederate States of America and everyone who believes in the truth rest in the power of Jesus Christ from the homosexual offprings of Satan.

The next holiday is the holiday of firstfruits, which call for the Hebrews to give their firstfruits to the Lord when they enter the Promised Land. Finally, the third holiday is the Festival of weeks.

The Tradition of the First 100-Day Comes from the Festival of Weeks

The tradition of the first 100 days comes from the festival of weeks, which begins on January 10 after the first Sabbath of the year. The first Sabbath of the month of January usually falls within January 10 and the count starts after the Sabbath, according to the instructions given in the Festival of weeks. After the Sabbath count seven weeks or 49 days, which, when added to the day after the Sabbath, equal to 50 days after the first Sabbath of the year. And then the instruction calls for the counting of an additional 50 days, totaling 100 days after the Sabbath before 13 animals can be offered as sacrifices; however outside of the real Israel, it is 13 human beings that are offered as sacrifices to Satan after the first 100 days of the year. **It is clear that after the first 100 days of the first**

Sabbath of the year, the Festival of Weeks asks for the offering of 13 animals as sacrifices.

The offsprings of Satan in their practices of moon worshipping for human sacrifices do not use January 10 as a firm date, they use the first Sabbath to begin the count. So from roughly about January 7 or 9 on a given year, depending on what date the Sabbath falls, when fifty days are added, it leads to February 26 through February 28, human sacrifices are offered and when the additional 50 days are counted it almost always leads to April 19 and April 20 when at least 13 human sacrifices are offered.

Beyond the sacrifices demanded by the Festival of Weeks, other sacrifices are offered to satisfy the rest of the Festival Calendar. Thus, by April 20, the 110th day of the year, additional human sacrifices are offered and 86 days later on July 15, more human sacrifices are offered from July 15 through July 23 to satisfy the Festival of Tabernacles. For example, Bill and Hilary Clinton murdered 230 people from the TWA flight 800 on July 17, 1996, they offered the victims as human sacrifices to Satan and they also murdered John F. Kennedy Jr. on July 16, 1999; they offered him as a sacrifice to Satan; 110+86=196 days, this concludes the first half of the year from January 1 through July 15.

The First 100 Days of 2013

I wish to invite the reader to use the guidelines from Leviticus 23 to plug in the numbers to see if they match with the events of 2013.

In 2013 the first Sabbath fell on January 5, 2013, fifty days from January 5, 2013 led to February 24, 2013. What happened in the world on that date? A number of incidents occurred all over the world where the American Empire killed people to offer as sacrifices to Satan, but the big news was the resignation of the Pope which he himself announced on February 11, 2013. February 11 was the same date Nelson Mandela was released from prison in 1990 after De Klerk announced it on February 10, 1990. The date

February 10 is significant because it was on that same date the living God spoke to Noah, telling him to get into the Ark because he was about to send the rain in seven days to begin the Great Deluge to punish the wicked. Barak Obama announced his candidacy for president on February 10, 2007. February 24, 2013 marks the fiftieth day after the first Sabbath and the Pope officially resigned on February 28, 2013. This is consistent with the February 26, 1993 bombing of the first world trade center under Bill Clinton, leading to the first engagement of the ATF and Tobacco agents with David Koresh on February 28, 1993 in which a number of people died, including 6 FBI agents—ultimately, a 50-day siege would bring the operation to a total of 86 deaths on April 19, 1993—they were offered as sacrifices by fire to Satan—a textbook 100-day human offering.

These religious dates fit like a glove in the Waco affair; from the bombing of the World trade center on February 26 to the April 19 explosion of the David Koresh's compound, which killed altogether 86 people. This is also consistent with the February 27, 1933 explosion of the Reichstag building, which brought Adolph Hitler to power in Germany.

The illuminati use the February 24-27 dates not just to satisfy the guidelines of the first 100-day after the first Sabbath of the year found in the book of Leviticus on chapter 23, but also because on February 27, the living God Spoke when he asked Noah to get out of the ark with his family because the earth had dried from the Great Deluge—February 27 is a power date. The 100th day after the first Sabbath varies in the satanic practices depending on which date the first Saturday of the year falls on, but it is firm when observed by the children of the living God who use January 10 as the first day, the day the lamb was chosen. The resignation of the Pope was big news, the like of which has not been heard of for close to 600 years—just as the news of the release of Nelson Mandela in the power of the February 10 date was big news. In addition, the same number 86 that is found in the Waco operation where 86 people died is also found in the news of the Pope's announcement; the Pope is 86 years old—this is significant because

Abraham was 86 years old when Ishmael, the illegitimate son of Hagar, the father of the Jewish nation was born—the number 86 is the key number in the Jewish voodoo practices of human sacrifices, along with the number 13, the age of Ishmael when Satan gave Abraham the covenant of circumcision on Ishmael's birthday. Hence the basis for the Bar-Mitzvah. Abraham was 86 years old when Ishmael was born, he received the covenant of circumcision at 99 years old—this explains why the number 99 is so ubiquitous in American commerce, Abraham was 99 years old when Satan made the covenant of circumcision with him.

Moreover, the Pope chose to address the people about his resignation on February 17, 2013, another power date, the same date Barak Obama signed the stimulus package in 2009. February 17 was the very date when the Great Deluge of Noah started, so the Pope, by speaking out in public on February 17, 2013 was acting as if he were god and Barak Obama was the new Noah as he schemes to provoke civil wars in Haiti and in the United States to shed the blood of the innocent Hebrews for the benefit of the Jews. Furthermore, the Pope went into sequestration on March 1, 2013, the very same day the budget sequestration took effect in the United States where every agency was to reduce expenditures by 85 billion of dollars, (the number 86 has surfaced again) except agencies that were explicitly exempted by the new statute. These are no coincidences or accidents; these events are part of an elaborate religious system used by the illuminati, but it is not going to work this time because Benedict is not god and Barak Obama is not the son of the living God; Barak Obama is a little liar who is going to prison for murders, thefts and massive crimes against humanity—there is not going to be another Civil War in Haiti and in the United States to shed the blood of the innocents for the benefit of the Jews. Benedict and Francis cannot help Obama and Bill and Hilary Clinton, and the entire charade they have orchestrated was for nothing, it will not work and the punishment of the wicked is imminent.

Chapter 3

The Boston Marathon Bombing Occurred Exactly 100 Days after the First Sabbath of the Year

According to the 2013 calendar, when fifty days are counted from February 24, 2013, it leads exactly to April 15, 2013; what happened in the world on that date?

Breaking News:

The Boston bombing occurred exactly on April 15, 2013, exactly and precisely 100 days after the First Sabbath of 2013 to comply with the biblical guidelines found in the book of Leviticus in chapter 23

There is no way the Boston bombing could have been perpetuated by the Tsarnaev brothers without the involvement of the U.S. government—this explains why the older Tsarnaev brother was killed precisely on April 19, 2013. The entire operation was conducted by Barak Obama to offer human sacrifices, but it did not work, at least 13 people were supposed to have died, but only three died, once again Obama failed.

So the first half of the year is 196 days divided as follows; 110+86=196

The breakdown:

1. The first 10 days of January, including the first Sabbath:

2. The 100 days after January 10 where the first 50 days after the first Sabbath usually lead to around February 24 through 28

3. The second 50 days usually lead to April 19-20:

4. And finally, 86 days from April 20, lead to July 15, the beginning of the Feast of Tabernacles. For example, in 2010 Barak Obama allowed the oil to leak in the Gulf of Mexico for precisely 86 days from April 20, 2010 to July 15, 2010. And this also shows that the Boston bombing was part of this ritual: the event occurred on April 15 and the surviving brother is scheduled to appear in court on July 10, 2013, the Day of Atonement according to Leviticus 23. This suggests that those who rely on human sacrifices for their salvation are sacrificing Tsarnaev for their salvation, but it is not going to work. It is also important for the reader to be mindful that in addition to the guidelines found in Leviticus 23, the science of the equinoxes and the solstices, which reflect the warring rotation between the moon and the sun, plays a part in the practice of human sacrifices as well. The equinox as the name suggests, is an equality, a balance during the day between the sun and the moon, whereas the summer solstice of the month of June, usually June 21 marks the time of the year when the sun rises to its highest point, making June 21 the longest day of the year and the shortest night of the year. This phenomenon gives the sun, which symbolizes the man, a very decisive advantage over the moon, which symbolizes the woman. The Jews who are the priests of the American empire follow the moon calendar because they worship the woman, the moon as depicted by the statue of Liberty—this explains why many cultures in the world worship a woman names Lucy or Lucia as in Lucifer during the summer Solstice.

The second half of the year

Why is there a second half of the year that mimics the first half of the year?

The answer is simple: Satan seeks to control the kingdom of the living God, so he attempts to pre-empt the children of God by following the guidelines given to Israel, but he does it in his own way; chiefly, he offers human sacrifices instead of animal sacrifices, but his own calendar is very different from that of Israel. This explains why the Jews have always pretended to have two different new years; as the offsprings of Satan, the Jews follow the guidelines Satan gave to the Hebrews through Moses. As God instructed Moses, the New Year starts in January for the children of God, especially on January 10 the day the lamb was chosen, but for the Jews, the New Year really begins in July. This explains why the American fiscal year begins on July 1st to celebrate the Festival of Trumpets, according to Leviticus 23. Thus, July 4 is not just America's independence, it is America's new year, just as January 10 is Israel New year—the Haitians, the real Hebrews celebrate their New Year and their independence on January 1, and this also explains why the living God decided to bring a new and lasting freedom to the Haitians on January 12, 2010 through the earthquake, by killing all the homosexuals occupying force of the United Nations in Haiti. Ban Ki Moon conceded that the UN suffered its worst loss of lives ever in Haiti on January 12, 2010. This also explains why July 1st is known as Canada day of independence and July 14 is known as Bastille Day in France. July 1st is the day of the Festival of trumpet according to Leviticus 23. It is a day of Sabbath for the Jews and the American illuminati when they should present human offerings to Satan:

Breaking News:

On the twilight of June 30 and July 1st, 2013, 19 firefighters were killed in a wild fire in Arizona—the fire was reportedly triggered by a lighting strike.

The firefighters were offered as human holocaust to Satan. It is reported that this significant number of dead firefighters is unusual and that it is the largest number of firefighters that died on duty since the events of 09/11/01 where the number of 19 was also featured in the 19 hijackers—the last time so many firefighters lost their lives was in 1933 when Hitler took power in Germany. The mandated offerings to Satan can be engineered from the spiritual realm where evil spirits take control of the offerings by orchestrating events that lead to the demise of the victims like in the unusually high incidence of deaths on American highways on significant dates like Thanksgiving Day and New Year Eve. Or Satan can leave it to his servants from the physical world to take charge of the offering like Barak Obama has done in the July 20, 2012 Aurora shooting—based on the guidance found in Leviticus 23, more offerings should be expected in the month of July—on July 10 and July 15 through July 23, 2013.

So July 15 through July 22 leads to the first Sabbath of the second half of the year—the Jewish Sabbath; the festival of Tabernacles is satisfied by offering sacrifices on July 15 through July 22 and 23. So from July 22, count 50 days to September 10, it falls on September 11 on leap years—this is precisely why there are always sacrifices offered on September 11, it is a Jewish holiday—consistent with the worshipping of the moon, the worshipping of Lucifer. This revelation means that the September 11, 2001 operation was conducted by Dick Cheney and the September 11, 2012 operation that killed Ambassador Christopher Stevens in Benghazi Libya was conducted by Barak Obama and Hilary Rosen Clinton who is the personification of Lucifer. And from September 10-11 the additional 50-day count leads to October 30 or 31; Halloween night. The week of Halloween includes the day of the dead on November 1; the 110th day of the second half of the year from July 15 falls exactly on November 2; these are all power dates.

Obama conducted the Fort Hood operation on November 5, 2009 to offer innocent Americans as sacrifices to Satan in the Fort Hood shootings just as he offered Americans as sacrifices in the July 20, 2013 Aurora, Colorado shooting to satisfy the Feast or the Festival of Tabernacles. Finally, 86 days from October 30-31 lead to January 26-27 of the following year when an American president either makes the State of the Union Address or the inauguration's speech. The second half of the year is largely satanic, it contains the winter solstice on December 21 when the sun rises the lowest and when the day is shorter and the night is longer, giving the woman a seemingly brief advantage in the astrological war between good and evil. This was the day the illuminati called the end of the world, meaning the day Satan had chosen to kill the servant of Jesus and to begin a Civil War in the United States in 2012 through the November 6, 2012 presidential election. December 21 is the reverse of December 12, 2000 when the U.S. Supreme Court stopped the Florida vote count, which brought America on the brink of a Civil War under Bill Clinton.

Moreover, after all the human sacrifices demanded by Satan during the month of July, from July 1, the day of trumpets, to July 10, the day of atonement to July 15, the beginning of the Feast of Tabernacles, which last through July 22, additional sacrifices are offered in the month of August as well. Starting on August 15, the date when Solomon finished the building of the Sans Souci Palace in Haiti after he had completed the construction of the First Temple of Jerusalem. Solomon celebrated this achievement for two weeks, through August 22 and then through August 29, this explains why the Moslem celebrate Solomon in August through Ramadan and this also explains why the U.S. Congress celebrates Solomon by taking off during the month of August. The American Empire, just like the Moslem, celebrates Solomon, the mulatto false prophet who built the temple of Satan in Haiti in the name of the living God in the power of a woman named Sheba. After Ramadan, the Jews celebrate Rosh Hannah in the first 50 days of the second half of the year.

It is based on these religious dates and practices and history that Obama have been attempting to murder innocent Americans around July 15 through 23, 2013 and to attempt to murder more Americans around September 10 and 11, 2013 and on Halloween in the first week of November to satisfy the guidelines from the book of Leviticus; this is a science and Obama has no choice, but to continue to observe these practices as long as he is in office, but Barak Obama will be removed from office very soon because the living God, the creator of the heavens and the earth is against him.

Chapter 4

The Mystic in the Boston Marathon Bombing

On April 15, 2013, at around 3:00 P.M. EST, two consecutive explosions shattered the festive mood in the city of Boston Massachusetts, the biblical city of Salem, the original capital of the Catholic Church, the homosexual Church of Melchizedek; the Church of human sacrifices. As soon as Barak Obama and the illuminati engineered the bombing of the Boston Marathon, the Korean crisis disappeared like a puff of air—it was all staged to overshadow the crimes of Obama around the world, especially in Syria where Obama sent American troops to Jordan to fight in the Syrian conflict. The media was pleased to find an excuse to stop fabricating the Korean situation as a potential nuclear crisis, the Boston bombing became the new terrorist event, an event they had hoped to use as impetus for Barak Obama to invade Syria and to take other actions in the Middle East. They quickly stopped covering any news about North Korea, except to report that very day that North Korea did not launch any missile as they have reported they might. If the fabricated crisis in the Korean peninsula between North and South Koreas gave the American media—all the media, including Television, Newspaper, Radio, and Social Media an excuse not to report the crimes of Barak Obama throughout the world, including in Syria where Obama has put the U.S. in direct conflict with Russia and Iran and where the U.S. is trying to get Turkey, Israel and Jordan involved in the conflict in the hope to remove Bashar Al Assad from power more quickly, then the media was hoping that the Boston bombing would have offered a new opportunity for Obama to offer human sacrifices to gain mystical powers to pass new gun laws and to find a new mandate to fight foreign wars like the events of 09/11/01 did for Dick Cheney and George W. Bush in 2001. However, this time

Obama and the homosexual vampires in the American media were severely disappointed as only three people died in the Boston Marathon bombing, not enough blood was shed to help Barak Obama.

Barak Obama is presently murdering innocent civilians in Afghanistan, a nation that has done nothing to the American people and has not invaded its neighbor like Saddam Hussein has done. Barak Obama has more than tripled the number of American soldiers in Afghanistan since he took office, he has increased the number of cowardly drone strikes in Afghanistan more than tenfold, he has increased the number of civilian deaths in Afghanistan, in Pakistan and even in Yemen at an alarming rate, yet the American media have remained silent in their desperate conspiracy with their mulatto loser whom they hope can save them from the incoming wrath of the living God, but he cannot and their punishment is imminent. Barak Obama is a homosexual invader, he has sent American troops to Syria through Turkey and Jordan, to Sudan, Somalia, Central Africa and other places in Africa, yet the American press has remained silent. Since Hitler invaded Africa, Barak Obama has murdered more black men than any other leader since Abraham Lincoln murdered hundreds of thousands of blacks through the American Civil War, a War that was fought to conquer the real biblical Israel, the land God promised to the black and the white children of Jacob—the real black and the real white southerner are brothers.

Barak Obama and the American freemasons, the illuminati are behind the Boston Marathon bombing and the evidence is found in the following:

1 **Human sacrifice within the practice of the first 100 days**

From Saturday January 5, 2013, the first Sabbath of the year, to April 15, 2013 when the Boston bombings occurred, it took precisely **100 days,** this is not a coincidence, it is the religious application of human sacrifices.

The victims of the bombing are expiatory victims; they are offered as sacrifices to Satan in the covenant of the mulatto Cain, which was established in the silent Passover of human sacrifice when the living God put a Mark on Cain's forehead with the blood of Abel. The Boston Marathon bombing is very significant because it is the very first official act of human sacrifice after the new Pope who calls himself Francis was appointed. The sacrifice was made precisely in Boston, the biblical Salem, the birthplace of the Catholic Church, the church of Melchizedek, the original Pope of Satan, the father of the Catholic Church. In addition, the human sacrifices were offered to help Barak Obama pass the gun control legislation; however, the bill failed to gain 60 votes on April 17, 2013. The vote took place shortly after the Boston bombing, which failed to produce enough blood to push the bill through the Senate and it failed. Every major piece of Obama's legislation has been passed after innocent American blood was shed. Most notably, the Health Care PPact with Satan, Obama's signature legislation was voted by the House on Saturday November 7, 2009 after the November 5, 2009 Fort Hood Shooting. Prior to this legislation, Tim Geithner, the Treasury Secretary unveiled a plan to transfer the entire American Wealth to the Jews on Wall Street on March 23, 2009 after Barak Obama signed the so called bailout package on February 17, 2009. Geithner's plan came on the backdrop of violence that shed the blood of American people throughout the month of March. In one incident, an Alabama man killed 10 people in a drive-by shooting, in another incident, a man shot 8 people from a nursing home in North Carolina and finally, six people were fatally shot in an apartment building in Santa Clara, California. It is clear that Obama is a vampire that sucks on the blood of the American people to advance the dark cause of the

Jews. After the gun law was defeated, Obama called a press conference to complain and to attack those who voted against the bill and he vowed to continue to fight for "sensible gun control".

Breaking News:

Waco all over again

Later that night, a huge explosion took place in West, Texas, near Waco, a fertilizer plant supposedly exploded, injuring close to two hundred people, but the number of fatalities was not known. It cannot be an accident if the explosions took place the very night after Obama vowed to continue to fight for "sensible gun control". It cannot be an accident when the incident took place on April 17, 2013, while the Waco incident took place on April 19, 1995 and in addition, a video footage has emerged on the internet to show the possibility that a missile strike had caused the big explosion from the fertilizer plant, but the voodoo did not work.

It was not an accident when Barak Obama used the power of the presidency to give his first official order to kill blacks from Somalia accused of piracy in international water in his first 100 days in office. A siege ensued and by April 12, 2009 a number of them were killed and on April 20, 2009, Obama brought a young black Somali teenager to Babylon, the modern city of New York to face trial. Clearly, that operation was conducted as a religious ritual to satisfy the tradition of the first 100-day liturgy through which human sacrifices are offered to Satan.

The entire American media was happy for Obama; they reminded the nation of the words of Joe Biden who predicted that Obama would be tested in his first 100 days in office. On April 20, 2009, Obama concluded the operation by bringing a black Somali teenager to New York to face charges—Obama's first act in office was to shed the blood of innocent black Africans. It cannot be an accident when Barak Obama engineered an 86-day oil leak in the Gulf of Mexico, killing a number of workers and millions of wild lives, exactly on April 20, 2010. It cannot be an accident when Obama attempted to kill his own wife Michelle on April 19, 2011. It cannot be an accident when Barak Obama directed the CIA to explode a Pakistani airplane on April 20, 2012, killing 131 people. It cannot be an accident when Obama gave the order to shoot down a small airplane in distress over the Gulf of Mexico on April 20, 2012.

It is clear therefore that the Boston Marathon bombing was staged by Barak Obama and the illuminati to offer human sacrifices, to find a mandate for new wars in the Middle East, to further restrict the freedom of all Americans and to pass dark legislations like the so called sensible gun control legislation, which is designed to provoke violence in America and the evil immigration law, which is designed to steal the wealth of the white and the black American Hebrews and to keep them in bondage forever. And to pave the way for the Mexicans, the cursed Canaanites, the Indians from India, the people from Saudi Arabia and the Chinese immigrants to take over the U.S. in a third wave of immigration like the European did after the American Civil war in which the blood of the white and the black Hebrews were shed for the benefit of the Jews and the Europeans who came to settle in America in the second wave of immigration at the expense of the real white and black American Hebrews who belong to the rich confederate nations of the south, the real biblical Israel.

The Boston Marathon operation unfolded like the international Somali operation and just like the Somali operation ended with the April 20, 2009 arrival in New York of a black Somali teenager who were taken alive, the Boston operation also ended with the killing of Tamerlan Tsarnaev on April 19, 2013 and the capture of Dzhokhar Tsarnaev, a white teenager on April 19, 2013. The numbers are too precise for all of this to have occurred by accident.

In addition, by closing schools, businesses and by imposing an order on the residents of Boston not to leave their houses, the police and the authorities in Massachusetts have essentially imposed a holiday on all the residents on April 19, 2013, which is a holiday that is traditionally celebrated in Massachusetts and in Maine every year to commemorate the battle of Lexington and Concord, which took place on April 19, 1775. So April 19 is Independence Day in Massachusetts. It is reported that "Since 1969, the holiday has been celebrated on the third Monday of April" and April 15, 2013 was the third Monday of April. In addition, The Boston Marathon has come to be known as 'Marathon Monday' because it has been held on the third Monday of the month to celebrate the April 19 Independence Day, so the Boston Marathon is a very powerful religious and historical symbol.

So the events that unfolded in Boston Massachusetts were totally scripted by the U.S. government as a huge human sacrificial offering to Satan. It was designed to reinvent a new independence for the American nation as the Lincoln Covenant has come to an end and the Barak Obama's 2008 Emancipation Call has not been accepted. First, the Pope resigned, an event that has not occurred in close to 600 years; this happened because the era of Christopher Columbus has come to an end after 13 generations or 520 years (13*40=520), from 1492 to 2012, which means the kingdom will return to the Haitians soon.

Secondly, the bombings took place on April 15, 2013 exactly 100 days after the first Sabbath of 2013 and April 19, 2013, the operation ended and the people of Boston celebrated, but it is not going to work because the living God will not sanction anymore human sacrifices from Satan—the covenant of human sacrifices has come to an end. Moreover, the Abel and Cain's symbolism has also been found in the two brothers that were accused; the one in the black hat, symbolizes Abel, he was killed; and the one in the white hat who symbolizes the mulatto Cain was taken alive, but this time the living God will not allow a criminal to exist at the expense of innocent blood. As the high priest of Satan, Barak Obama went to a Boston church to offer the victims of the bombing to Satan in the hope that the living God would accept them, but it will not happen. It is also important to note that the events of 09/11/01 also originated in Boston where the airplanes supposedly took off for New York, Pennsylvania, and Washington D.C. The entire event occurred on the land of Shinar: Boston is the head of the Kingdom, the biblical Salem, the home of the Catholic Church and Melchizedek is the priest of Salem; the first Pope of the Catholic Church. New York is the biblical Babylon nation; and Pennsylvania is the Jews' first home away from Palestine, or San Diego, the biblical Philistine nation. Pennsylvania is the birthplace of the American Constitution, which means the document was produced by the Jews—the priests of Satan; and finally Washington D.C. is the place where the Chinese congregation was more pronounced on the land of Shinar—Shinar is an early spelling of China.

The original mystic of the 'Scapegoat' concept

"Aaron is to offer the bull for his own sin offering to make atonement for himself and his household. Then he is to take the two goats and present them before the LORD at the entrance to the tent of meeting. He is to cast lots for the two goats—one lot for the LORD and the other for the scapegoat. Aaron shall bring the goat whose lot falls to the LORD and sacrifice it for a sin offering. But the goat chosen by lot as the scapegoat shall be presented alive before the LORD to be used for making atonement by sending it into the wilderness as a scapegoat."

(Leviticus 16: 6-10 NIV)

The concept of the Scapegoat according to the guidance given to Moses by Satan in the above quote is for one person to kill another, two victims, but the one that remains alive is to bear the sins of the nation, he is to be used to make atonement for the people by going into the wilderness.

This concept first surfaced when Cain murdered Abel and after which the living God cursed him and sent him in the wilderness with a 'Mark' on his forehead to protect him from getting killed—that 'Mark" was made with the blood of Abel, his own victim—this established the covenant of human sacrifices, the Cain Passover. Cain was the original Scapegoat; he murdered Abel, but he escaped in the wilderness by making atonement for the rest of the criminals; thus, everyone who believes in unrighteousness can find protection, or coverage through Cain in the blood of Abel, but this has to be repeated every year because it is an imperfect sacrifice. The way the term scapegoat is currently used suggests that the person who is the scapegoat is an innocent person who bear the sins of others, but that is wrong. The scapegoat is actually a guilty person, a criminal who gets away with murder for a time because of the mercy of the living God who put a Mark on him with the blood of his own victim.

The entire Boston Marathon bombing event was orchestrated by Barak Obama to establish a renewal of the Cain Passover by using the Tsarnaev brothers as the two goats, but it did not work because the Tsarnaev brothers are white and the symbolism of the white and the black hats is not strong enough to recreate and recapture the mystic of the original voodoo.

Breaking News:

The freemasons in Washington D.C. decided to use Aaron Hernandez and Odin Lloyd in their plan B as the new goats to implement the Boston Marathon Voodoo

The fact that Odin Lloyd is black like Abel and Aaron Hernandez is white Hispanic; he closely resembles the mulatto Cain. Aaron Hernandez fits as a beast with the profile of a Scapegoat, the name Aaron gave him the spirit of the priesthood of Satan just as Aaron, the brother of Moses became the priest of Satan as it is shown in the above quote from the biblical book of Leviticus. In addition, Aaron also has an Italian background and since the church of Satan is now in Vatican, Italy, that also makes him a natural priest of Satan from the church of human sacrifices, the Catholic Church.

Aaron Hernandez was first arrested on June 26, 2013 for the murder of Odin Lloyd, a power date that is consistent with the voodoo of the illuminati; June 24 is observed by the Catholic Church as the Feast of Saint John, but June 26 was a very important date since the number 26 is the number of the woman, the original Eve, the mother of the mulatto Cain who murdered Abel to become the original Scapegoat. The number 26 is featured prominently and strategically in every document of the illuminati, including the Obama's Health Care PPACT with Satan in which a child is allowed to remain on his parent insurance policy until the age of 26 years old and this also explains why Tamerlan Tsarnaev was killed at the age of 26 years old and it is no accident that the black Trayvon Martin was killed on February 26 by George Zimmerman, a white Hispanic who closely resembles Cain, Barak Obama and Aaron Hernandez, it was the work of Satan.

In addition, Aaron Hernandez was officially indicted, meaning formal charges were brought against him in a court of law on August 22, 2013, another power date. The date August 22 is hugely important in the tradition of Satan; it was the end of the first week of celebration of the completion of the Solomon's temple and his palace; Solomon finished the palace on August 15 and celebrated the achievement for one week until August 22, but the people were so happy and elated, he decided to extend the celebration by another week until August 29. This explains why the Catholic Church celebrates the Lady of Assumption on August 15, the accomplishment of the Solomon's temple was achieved through the power Satan gave to the disobedient black Eve in the Garden of Eden when he promised her she can become like God if she eats from the tree of the knowledge of Good and Evil. However, that original power was later transfer to Lucifer, a white woman like Hilary Clinton or Angela Merkel of Germany.

Consistent with this biblical understanding and the practice of human sacrifices, the plan of the freemason in Washington is to find a way to help Aaron Hernandez be released sometime in April 2014. He could either be released on technicality or he could be tried and found not guilty of murder so he could be sent free into the wilderness as the scapegoat that makes atonement for the Jews, the Catholics, the Freemasons and the rest of the people, but it is not going to work; the living God will never accept Aaron Hernandez as a legitimate scapegoat like he accepted Cain for a time and Satan surely, does not have the power to act unilaterally in the world.

In their desperation and because this archaic practice has been going on for such a long time, the offsprings of Satan seem to have forgotten that it was the living God who actually put the blood of Abel as a 'Mark' of protection on Cain's forehead, it was not Satan; therefore, without the blessing of the living God evil cannot exist. God allowed evil to exist because he wanted to keep the promise that was destined from the tree of the knowledge of good and evil; the legitimate and obedient white and Asian men and women who would come forth from the tree of the knowledge of good and evil.

Satan established the doctrine of pre-emption by making an untimely and an illegal entry into history by coupling with Eve while he was still in the serpent stage. He metamorphosed into an attractive man who appeared good looking and bright to Eve and she succumbed to his charm and to the promise of becoming a goddess.

However, God still secured the good seed from the tree of the knowledge of good and evil when he said; "no one descended from a forbidden marriage (coupling) would be admitted in my assembly until the tenth generation." This means after ten generations someone would emerge from an evil lineage as a good seed, totally healed by God with a different genetic make-up and a fundamentally different spirit from that of his parents.

God allowed evil to exist for a time to secure the good seed that he intended to come out from the tree of the knowledge of good and evil, and now the living God is prepared to phase out for good the covenant of human sacrifices, the Passover of Cain is over.

Therefore, the blood of Odin Lloyd will not be allowed to be used for the atonement of the Jews and the other Obama supporters, the Catholic, the homosexuals and all who do evil. The blood of Trayvon Martin will not be allowed to be used as atonement of sins for evil doers and certainly, the blood of Tamerlan Tsarnaev will not be allowed to be used to atone for the sins of criminals and the blood of the children that died in the Newtown, Connecticut massacre will not be allowed to be used to atone for the sinful ways of the offsprings of Satan: Barak Obama, Bill Clinton, and Hilary Clinton will be judged and evil is about to be punished very soon—the earthquakes and the fire from heavens are coming to punish America and the Obama supporters, especially those from the media.

2 the date April 15, 19 and 20

The liturgy of the first 100 days:

April 19 and April 20 are respectively the 109th and 110th days of the year; however, they represent the 100th day after January 10, the date when the lamb was chosen by the people of Israel shortly before they left Egypt (Mexico) in the Great Exodus.

According to the book of Leviticus, the people of Israel were commanded to observe the Feast of Weeks, or the Feast of the first 100 days, which start after the first Sabbath and lead to April 19 or 20, 100 days later and to offer sacrifices.

The human sacrifices that are offered on and around April 19 and April 20 are offered to Satan, consistent with the guidelines found in the biblical book of Leviticus, in chapter 23. One way to discern if a set of instructions comes from God or Satan is to check whether the guidelines call for the observation of a particular event based on a firm date or based on the position of the moon. For example, the guidelines that call for counting 100 days after the first Sabbath come from Satan; they do not involve a fix date. This explains why American holidays are usually set based on different dates. For example, Thanksgiving is celebrated on the fourth Thursday of the month of November.

The date April 15 is a very significant date because it is the 105th day of the year, **exactly 100 days from Saturday January 5, the first Sabbath of 2013** and only 4 and 5 days away from the most important April 19 and April 20 dates; the 109th and the 110th day of the year. The living God used the 110th day of the year, 101 years after the Great Deluge to divide the earth, giving to Satan temporary control of the eastern hemisphere and keeping for himself the control of the western hemisphere until the time comes for him to consolidate complete control of the earth again. And ever since, Satan, in his imitation of the living God has used the number 110 to make statement of power in the world. The number 110 is also the number of 11 with the 0 silent. The number 110 is also the number of the Messiah; Joseph, the son of Jacob who brought the 66 offsprings of Jacob to Egypt where they became a nation died at the age of 110. And Joshua, the faithful servant of the living God who brought the nation of Judah and Israel out from the desert to the Promised Land also died at the age of 110.

Chapter 5

The Mystic in the Resignation of Pope Benedict and the Re-selection of Barak Obama

Barak Obama and his illuminati supporters, including the Republicans conspired to steal the November 6, 2012 Presidential election. They are desperate in their desire to gain magical power in the historical mystic of Solomon—the antichrist—the builder of the house of Satan. This mysticism makes it possible for other antichrists to assume the full power and authority of Solomon when they enter their fourth year in office. Solomon began to build the temple of Jerusalem in Milot, Haiti in his fourth year in office. And like many other antichrists before him, Barak Obama needed to win re-election so he could enter his fourth year in office in the hope he would assume the full power and authority of Solomon in order to build a house of blood by provoking a civil war in the United States, just like Lincoln built a house of blood by provoking and prosecuting the American civil war. However, when Obama and his supporters, those at the upper echelon of the illuminati realized that they have been upstaged by Jesus in Syria where Bashar Al Assad is still in control of the government, in defiance to Obama, they decided to write a completely new spiritual voodoo script. That new script called for the "sequester" of the "Faithful Servant" of Jesus. In order to achieve this voodoo, they decided to stage the resignation of Pope Benedict and to sequester him because the penitence of Pope Benedict symbolizes the neutralization of the "Faithful Servant" of Jesus. And the illuminati have chosen a Pope from Argentina and gave him the name of Francis—the English version of Francois—the name of the Faithful Servant of Jesus—to assume his power and natural authority—but it is not going to work—the new Pope will fail. Pope Francis is a liar and a deceiver who practices the art of speech without action—

he is committed to the cause of human sacrifices and homosexuality—his mission is to further the reality of half free and half slaves that now exists throughout the world. But that strategy will not work because the Church, the House of the living God belongs in Haiti, the real biblical Jerusalem, not in Argentina, not in the Vatican, and not in Saudi Arabia. However, God lives in the body of Jesus. From the time Pope Benedict was sequestered to the time a new Pope was elected, the American Congress also passed a measure called "The sequester" and soon thereafter the American stock market made exceptional gains by setting record highs after record high. And soon after his re-election, Obama travelled to a place called "Israel", in the Middle East, in the hope to return with the new powers of Solomon, but Barak Obama embarrassed himself, he did not return with new powers and by April 19, 2013 Bashar Al Assad was still in power in Syria and on that very day, a U.S. Court nolled a criminal case against the "Faithful Servant" of Jesus who was about to be murdered in Norwalk, CT as a patsy of the CIA. Barak Obama and his supporters, in their desperate quest to remove Assad from power and to stop the war in Syria, have announced several strategies: they have announced a new commitment by EU nations to arm the Syrian rebels who are fighting against Assad; they have also announced a new investigation by the UN into reports that Assad has used chemical weapons against his own people, a move designed to give an excuse to the US and NATO to officially invade Syria, if the rumors were to be substantiated by the UN. And finally, the U.S. has announced the formation of a special military invading force that could be quickly deployed on the ground anywhere in the Middle East in the event of trouble. This announcement was made in the shadow of the fabricated crisis in the Korean Peninsula so the American people would not really know the extent of the U.S. involvement in the war in Syria. There is no Korean crisis. The U.S has done the same thing in November 28, 2010 before a scheduled presidential election in Haiti, that same day, Julian Assange, a CIA operative published the so called WikiLeaks cable for the first time to create news in order to overshadow the crimes Obama and Hilary Clinton were about to commit in Haiti and in the Ivory coast, where a runoff presidential election was also scheduled that very day. This strategy stems from a dark spiritual principle; to use fabricated news as a diversion to cover up a real and more important story that is going at the same time. This was the principle used by Hilary Clinton and Barak Obama in the murder of Christopher Stevens. The September 11, 2012 deaths of Ambassador Stevens and three other Americans in Benghazi, Syria were used as news decoy and human sacrifices to cover up the September 13, 2012 announcement by Ben Bernanke that the Federal Reserve had decided to print money to purchase up to $86 billion worth of Mortgage backed securities and treasuries, every month, indefinitely. It is important to note that the actions of the Federal Reserves are criminal, treasonous and completely unacceptable. A government should not print money if the money is not backed by gold or another currency with intrinsic value. Moreover, the money is used to wrongly enrich a few actors on Wall Street—it is used to purchase worthless Mortgage Backed Securities, the toxic assets of private enterprises. The Federal Reserve has not printed money to promote an expansion of economic activity in the real economy, but instead, the Federal Reserve decided to purchase worthless and toxic securities as a way to restore the heavy losses that private bankers and investment firms had incurred in the 2008 financial debacle and they expect the American people to pay for it by driving them into debt. And in return, the firms and the banks that received money from the Federal Reserve pledge to drive up the stock market prices by buying equities—this way, every investor gains, including those in the Middle Class with (401K) investments. The Obama administration also uses the $ 86 billion bond buying program to bail-out European banks and European nations, including Greece and Italy, while the American people, especially the blacks and the underclass, suffer without jobs and without opportunities.

The American media and the Obama administration have used the 2013 Korean crisis to overshadow the crimes Obama is committing inside Syria by supporting every criminal group in the Middle East that has been armed and sent to overthrow Bashar Al Assad, but Obama is losing the Syrian war. And ultimately, the Syrian crisis will cause new wars to erupt all over the Middle East, including Egypt, Israel, Turkey, and others. Obama and John Kerry are now engaged in a great struggle inside Syria where Russia and Iran are fully committed to protecting the government of Syria by providing arms and personnel to Bashar Al Assad. Obama is also engaged in a great struggle in Africa. He has sent soldiers all over Africa to murder innocent Africans in Libya, in Sudan, in Central Africa, in Uganda, in Somalia, in Mali and every place where the spirit of resistance against Satan has been kindled. The great struggle begins in Haiti: The Haitian struggle is not an overt military struggle, but rather a contest of will regarding the direction of the country, which in turn decides the direction of the world. This is why the capital of Haiti is called Port-au-Prince, meaning the city of the Great King as Jerusalem is known in the bible—whoever controls Haiti, controls the world. Obama, Bill and Hilary Clinton invaded Haiti after the January 12, 2010 earthquake because they were desperately trying to hold on to the control of the Roman Kingdom, but the era of Columbus has come to an end.

Barak Obama and the illuminati have attempted to reinvent themselves with the appointment of a new pope, but it is not working.

The Pope used to be the king in former times, but after the separation of church and state, the Pope has come to play a behind the scene role, but remains firmly involved in the management of the kingdom of Satan.

This is done in imitation of the holy history of the priests of the living God. For example, the law; the Ten Commandments were given to Moses who was the leader of the people of Israel during the Great Exodus when they first became a nation, but God does not allow his priests to be called Pope, because God is the Pope, the Papa of the holy people. Later, King David himself was called a prophet, so David was both, King and prophet. The tradition of the papacy comes from the rise of Melchizedek in Salem, Massachusetts—he was the first Pope of the Catholic Church. That tradition continued until the servants of Satan abused their people in Europe and after the French revolution the church was separated from the state to placate the people. But the freemasons of Europe continued in their deceptions; they gave the impression of separation, but from behind the scene they continued to work as one entity. However, the Vatican admits that the power of the Pope comes from the Chair—the Chair on which Abraham Lincoln seats in Washington at The Lincoln Memorial. The power of Satan flows from Washington to the Pope in Vatican, this is why Pope Benedict was forced to be sequestered. The "sequester" is also a strategy of penitence used in the hope to placate the living God and to please Satan, but it is not working. God will not be placated just because one homosexual has decided to sequester himself in excessive luxury, while another, Pope Francis pays lip service to the idea of righteousness. In this Sabbath, the living God has gained the upper hand through the blood of his son Jesus, he will be the one who does the judging and the punishing and he has certainly found Pope Benedict and Francis along with Barak Obama, Hilary and Bill Clinton and those who follow their ways, guilty of murders, human sacrifices and of promoting a world of homosexuality, a world of half free and half slaves—and a world without peace and without justice.

Chapter 6

The American National Landmarks Are Religious Satanic Symbols Found in the Bible

The secular is the religious: the national symbols that confirm the United States is a Satanic Theocracy—a nation that follows the ways of Satan

The following 8 national symbols show a shocking correlation with religious biblical symbols—Satan is using these symbols in the American Kingdom to assume the authority of the living God of Jacob—these symbols show beyond any doubt that the United States of America is a Satanic Theocracy.

1 The Lincoln Memorial. The Lincoln Memorial is in part a replica of the Ark of the Covenant that Moses built in the desert of Sinai, the desert of South Dakota one of the places where the children of Jacob lived after they left Mexico. The Ark of the Covenant was built like a box to house the two stone tablets on which the Ten Commandments that were given to Moses on Mount Sinai were inscribed. The Lincoln Memorial is also built like a box. The interior of the Lincoln Memorial, like the Ark of the Covenant, contains two speeches given by Lincoln and just like the Ten Commandments are carved on two stone tablets, two speeches given by Lincoln; the Gettysburg Address and the Second Inaugural Address are also carved in stone on the wall of the Lincoln Memorial—a perfect religious match. In addition, the outer court is built like the White throne of Solomon. A big white throne is built for Lincoln like Solomon built in Haiti. The biblical account made it clear that six steps of gold led to the Solomon's throne with six lions on either side of the steps. The same thing is done for Lincoln. The Lincoln white throne is framed among 12 pillars; six on either side, instead of 12 lions; however, to capture the animal spirit of the 12 lions in the Solomon's white tower of justice the images of the lions are sculpted at the very entrance. And like the Solomon's throne, the Lincoln's throne also has six steps leading to Lincoln. The last six steps that lead to the throne of Lincoln are not made of gold because this current American kingdom is not as rich in gold as the original Haitian kingdom was under King David and King Solomon, Haiti is the gold standard. The American kingdom, the fourth and last kingdom of Satan is a kingdom of clay mixed with iron.

Moreover, Solomon built the temple, the first Haitian Citadelle, in seven years in the blood of the white Canaanites and the U.S. invaded Haiti in 1915 to build the Lincoln Memorial in the blood of the Haitians. It also took seven years to build the Lincoln Memorial from 1915 through 1922 and soon after the construction of the Lincoln Memorial in the blood of the Haitians, the period known as the "**Roaring Twenties**" began to bring unprecedented prosperity to the American elite; the offsprings of Ham, Irad, Egypt, Nimrod, Ishmael, among others, but the dark prosperity did not last, the living God punished those who did evil to the Haitians and precisely seven (7) years from 1922 when the Lincoln Memorial was inaugurated, the American Stock market crashed in 1929 and the American prosperity was gone for a time. The comparisons go on and on—the evidence is compelling, the Lincoln Memorial is a religious temple, not a secular construction. Finally, just as the Solomon's temple was built with two pillars that stand for Joachim and Boaz, the other side of the Lincoln Memorial is reserved to honor Barak Obama if he were to succeed in provoking a Civil War in America to complete the vision of Satan, but he will be denied.

2 The Pentagon. The American Pentagon is also a religious temple. It is built like the **Pillar of Offerings** in the second temple of

Jerusalem, the Haitian Citadelle (please see "A Pictorial Presentation of the Seven Holy Books".

The American Pentagon is designed like the top of the Pentagon design that is found on top of the Haitian pillar of offering, the front of the Cidatelle where the gold dome used to be. The American Pentagon is a pillar of offerings without a dome—it is a religious building just like the temple of Mecca and the Taj-Mahal, which are copied from the Haitian Citadelle. This explains why during the events of 9/11/01, the Pentagon was one of three religious places that were affected in the land of Shinar. The land of Shinar is located in the Northeast of the U.S., from as far north as Massachusetts, all the way down to Washington D.C.—Shinar is an early spelling of China. The land of Shinar includes cities like Babylon or New York where the Towers of the World Trade fell like the original Tower of Babylon. Pennsylvania, the birthplace of the American Constitution and Washington D.C., the American Capital, D.C. stands for the city of the Dead Christ—the Pentagon, as the pillar of offerings is used by Satan to offer human sacrifices through wars, foreign and domestic every Sabbath—most of the religious mass shootings in America originate from the Pentagon.

3 The American White House is also part of the religious design found in the Haitian Citadelle; it is built like the Haitian Citadelle with three floors, not counting the basement. The three floors signify the three stages of development. In the first stage, the serpent is the guide of man and the tree is the primitive home, the primitive temple of the serpent. In the second stage, the serpent continues to be the savior of men, but his new home is the temple of cedar or the building of concrete that Solomon built with the two pillars like the former twin towers from the World Trade Center. Finally, in the third stage of development, the man became the living temple of the living God and the serpent is no longer the savior of the man, but Jesus himself becomes the savior of man—

this is precisely why it took 46 years to build the second temple. The number 46 signifies a man as it takes 46 chromosomes to create a human being; 23 from the mother and 23 from the father. The second temple of Jerusalem symbolizes a man, but the real temple of God was built by Jesus through his death and resurrection—he created a living temple for a living God. Those who practice the art of Solomon have the serpent for savior, an animal with limited knowledge and authority—this explains why some in the medical community are changing their medical logo from the two serpents from the tree of the knowledge of good and evil to the one black serpent Moses used to cure the Israelites in the desert. They have decided to do this because they want to come closer to Jesus. Jesus was raised like a serpent on a cross in the same desert of Arizona to save those who believe in him from the judgment of God and to cure their diseases, including cancer, AIDS, diabetes and more. Satan rebelled against God and God cursed him, as a result, he never became all he could be and thus, he remains a serpent, an animal with human mask, like Barak Obama and Bill and Hilary Clinton. The medical community treats its patients, but Jesus cures the sick by taking away their illnesses for good—this explains why Jesus promises life, but Satan can only promise Health Care insurance, no cure.

4 The number of the White House is 1600; the number 1600 represents prosperity because it took exactly 1600 years for prosperity to return to earth after the original sin. Noah was born 1000 years after the fall of Adam, and when Noah turned 600 years old, the flood came and destroyed everyone, except Noah and his family. The Great Deluge was the Great Baptism of the earth; the water lifted the curse of poverty that God pronounced on Adam as a result of the original sin to bring a new world of prosperity on earth. The Great Deluge also gave birth to the notion that wherever there is a great crisis, there is also a great opportunity, as the Great

Deluge destroyed the wicked and at the same time brings abundance and prosperity back on earth.

5 The American eagle: the symbol of the black eagle—the black bird Noah released after the Ark landed on Mount Ararat on July 17, on my birthday. The eagle stole the green olive tree from the white Dove, 7 days after the Dove had brought the olive branch to Noah. This set up a Sabbatical duel between the white Dove and the black eagle; each seeking to control the prosperity of the earth for seven years. The elite illuminati simulate this spiritual duel through the game of golf by featuring the 'birdie' and the 'eagle' on the 'green'. The black eagle is also a vampire who dwells in high places with powerful piercing vision; the young eagle drinks blood to survive and to grow—this explains why the United States always seeks to shed the blood of the innocents every Sabbath.

6 The White House is located on Pennsylvania Ave because Pennsylvania was the place where the American Constitution was produced—it is the birthplace of the American nation. This also explains why Pennsylvania was also affected by the events of 09/11/01. Philadelphia, Pennsylvania became very prominent in American history because the Jews, as the satanic priests of the American nation, first settled in Philadelphia after they left their original home in San Diego, California. San Diego is the original biblical Philistine, the place where fightings were going on at the time when the black Hebrews were leaving Mexico, the biblical Egypt in the 'Exodus.' The city of Philadelphia was founded after the Philistines or the Jews had settled there from San Diego. This explains why the same violent characteristic that had existed in San Diego, California since biblical time now exists in Philadelphia; the city of Philadelphia has a very violent history, it is the strike capital of America. The same violent characteristics is also found in the Middle East nation the Jews are calling Israel, it is a very violent society, this trait is found wherever there is a large concentration of Jews like New York and Chicago.

7 The statue of Liberty in New York, the ancient city of Babylon.

The statue of Liberty symbolizes Lucifer to whom the authority of the original black Eve was transferred. Eve was the original "**Lady of Assumption** "she later became **Ave Maria, or Eve Maria**; she defeated Adam when she accepted the seduction of Satan who told her that she will not die if she ate of the tree of the knowledge of good and evil. Satan lied and Eve and Adam died, but Eve became the Queen of the damned, the Lady of Assumption, the Statue of Liberty.

The Statue of Liberty is designed based on a biblical angel, Jesus Christ himself

According to the biblical account, it is written in Revelations 10 that the mighty angel of the Living God stands with his right foot on the Sea, yet the Statue of Liberty stands on the Sea. The mighty angel is described by the Bible as "robed in a cloud with a rainbow above his head; his face was like the sun; his legs were like fiery pillars". This description matches the Statue of Liberty, which displays a woman in a robe in the cloud, high in the skies of Babylon or New York. The sun shines in the face of the statue to attempt to match the description of the biblical angel. Moreover, it is written that the angel had a rainbow above his head, yet, the statue of Liberty has seven crowns above her head to match the seven crowns on the head of the dragon, or the seven buildings that made up the former World Trade Center. And the legs of the Statue of Liberty are sculpted like fiery pillars, like the legs of the angel from the biblical book of Revelations. These veins are expressed through the legs of Hilary Clinton who has the spirit of Lucifer, the Statue of Liberty—this explains why Hilary Clinton usually wears pants; her legs are like fiery pillars—the vein may not look good, but they are the symbols of satanic power. Furthermore, the biblical account states, "**The angel that I have seen standing on the Sea and on the land raised his hand to heaven." (Revelations 10: 5 NIV),** yet the Statue of Liberty also raised one hand with a torch of fire to the heavens—again, a perfect match with the biblical version of the mighty angel. Finally, the following entry is found in Revelations 10;

"Go; take the scroll that lies open in the hand of the angel who is standing on the sea and on the land." Again, the reality of the Statue of Liberty matches with the biblical reality as she too has an open book in her hands with the following inscription: '**July 4, 1776**', which confirms that the American nation is a satanic theocracy that worships Eve as their god, the Queen of the damned. This is not an opinion; this is a scientific presentation that shows that all the major American landmarks are in fact religious symbols, which leads to the conclusion that the United States government is in fact a Satanic Theocracy where Barak Obama, the antichrist would rise to power before he is humiliated and defeated by Jesus.

8 The World Trade Towers

The former Twin Towers of the World Trade Center symbolized the two pillars from the original temple of Solomon; they stood for Joachim and Boaz. Solomon built the temple of Jerusalem for Satan, in the name of the living God—he built it with the wrong dimensions and design. The two pillars in the temple of Solomon represent the legs of a man because in the camp of Satan, the temple of cedar is the last stage of evolution because Satan was cursed never to become a man; thus, the temple of Solomon represented a man, not a snake. The living God was angry at Solomon, the antichrist and destroyed the temple after 430 years.

However, those who worship Solomon continue to reproduce different versions of the temple. The person in the temple of Solomon can be a woman as well, as the four pointed star that is often captured in churches is based on the natural formation from certain maple trees—this natural formation is designed perfectly like a woman's vagina, a four pointed star, which the Jews turned into a six pointed star which they refer to as the Star of David. The four domes of the Taj-Mahal are like the four pointed stars from the tree of knowledge of good and evil from the Solomon's temple. The pillars of the temple are like the twin towers of the Champs Elysees in France and the twin towers of the Tower Bridge on the River Thames in London. However, in these last days, more and more buildings are being built with the architecture of the second temple, featuring the round or oval look of the pillar of offerings in the present Haitian Citadelle, like many churches and Universities are built to seduce the Haitian God. But, the way to please God is not to build a temple of cedar that is acceptable to him, but to do justice by treating everyone equally and by respecting and obeying his laws, his commandments and statutes. The totality of the evidence shows a perfect correlation between the American landmarks and the biblical landmarks—the American landmarks are in reality religious duplications of biblical landmarks. The reader must concede that this presentation shows a perfect correlation between biblical landmarks and American landmarks, which in the aggregate of the preponderance of the evidence helps conclude that in fact, the U.S. government is a Satanic Theocracy. The honesty of this evidence must be respected; if the evidence fits you must believe.

Chapter 7

The values of the Kingdom of God and those of the Kingdom of Satan

The American Constitution

The American Constitution is the most evil constitution that men have ever devised against the living God. It is the most evil document in the history of humanity. Solomon institutionalized white slavery in Haiti against the Law of Moses, which clearly stated that the alien and the Israelite were the same before the living God in the eye of the law and the alien needed to be treated the same as the Israelite, like King David did. King David treated everyone equally in Judah and Israel, including the aliens, the white Canaanites. And God found King David to be the best King in the history of the world and decided to give his throne to Jesus, his son. However, King Solomon violated the law of the living God, the Haitian Constitution, which was also the Constitution of the other Caribbean nations and the Constitution of the Confederate States of America, by turning white Canaanites into slaves. George Washington, Thomas Jefferson, Benjamin Franklin and the other founders of the American nation institutionalized slavery by making it part of the American constitution, making the American Constitution the most primitive, and the most evil document in world history. Just imagine that the U.S. Constitution makes slavery legal in America—slavery is the law in America—racial profiling is the law in America. According to article four of the U.S. Constitution, the nations of the north agreed to return all runaway slaves to the south by engaging in racial profiling. Every American institution recognizes and accepts the unequal treatment of blacks and some poor whites and other minorities in American societies. However, prior to the drafting of the U.S. Constitution, it has always been illegal to treat foreigners and aliens as slaves and second class citizens and wherever these practices had occurred within an Empire, they have always occurred in violation of the law, except in America. George Washington signed the first Runaway Slave Act during his second term as President to make 'Stop and Frisk' legal in America. And later Lincoln would continue the practice by pretending to free the slaves through the 13th Amendment, yet anyone who can read understands that the language of the 13th Amendment is not a language of freedom; it is the language of conditional slavery, which prompted Martin Luther King to say in 1963; **"100 years later, the negro is still not free."** Just because the American constitution is celebrated every day in the mainstream of American life, does not mean it is a good document. The American media often glorifies the evil and vilifies the good like they have vilified George W. Bush and glorified Dick Cheney, the author of all the evil policies of the Bush administration. Had George W. Bush not said, "I AM THE DECIDER" to stop Dick Cheney, the world would have been in worse shape than it is today. George W. Bush went to war in Iraq to stop Saddam Hussein, a true evil entity who had unleashed 22 years of non-top wars on humanity after he had invaded Iran, his neighbor to the east, to provoke a war that lasted from 1980 through 1988. And less than two years later in 1990, he invaded Kuwait, his neighbor to the south east, which led to the 1991 Gulf War against the United States. Saddam Hussein survived the 1991 war, but he allowed Bill Clinton to cowardly bomb Iraq from 1993 through 2000 in the doctrine of 'no boots on the ground'. Saddam Hussein did not back down from military conflicts with the U.S. and he did not resign—his actions caused the death of millions. The carnage continued until George W. Bush finally stopped the 22-year cycle of violence. But, instead of being honored for removing an evil man from the world scene, the American media vilified George W. George; however, when Obama and Hilary Clinton invaded Libya in 2011, and murdered hundreds of thousands of people and executed Qaddafi in the street, they were glorified, even though Qaddafi never invaded his neighbors and never represented a threat to the United States.

Everyone complains about the evil IRS and its power to tax Americans, but when George W. Bush gave a tax cut to everyone—they vilified him, but no one returned the money they had saved from his policies. Instead, they claimed that the tax cut was for the rich; they have corrupted the truth and the way of righteousness. To give a tax break to the rich is a good thing, it is not evil. To give a tax break to everyone is good because taxing anyone is evil. A real government does not tax its citizens because the king of the nation should use the natural resources of that nation to create revenue to meet the national budget. For example, the huge profits Exxon Mobile is making from its oil revenues actually belong to the American people—the American government leases the oil rigs from the Gulf of Louisiana and other places to domestic and foreign companies instead of operating the rigs themselves to create wealth for the American people—that is really evil.

It is not wrong to be rich and to receive a tax cut. There is a fundamental difference between a rich person who earns his fortune and a criminal who makes his fortune by stealing from the government, like the banker Obama has given the stimulus money to—this is the practice that should be opposed, not a tax cut. Slavery, racial profiling and discrimination are encouraged by the American Constitution as a matter of law.

The Values of the Living God versus those of Satan

God creates all things, but Satan seeks to amend the creation and the commandments of God;

God prefers honey Satan prefers milk;

The Values of the Kingdom of God and Those of the Kingdom of Satan

The children of God are fishermen—they eat fish, but the offsprings of Satan are hunters—they eat meat;

God prefers the trumpet, but Satan prefers the flute;

God wants each nation to live freely and independently, but Satan wants every people and every nation to live together in a global village;

God is loving and forgiving, but Satan is judgmental and unmerciful;

The true priest of God is a man, but the woman is the priestess of Satan;

God wants freedom for everyone, but Satan seeks to enslave everyone, even his own servant;

Chapter 8

The Ten Amendments of the Bill of Rights

The American Constitution is a document that supports slavery to create a world of half free and half slaves. To this end, everything about the American Constitution is the opposite of the freedom that is promoted in the Law of Moses. American historians have always advanced that American slavery was a southern institution to justify the Civil War, but in reality, American slavery has always been a partnership between the nations of the North and the Southern States. This partnership called for the Northern states to collaborate with slavery by returning all runaway slaves to their owners to the south. If the northerner agrees per the American Constitution to uphold slavery by returning runaway slaves to the south, then both, the northerner and the southerner are engaged in the promotion of slavery. Furthermore, American historians have also downplayed the fact that after the "Louisiana Purchase", which significantly expanded the boundary of the United States, Thomas Jefferson allowed the promotion of slavery in the new territory—this makes slavery an American institution, not a southern institution and slavery still exists in the United States today—the prisons have become the new plantations per the language of the 13th Amendment.

Moses gave the Hebrew Israelites the **Ten Commandments**, but the founders of the American Constitution gave Americans the **Ten Amendments**.

God commands, but Satan Amends.

The original commandment of God was given to Adam, but Eve amended it when she decided to listen to Satan who told her that she will not die if she ate from the Red Maple tree of the knowledge of good and evil. An amendment is usually a corruption of something good. It is the way of Satan, the way to perdition; it comes from Eve, Lucifer or the Statue of Liberty. However, God sometimes may decide to amend his own decrees. For example, God amended the decree that holds the son responsible for the sins of his father when he declared; "The soul that commits the sin is the soul that will die."

3 Amendment 1: the first amendment to the U.S. Constitution is an assault on the first commandment Moses gave to the Israelites, which states, **"Thou shall not have no other gods before me"**, but the first Amendment to the U.S. Constitution states that Congress shall make no law, respecting an establishment of religion, which means Congress shall not accept or recognize the First of the Ten Commandments of Moses as the laws of the United States and that every U.S. citizen could engage in the worshipping of any god he or she wishes, contrary to the commandment of God. Hence, the first amendment to the U.S. Constitution promotes polytheism, the worshipping of many gods, while the First Commandment of Moses emphasizes monotheism, the worshipping of the only true Haitian Living God. This also explains why the study of world religions is heavily promoted in America, while the study of the Bible is virtually forbidden in American class rooms and completely corrupted in American churches by homosexual pastors.

The first Amendment to the U.S. Constitution gives to the U.S. citizen the right of free expression, but in reality, this is not possible because a government cannot really survive if the values upon which it is founded are allowed to be openly attacked and criticized by its citizens. Freedom of expression is allowed in America only when that expression is in accordance with the values of the American government, which is a satanic theocracy constitutionally designed and committed to promote and reward the practice of polytheism. The U.S. government is in fact fundamentally opposed to the teachings of the living God. There is no real freedom of speech in the U.S. since it is forbidden in U.S. colleges and universities to speak about Jesus, the laws and the principles of the living God, it is the corrupted version of the Jews' Christianity, which is referred to as Judeo-Christianity that are being promoted in American academic life.

4 Amendment 2: the second Amendment is the right to bear arms. This amendment is the reverse of the silent commandment that promoted peace in Judah and Israel. Every nation has an army or should have an army of well armed men to protect the sovereignty and the freedom of that nation in times of war, but in times of peace, regular citizens should not be armed to protect themselves against their own neighbors and countrymen. This amendment to the U.S. Constitution was conceived to create a violent confederation, a confederation made of alliances among different people and nations where riots and mini Civil wars would break out among the people along racial lines every Sabbath. The second clause of the second amendment gives to the U.S. citizens the right to bear arms because Satan intended to create a violent and evil society to make it easier for human sacrifices to be offered through violence every Sabbath for the atonement of sins. This explains why there has been such a long and disturbing history of riots in the United States.

5 Amendment 3: the third Amendment to the U.S. Constitution states that military troops may not be sent to the private homes of American citizens without their consent in time of peace, but the government may do so in time of war. Again, this is no different than any other circumstance where private citizens are forced to sacrifice during the tragedy of war. If a government promises its citizens not to send troops to their homes in times of peace, but may do so in times of war, this is not really a right—again, this is a hoax.

6 The rest of the document, amendments 4 through 10, like 1 through 3 focuses on what the government will not do to the American citizens, even though they have done them any way; for example, the 4th Amendment promises to protect Americans against unreasonable searches and seizures, yet that promise, that American right is routinely violated, not just against blacks, but against other American citizens who are not rich and cannot afford the high price of American justice. And in many cases, the government uses its authority and power to violate the right of defendants who are rich and well represented.

The Ten Amendments tell Americans of the narrow ten rights they supposedly have and the rest belongs to the government, but the Ten Commandments tell the Hebrews ten things not to do and beyond that they are totally free to live as they please, as their God inspires them to live. The government of biblical Israel does not tell the Hebrew Israelites what rights they have, that is evil, it only tells them what not to do to avoid offending God so they might live and so they might prosper. Beyond the Ten Commandments, the living God gave Moses a number of regulations, decrees and statutes that all Hebrew Israelite citizens must observe; however, any law, regulation, statute or decree not expressed in the Israelite Constitution are reserved as total freedom to the average Hebrew Israelite.

7 Satan believes in a melting pot where everyone, every nation and every race live together, but God believes that each nation, people and tribe should live separately in their own land, their own nations and in their own communities. Before the framing of the U.S. constitution, there were the Articles of Confederation, which clearly meant that America was not a nation, but a coalition, a confederation of 13 states. These states came together primarily to form a military alliance against a common enemy—that enemy was supposedly England, but in reality, England was not the enemy of the Northern nations, it was and remains today the enemy of the southern nations. However, after the U. S. constitution was produced and adopted, America became an artificial nation as the former nations of the confederation were now forced to adopt and live by the values of the new constitution. The U.S. constitution creates a central government with supreme authority over the 13 nations and they each pledge to submit to that new authority and to also submit to its values. The 13 nations that made up the confederation, especially, the nations of the south, made a catastrophic error in assuming that they could embrace the new U.S. constitution and still remain sovereign and independent, but that was not possible. And ultimately, this mistake became evident when Abraham Lincoln told the Southern Confederate States of America that the U.S. constitution is supreme and that no state had the right to leave the union because the union is supposedly perpetual. To create this new nationalism, the U.S. engages in affirmative actions, forced bussing of blacks away from their own neighborhoods to white schools, and in many cases, the government has established different standard for different people in order to promote a multi-culturally society, but it is not working. The government cannot force people to love—social engineering does not work, which explains why blacks often score lower than whites in standard tests and why black poverty has increased in this apartheid experiment.

8 Satan believes in a pyramid where people are ranked from top to bottom—those in the bottom are slaves and second and third class citizens and those at the top are the overlords, but God wants a society without slaves where everyone can use his talents to climb the extreme heights of the pinnacle of success. God had not created everyone equal; everyone is unique and God has different relationships with different people and he uses his priests, his prophets as mediators between himself and the rest of the people. However, God wants a society where everyone is treated equally in the eye of the law. As God told Moses, "**you and the alien are the same before me**".

Chapter 9

The built-in duality of the universe—the nature of the Living God and Satan

1 The universe is created with a built-in duality. This duality has served to create a fusion of the elements of creation to ultimately produce a perfect creation over time. The original creation in fact, was only a platform for the evolution of many other creations, up to the ultimate and perfect creation, consistent with the scientific view of multi-verse.

The world was created and the world evolved; the story of creation is very clear—God created Adam the man and the woman Eve—evolved from his rib. The man is given control of the kingdom, but without the woman, he cannot succeed because she was made to complete him—the biblical account makes it very clear, **"it is not good for man to be alone**." This is a highly significant statement because prior to the creation of Adam, everything God created was good, including the creation of Adam. God created Adam in perfection and God was with Adam for the first 30 years of his existence, Adam was the perfect servant of God. In fact, the name Adam means my servant. Adam was full of life and he was fulfilled because God was with him and Adam took care of the Garden of Eden in Haiti as God commanded him. And Adam also named all the animals and did other works for God. However, as God was getting ready to withdraw from Adam, he made the observation that it is not good for man to be alone. This means a man is either with God in perfection as a holy servant of God or with a woman in near perfection. Thus for a man to achieve the holiest of tasks, he must leave the woman and must be totally devoted to God like Enoch, the seventh generation from Seth walked faithfully with God for 300 years after he had turned 65 when he had fathered Methuselah. The 300 years of faithful devotion Enoch had shown to God not only confirm that Adam served God faithfully for 30 years before God created Eve as a partner for him, but the number 300 also explains why the Jews pay 30 pieces of silver for the life of Jesus—the number 30, or 3 or 300 is the number of perfect servitude to the living God. Eve was supposed to complete Adam in the absence of God, but she decided to go rogue by listening to Satan. The evil woman serves Satan to satisfy her selfish and personal ambition of power, but the good woman works with her husband in a partnership that makes it possible for them to achieve whatever God put in their hearts and minds. Ultimately, the good woman is a mother because her relationship with her son is holy. In a perfect partnership, the CEO of a corporation should use his wife as the COO or in a very significant capacity to help the corporation succeed. The argument that a woman serves her husband by staying home is a corrupt argument and it should be dismissed completely. A woman should be involved in the affairs of her husband if he is to fully succeed in all his undertakings. God actually created Eve to play the same role that he himself played in the life of Adam prior to her creation. This means in fact, that the woman is a de facto god in the life of a man, but the man remains the priest of God, the leader of the partnership. A real partnership between a man and a woman is living together, raising children together, building together, dreaming together and succeeding together through the idea of natural duality between the man and the woman.

The duality is also expressed in the reality that each place in the western hemisphere is mirrored by another place in the eastern hemisphere. For example, the map of the United States is the perfect mirror image of the map of China, the map of Canada is the perfect image of the map of the former Soviet Union, the map of Russia and among others, the entire African continent is the perfect mirror of the South American continent—the duality of the universe continues.

This geographical duality helps give rise to the scientific concept of **"Entanglement of identical particles"**, which scientists explain as two identical particles of light that are separated by a vast distance and still whatever affects one instantly affects the other, like twin separated at birth chose the same career and the same lifestyle, even though, they are far apart. This duality is now very manifest in the events in Libya and Syria, whatever affects Syria also affects the United States because the Syrians and the Libyans are genealogically pegged with the American and the Caribbean Hebrews and as long as the Civil Wars are going on in Syria and in Libya, Obama and Hilary Clinton cannot provoke a Civil War in America or in Haiti.

The duality in the universe suggests two creations as expressed in the following:

2 The light and the dark; in the beginning there was darkness and God spoke saying, **"let there be light and there was light."** The nature of God and Satan is like a car battery where the servant of the living God is the positive pole, the light and Satan is the negative pole, the darkness. And God himself is the alternator, the source of the energy that powers the car battery. And as the battery emits enough balance electricity to power an engine through the positive and the negative poles, the forces of light and dark create a fusion over time to create a more perfect universe. However, the positive pole is the superior pole because the universe was created with the light of its spoken words.

3 Day and night: this duality expresses the same idea of light and darkness. There are 12 hours of day and 12 hours of darkness just as there are 12 children of Jacob and 12 princes descended from Ishmael—the kingdom of God comes from the 12 children of Jacob, the son of Isaac—the only legitimate child of Abraham. The children of the living God are the children of light, they are born during the day, but the offsprings of darkness are born at night. This also explains the fundamental flaw in the deception of the Christmas culture as we know it today in which the people of the world pretend to worship Jesus the son of God by singing "O Holy Night". This is a fundamental flaw because Jesus as the son of the living God was born during the day, not at night and there is nothing holy about the night. The night is naturally unholy, which also explains why Barak Obama, the antichrist signs every legislation at night—this is so because his deeds are the works of darkness and they must be accomplished during the night.

4 heavens and earth: the heavens are the world above and the earth is the world below. The heavens, up to the seventh heaven, the home of God are superior to earth because God rules over men and the armies of heavens are superior to all earthly armies. **Satan, the negative pole and his stars, his angels also lived in heavens before they were thrown down to earth by force in 1947.**

5 The sun and the moon: in this duality, the sun represents the man, the positive pole; life comes from the sun, and the moon represents the woman, the negative pole—the cycles of the moon directly correspond with the menstrual cycle of the woman.

6 the man and the woman: the man was created and God gave him one Commandment and later the woman Eve evolved from the man's rib and Satan gave her one Amendment by corrupting the commandment of God. Thus, the man Adam started his walk in the universe with God, but fell and the woman assumed the kingdom from him, but the kingdom she assumed was a kingdom of poverty and darkness—it took 1600 years (1600 Pennsylvania Ave) for the curse of poverty, the curse of Adam to be lifted. The woman started her walk with Satan, but later God secured good women like Sarah, Rebecca, Rachel, Ruth, Esther, the Virgin Mary, the mother of Jesus and many others to help bring great blessing to humanity, but they have all respected their roles.

7 a human being is formed by the contribution of 23 chromosomes from the mother and 23 chromosomes from the father—the duality creates a fusion.

8 the duality also extends to the human body; the human body is divided between the upper chamber and the lower chamber. The upper chamber is the part that contains the heart and the spirit of man or the woman. When a man or a woman is governed by the spirit from the upper chamber of the body, he or she is able to display the superior qualities and ideals of men. However, the lower chamber of the man or the woman contains the sexual organ and is primarily physical—the sex and the sexual activities are very important in the production of the things of the flesh and to make babies, but they are secondary to the spirit, which powers love, compassion and other virtues. The physical love of the flesh as expressed between a man and a woman is very different and subordinate to the love of the spirit as expressed between the mother and a son and between a father and a daughter.

9 This duality also extends to the right side and the left side of the man and the woman. The right side is the sign of life. The right side of the heart is much stronger than the left side of the heart. If a stroke originates from the right side of the body, it is more likely to cause more devastating damage than if it had originated from the left side of the body. The same goes to a heart attack that originates from the right side of the body. When people give blood, the blood should be drawn from the left arm, not the right. One should rarely allow any physician or medical personnel to draw blood from his right arm—it can be very damaging to the heart and could lead to death. The psalmist says to God; "**I know you will protect my right side**."

10 God separated the water above or fresh water from the water below or salt water:

God allowed Moses to lead the Hebrew children of Jacob out of slavery from Mexico by parting the salt water of the Red Sea, which is the Gulf of California, but Moses could not lead them to the Promised Land beyond the Mississippi River. 40 years later, God empowered Joshua, a more faithful servant to lead the children of Jacob through the fresh water of the Mississippi River to the Promised Land—the duality continues. The power of life is found in fresh water, not in salt water—the fish of the Sea are sustained by the oxygen from the fresh waters that travel within the Sea from the rivers of the Caribbean, from the triangle of Eden between Haiti, Cuba and Jamaica, including the true biblical Euphrates River, which is now called the Caribbean Sea. The Caribbean Sea is not really a Sea, but a river—this is why the waters of the Caribbean are so crystal clear,

The Atlantic Ocean crashes into the rivers of the Caribbean and this reality also explains why so many fish have been found dead all over the world in recent days—it is because Bill Clinton and Barak Obama have been poisoning the Haitian rivers with Agent Orange to kill Haitians with a disease they are calling cholera and to replace them with people from the Middle East, Europe and New York. Every intellectual from all American universities pretends to be smarter than everybody else in the world, but when fish started to die by the millions, everyone remains silent and pretends not to know the cause. The cause is simple; the rivers of the Caribbean travel from the triangle of Eden between Cuba to the west, Jamaica to the south and Haiti to the east—all the way to Africa, California, Europe and the Middle East. The Garden of God is located east of Eden, in Haiti as reported by the Bible and whenever Bill Clinton, Hilary Clinton and Barak Obama poisoned the rivers of Haiti to kill the Haitians, the waters travel and kill the wild lives within the Sea Dead fish have been found on many shores around the world recently including; Arkansas, Norway, Brazil, and California among many others. And countless human beings have been made sick or killed by eating contaminated fish and other products of the Sea and through contacts with the waters. The Haitians know the crimes of Bill Clinton as they have caught U.N. soldiers, poisoning the waters of Haiti. In addition, after a huge number of fish was found on the shore of a lake called Lake Azuei in Haiti; dogs in the area ate the fish and the dogs died because the fish were toxic. So if the scientists in the United States wanted to find out what is causing the fish of the Sea to die in such massive numbers they would have simply tested them—especially since a big number of black birds have also being found dead in many places. The birds died after they ate the fish—they died just like the dogs died in Haiti. The law is very clear and there is no law anywhere in the universe that gives Barak Obama, Bill and Hilary Clinton the authority to murder so many people and so many animals in the universe—and soon they will have to pay for their crimes.

11 The duality extends to the light of the stars in heaven—the brighter light of the 66.666% of the stars that remained in heaven after the fall of Satan and the smaller light of the 33.333% of the stars that came down to earth with Satan—the duality of creation continues. The 33.333% of the black stars of Satan are the animals, the dinosaurs that fought against the 66.666% of the angels of God in heaven as it is written, in the biblical book of Revelations 12, **"There was war in heaven. Michael and his angels fought, [but the evil beasts of Satan] fought back, but there were not strong enough and there was no place found for them in heaven."** This explains why planet Mars is as red as the Grand Canyon, the ruins of the biblical Sodom and Gomorrah. Just as the twin cities were nuked by God overnight, Mars was also nuked by God in an inter-galaxy war in which nuclear weapons were used to destroy Satan and to overthrow the dinosaurs from space to earth in 1947. The leaders of the American nation are the offsprings of the dinosaurs that crashed in Roswell, New Mexico and other parts of the world in 1947—these are the people that are being referred to as the 1% in American society, the people that have enslaved the world since they had arrived on earth.

The world is full of mysteries and just because someone appears to look like a human being does not mean he or she is a human being. People like Bill and Hilary Clinton and Barak Obama are not humans, they are animals. They are primarily dinosaurs camouflaged in human likeness to deceive the world. The original sin was in fact an animal takeover of the kingdom from a human being—Eve slept with an animal. This explains why the Bible states that after God had driven away Adam and Eve from the Garden of Eden, he made clothes for them from animal skin. This is a huge mystery. It means that they were bitten by the venom of the animal, the serpent and they were no longer human beings, they became animals, but God allowed their shame to be hidden in animal skin. This in turn really means that they were allowed to remain looking like human beings even though they had become animals. I was born in Haiti where life begins and where every event that occurred from the very beginning of time as recorded in the Bible is consistently repeated, therefore I make this revelation with a high level of authority and assurance as every Haitian knows that voodoo practitioners have turned ordinary people into animals—and in many cases, they have turned themselves into animals as well. In addition, the Haitian culture is rich with the testimonies of people who have experienced or have seen people turn into animals and animals turn into people. I know beyond any shred of doubt that Bill Clinton is an animal, otherwise why would the punk murder so many human beings to shed their blood as human sacrifices to Satan. For example, a Haitian woman who was living in Connecticut with her husband told the amazing story how one morning she woke up from her bed with her husband and she went to the bathroom, but when she returned to the bedroom she saw a donkey on the bed. Apparently, the man had neglected to take the usual measures on the night before to hide his real animal nature from his wife. The woman was horrified, but God helped her keep her composure and she quickly and quietly left the home and she never returned.

I could easily write a book to showcase the testimonies of Haitians that have experienced the most shocking spiritual episodes ever recorded. In another example, A Haitian woman who lives in New York personally told me that a serpent came to her at night and had sexual intercourse with her in her sleep, but she cried to him saying; "I am afraid of snakes"! Then he metamorphosed into a white man as he continued to have sexual relation with her. When she woke up, she found the physical evidence that showed that it was not a dream—his semen was still inside of her. This story is a classic repetition of the original sin where a snake metamorphosed into a white man to have sex with the black Eve. Again Bill Clinton, Hilary Clinton and Barak Obama are animals, they are not humans—they are inferior and the world they have created is an inferior world of violence, theft, lies; a world of half free and half slaves where animals live at the expense of human beings.

Exactly 13 years after these dinosaurs were overthrown to earth in 1947, John F. Kennedy was elected president of the United Sates in 1960. And soon he announced that the U.S. would launched a space program that would make it possible for Satan to return to heaven—this explains why the living Haitian God had engineered the demise of John F. Kennedy as punishment for the space program. The dinosaurs came from heaven with a lot of knowledge and between 1947 and 1961 the first manned space flight took place under John F. Kennedy, but from 1961 to 1975, just close to 30 years since the dinosaurs came to earth, a number of generations of space vehicles came to existence and the first international docking station was created, but Satan will once again be overthrown from space.

12 The western hemisphere and the eastern hemisphere. The word duality comes from the word duel, which suggests a struggle between two forces; the forces of light and the forces of darkness. This duel, this duality was expressed 101 years after the Great Deluge of Noah when God divided the earth; given Satan temporary control of the Eastern hemisphere and taken for himself control of the western hemisphere. The western hemisphere represents the man. It is richer and much less populated—the biblical Promised Land is on the American continent, in the western hemisphere. The eastern hemisphere represents the woman—it is larger in physical size and immensely populated, which means that the nations from the eastern hemisphere can never, ever catch up with the wealth of the U.S. and the Caribbean.

Haiti is the richest place on earth. This reality will never change. The southern nations of the Confederate States of America, like Texas, Louisiana and North Carolina are the richest nations within the United States as measured by their natural resources, not by their GDP. China could not compete with the United States, unless American businesses, together with the American government, conspire to transfer the wealth of the American people to China in the east, the eastern hemisphere. This shift began in 1972, after Nixon went to China to make a secret deal with the Chinese government to transfer the wealth of the United States and the control of the Confederate States of America to China. The traitorous goal of the American government is to steal from the western hemisphere to give to people of the eastern hemisphere—this explains why the welfare and the prosperity of the Jews and the Europeans have always been more important to the American government than the welfare and the prosperity of the American people and it also explains why America has always downplayed the existence of the other nations from the American continent, except Canada and Mexico, but overplayed the existence and the importance of the nations from the eastern hemisphere, especially Europe and Asia.

Consider this reality: The European immigrants came and got rich at the expense of black and white American Hebrews from the south. And then the Japanese immigrants came—after World War 2, the Japanese were allowed to produce cars that resembled Chrysler cars and to sell them to Americans.

Japanese car makers like Toyota decided to open auto manufacturing plants in Brazil and in the United States very early on because Japan does not have enough of the raw materials needed to produce their automobiles. Japanese automakers succeeded only and only because they were given cheap access to raw materials from the American continent and they were given access to the American car market. And worst of all, Japanese finance companies like Toyota credit were given full access to the American consumers. The American consumed foreign products like third world consumers and the Japanese prospered at the expense of the average American. The Japanese were the first to benefit from the wholesale transfer of American wealth to Asia after 1972; however, by the early 1980's, after American economists were sent to China to teach them about the American economic system, the ways of capitalism and after a number of Chinese began to arrive in America to study business management, economics and finance, American jobs started to shift to China. Japan brought its car factories to America to take advantage of the abundance of natural resources in America to make it easier and more cost effective to build their automobiles, but conversely, the American manufacturers have moved their factories from America to China to give the jobs, the prosperity of the American people to the Chinese and to take advantage of the cheap labor in China in the short-term. Interestingly enough, as the massive transfer of American wealth to China escalated in the 1990s, the economy of Japan has reached a maturation stage, which they called the 'lost decade', but the reality was simple—the continuous transfer of wealth from America to Asia had shifted from Japan to China. And as China grew economically at the expense of America, the Japanese economy has leveled. And now it is South Korea that is taking advantage of the American consumers by flooding the American auto market with Hyundais and Kias. The American workers have prospered because they have enjoyed the benefit of increasing wage growth from the early 1920s when Ford doubled the wages of his workers and the trend of sustained wage growth continued through the Second World War. However, after 1972, the trend has reversed and the American workers have faced an era of declining wages, up to the severe and terrible downgrade of American autoworkers 'wages in the Obama's negotiated General Motors bail-out, in which new autoworkers are paid wages as low as $14.00 an hour, while older workers' wages have been cut drastically. All of this happened because the American government is the enemy of the American people—they have willingly allowed foreigners from the east to dominate Americans and loot their wealth.

Chapter 10

The Numerology of Judgment and the Numerology of Kingdoms and Empires

The understanding of numerology is crucial to understand the ways of God, the judgment and the science in the war between good and evil. The numerology is the science behind the astrological struggle between God and Satan, it is precise and reliable. This is why it is written "there is a time for everything." For example, the Sabbath is the time when God personally interferes in the affairs of men on earth, without asking anyone's permission because he created the earth and the earth belongs to him. The inhabitants of the earth are the tenants of God, including Barak Obama, Bill and Hilary Clinton and they are about to be made to respect the creator of the universe.

The following are some of the key numbers found in the evil practice of human sacrifices by the illuminati in Washington D.C.

The #3; the number 3 is the number of slave, or the servant of God. In the science of numerology, when one or more zeros, like 30, 300, 3000, or more are added to the number 3, the voodoo still works. For example, the Jews paid Judas 30 pieces of silver for Jesus; Enoch walked with God in a slave like faithfulness for 300 years; he did not die and like Jesus, his body did not see decay, he was taken away alive to heaven.

#4 signifies a level of completion, a time of enlightenment. God created the sun, the moon and the stars on the 4th day. Isaac, the only legitimate son of Abraham was weaned on the 4th day—he no longer needed his mother's milk.

#5 God created living animals like the fish and the clean birds on the 5th day.

#**6** God created other animals on the 6th day and he also created man on the 6th day and the creation was completed and God rested on the 7th day.

#**7** the number 7 is the number of the Sabbath, the time when God personally interferes in the affairs of men to administer justice—to free those who have been taken captives as slaves and to restore their properties, their homes and their land. The fight that takes place between God and Satan on every Sabbath or every 7-year cycle is about freedom and the restoration of properties. God gave Moses instructions; telling him, if someone becomes a slave because of debt, he should not be slave for more than 6 years, on the 7th year he should be freed and his properties should be returned to him if he had lost or sold them. The bankruptcy concept of chapter 7 is based on the instructions God gave to Moses regarding the discharging of debt during the Sabbath, but the way it is used in the U.S. is largely satanic. This explains why many of the most powerful companies, including most of the companies Obama gave money to from the bail-out package have filed for bankruptcies—they have sought to eliminate their debts even though they are not poor and they can afford to pay their debtors who are often less well-off than they are. They have waited until the Sabbath year to shield themselves from their small creditors—these companies include American Airlines, General Motors and others—they have refused to pay their debts because Obama is their homosexual god and he has supposedly forgiven their debts, but Obama does not have the power to forgive the debts of criminal corporations and bankers on Wall Street. The number 7 is also the number of judgment and punishment; God said if anyone killed Cain he would avenge him 7 times, but he would punish Cain on the Sabbath for killing Abel. People often say that the number 7 is the number of completion but this is not the case since the Living God completed the creation on the 6th day.

The number 6 is the day of completion and since the Living God rested on the 7th day, on the day of the Sabbath, then the number 7 is the day of power, judgment and the worshipping of the Living God. This explains why God asks everyone not to do any work on the day of the Sabbath because this is the day for him to act and to do justice in the world he created.

#13 the number 13 is the number of a new beginning, a new covenant. It may also mean a break from domination, the kings of Sodom and Gomorrah revolted from Amraphel after serving him for 12 years. Ishmael, the illegitimate son of Abraham was 13 years old when he entered the covenant of circumcision in the first Bar-Mitzvah in history.

#26 the number 26 is a very important number. It is arrived at by 2*13 =26, Eve was 26 years old when Satan approached her in the Garden of Eden. This explains why some in the scientific world advance the view that a human being is fully developed at the age of 26. However, this only applies to the disobedient woman who would become the official priestess of Satan at the age of 26. This also explains why Barak Obama; the false prophet of Satan allows for young people to remain on their parents' insurance policy up to the age of 26. And this also explains why the number 26 is ubiquitous in the Jewish and the freemasonic voodoo used in Washington D.C.

#49 the number 49 is the number of the 7th Sabbath or 7*7=49; the year after the 7th Sabbath is the 50th year, the year of the Jubilee

On the year of the seventh Sabbath, God engages in a big fight with Satan, whoever prevails in the fight gets to judge during that Sabbath. The Sabbath is a time of war between God and Satan for the control and the direction of the universe until the next Sabbath. God wants justice and Satan seeks to advance the cause of darkness. This explains why there is an economic recession in

America every 7-year, but the recessions are more significant in the seventh Sabbath, like the 1930s' recession from the 1929 crash of the American stock market. And this also explains why every time there is an economic recession in America, it is accompanied by a housing crisis, the properties of the slaves—the innocent Americans—the blacks and the white Hebrews and other good and decent Americans. Again, the number 49 is the number of judgment, the judgment of the seventh Sabbath.

#50 the number 50 is the year of the jubilee, the year after the seventh Sabbath, the year of deliverance. In the year of the Jubilee, God proclaims a deliverance from bondage; every prisoner, every slave that has been held captive is released from bondage and their properties are returned to them.

Hawaii, the place where Obama grew up is the 50th state of the American union, the jubilee state; it symbolizes the final triumph of Satan. This has been heavily underscored in the American Television show Hawaii-5-0. Hollywood uses television shows and movies to communicate religious messages to Americans; T.V. shows like 'I love Lucy', as in Lucifer, to pave the way for the rise of Luciferian women like Madeleine Albright and Hilary Clinton in American politics; and movies like 007 as in the 700 women of Solomon; who, as the builder of Satan's temple, is really the real Bond, the action hero of Satan. Hawaii became the 50th state of the union on August 21, 1959 and precisely seven Sabbaths and seven days or 49 years and seven days later on August 28, 2008, Obama, the son of Hawaii received the Democratic nomination for president of the United States and a year later, on the 50th year, the year of the jubilee, he became president in 2009 to shed a jubilee of blood in America for the atonement of the people of the east, but he has failed because this Sabbath belongs to God, not to Satan.

The now classic movie entitled "Guess who is coming to dinner"; starring Sidney Poitier is about the story of Obama's father and his white Jewish mother. The movie points to the fact that the two met in Hawaii and the fact that the black man was an educated man as Obama's father attended Harvard University, but he was not as accomplished as the movie suggests.

Obama was born in Haiti to steal the wealth of Haiti for the people of Hawaii and the rest of the east. The words HAITI and HAWAII are almost the same: when the T is removed from HAITI and when the W is removed from Hawaii, the two words became respectively, HAII and HAAII; HAII means Eden or paradise and HAAII means hell.

#490 the number 490 is the number of the Super Jubilee—it is the number of judgment, but this judgment is for the control, the transition of one kingdom to another

Lamech, the 7th generation of Cain said to his wives that he had murdered someone and if Cain was forgiven 7 times, he will be forgiven 70 times 7 or 490 years—the notion of forgiveness has escalated.

#480 the number 480 is the most important number from 490 as the war; the contest for the kingdom begins on the 480th year, 10 years before the transition of one kingdom to another. The Hebrews spent 430 years, 400 of them as slaves in Mexico, the biblical Egypt, they also spent 40 years in the desert of the American Midwest and they spent ten years conquering the major part of the Promised Land and finally, they spent ten years, conquering and dividing the rest of the Promised Land, it took 490 years. It is also written that Solomon started to build his temple on the 480th year after the Hebrews left Mexico—the kingdom had changed hand from King David to Solomon. The evil temple Solomon built stood for exactly

430 years, the same number of years the Hebrews spent in Mexico mostly as slaves before God delivered them and punished Mexico.

The #600, like the number 6 is the number of completion. It is also the number of a profound transition from a significant punishment. Noah was 600 years old when the Great Deluge occurred. 600 is also the number of sacrifice—King David paid 600 shekels of gold for the site where Solomon built the temple of Jerusalem—Solomon paved the holy of holies of the temple with 600 talents of gold.

#40 the number 40 is the number of transition—a transition from one leader to another—from Moses to Joshua after 40 years. Goliath defied the army of Israel for 40 days and 40 nights before the young David killed him, hence assuring his eventual rise to the kingship of Judah and Israel by replacing Saul. Satan tempted Jesus for 40 days and 40 nights before Jesus defeated him, thus assuring Satan's eventual overthrow from heaven. Barak Obama accepted the Democratic nomination for the presidency of the United States in August 2008, exactly 40 years after the murder of Martin Luther King Jr. in April 1968, however, Obama was mistaken and presumptuous, he is not the one who is sent by God to further the work of Martin Luther King Jr. I, Harry Francois, am the one who is chosen by the living God—I am the faithful servant of Jesus, the only begotten son and the only Christ of the living God. And finally, among so many examples, it rained for 40 days and 40 nights during the Great Deluge which brought about prosperity back to earth.

#86 the number 86 is the number of transition from one priest to another or one covenant to another. 602 years after the birth of Noah on the 86th Sabbath (86*7=602) and two years after the flood, Arphaxad, the black son of Shem was born and a new covenant was made with Noah. Abraham was 86 years old when Ishmael was born. The number 86 is the number of the Jewish priesthood from Ishmael—this is precisely why the Jews play a significant role in American and world affairs, they are the descendants of a black man named Abraham, but they are illegitimate because Sarah, the black woman is the legitimate wife of Abraham, not the Jewish woman named Hagar and Isaac is the only legitimate son of Abraham. The number 86 is featured in all the significant moments in American history. For example, from 1776 when America was born as a nation to 1862 when Lincoln changed America forever as a nation by issuing the "Emancipation Proclamation" to shed the blood of the black Hebrews, it took exactly 86 years. From 1861 when the American Civil War started for the conquest of the Confederate States of the South, the real biblical Israel to the time the satanic version of Israel was created in the Middle East, it took exactly 86 years. From 1862 when Lincoln issued the "Emancipation Proclamation" to 1948 when the United Nations finally recognized the Middle East state of Israel, it took precisely 86 years and among so many other examples; from 1915 when the construction of the Lincoln Temple, the Lincoln Memorial began to 2001 when the towers of the World Trade center got destroyed it took exactly 86 years. This signals the beginning of the end of the American Empire. And perhaps most significantly, from 1922, when the Lincoln Memorial was inaugurated, to 2008, when Barak Obama received the Democratic nomination for president, it took precisely 86 years; which signals the end of the Lincoln era, but Barak Obama as a loser will not be allowed to replace him—Obama was born to lose and the Jews and the freemasons are now left without a god.

46 and 64 the numbers 46 and 64 are spiritually the same, but the key number is 46. It took 46 years to build the second temple of Jerusalem just as it takes 46 chromosomes to build a human being—23 chromosomes from the father and 23 from the mother.

The second temple of Jerusalem took precisely 46 years to build. A human being becomes truly completes at the age of 46 years old. And his body can now become the true temple of the living God. This revelation also confirms that Jesus did not die at the age of 33, he was over 46 years old when he died, but quickly got resurrected.

#99 and 66 the number 99 is the inverse of 66, Satan made the covenant of circumcision with Abraham when Abraham was 99 years old, the year Ishmael turned 13 years old—this explains why merchandises are often priced at $13.99 in the economic matrix of Satan. Jacob took 66 of his offsprings to Mexico, the biblical Egypt and from 66, they grew to become a nation when the number of male of fighting age reached 600,000, the same number of blacks Obama called to join his campaign when he accepted the Democratic party nomination in Denver, Colorado on August 28, 2008 and the same number of soldiers Lincoln murdered in the American Civil War. To murder 600,000 black men is to murder the nation of Judah and Israel because the nation was formed when the number of males of fighting age (20 years old) reached 600,000

#100 the number 100

The number 100 is vitally important. It is the number of Covenant between God and the black children of Shem—Shem was 100 years old, two years after the flood, on the 86th Sabbath after the birth of Noah when his son Arphaxad was born. Abraham was 100 years old when Isaac, his only legitimate son was born and the living God made a lasting covenant with Abraham through Isaac.

#110 and 101 the numbers 110 and 101 are one of the same; they represent power and authority—God divided the earth exactly 101 years after the Great Deluge of Noah and both Joseph and Joshua, each died at the age of 110. April 20 is the 110th day of the year and

April 19 is the 110th day of the year during leap years—sacrifices are offered on these days. In the movie the 'Terminator', the number of the robotic terminator played by Arnold Schwarzenegger was 101.

The number 480 is broken down as follows; **236+244=480** and

110+86=196+40=**236**+8=**244**

1176+86=1862+110=1972+40=2012 or 236 years

#19 the number of 19 is the number of betrayal—King David was betrayed by 19 soldiers plus a leader, a general. Francois Duvalier who typified a second coming of King David was also betrayed by 19 officers, but he executed them in public. The events of 09/11/01 were said to have been committed by 19 hijackers, but spiritually that can't be true—since 19 is the number of treason, it has to have been an inside job; it follows therefore that the events of 09/11/01 were perpetrated by Dick Cheney and 19 other personalities who made up a shadow government during the crisis, each taking the alias of an hijacker—these people must be found and they must be punished—they have murdered innocent Americans to advance the cause of darkness.

Haiti was betrayed on the 19th year of Nebuchadnezzar of New York or Babylon when he invaded Haiti and destroyed the Solomon temple—this explains why occupations of Haiti usually last no more than 19 years as a spiritual principle. The first American occupation of Haiti lasted 19 years from 1915 through 1934 and this latest Bill Clinton's occupation of Haiti has lasted from 1994 when Clinton invaded Haiti under the guise of returning Jean-Bertrand Aristide to office through the present, it would be exactly 19 years in 2013, but the last Haitian revolution has already started on January 12, 2010 when the earthquake hit Haiti and killed all the UN troops in Haiti. Obama has reinvaded

Haiti but these new troops will soon be defeated. Bill Clinton is desperately looking for a way to provoke a Civil War in Haiti at the end of 2012 because it has been precisely 19 years since he took office in 1993—this explains why he sought a ceasefire in Syria from October 26 through October 30, 2012, but no one listened to him, as fighting continued in Syria. Bill Clinton has been running America for 19 years, through Dick Cheney and through Obama. Bill Clinton thought Hilary was the false prophet and would be president in 2009, so he made a deal with Dick Cheney during the 2000 Florida disputed presidential election, in which they agreed that Dick Cheney would not seek the Republican nomination in 2008 to make it easier for Hilary Clinton to win the presidency and in return, Clinton would allow George W. Bush to win the election of 2000 and Dick Cheney were to become the most influential vice-president in American history and he was until George W. Bush said, **"I AM THE DECIDER".**

The numbers in the American experience are broken down as followed;

1776+86=1862, the year Lincoln signed the "Emancipation Proclamation"

1862+86=1948 the year the State of Israel in the Middle East was created. Bill Clinton and Barak Obama have exhumed the body of Yasser Arafat, the dead Palestinian leader on November 27, 2012 to find mystical satanic power to create their own version of Judah by giving the Palestinians their own state, but it will not work—the power and the authority of the Haitians will not be transferred to Palestine.

1948+46=1994, the year Bill Clinton invaded Haiti under the guise of returning Jean-Bertrand Aristide to office—46 years after the

Jewish State was created in the Middle East, Satan initiated a new occupation of Haiti, another 19-year occupation of Haiti.

1948+64=2012 from 1948, after the creation of the state called Israel in the Middle East, Bill Clinton invaded Haiti in 1994 to initiate another 19-year occupation of Haiti and 18 years within the occupation in 2012, Bill Clinton, Barak Obama and Hilary Clinton hope to take over Haiti like the Jews took over Palestine after the second World War. Bill Clinton and his people have already informed the Haitians that a "massive group of investors" are about to come to Haiti, but in reality every foreigner who has gone to Haiti under the advice of Bill Clinton after the January 12, 2010 earthquake will have to leave Haiti very soon or they will perish—the last Haitian revolution is about to begin without apologies.

1862+60=1922, since the number 60 or 600 is the number of a profound transition from a significant punishment like the deluge of Noah; the Lincoln Memorial was completed exactly 60 years after the 1862 Emancipation Proclamation through which Lincoln murdered the people of the Confederate States of America.

1922+86=2008, the year Obama got elected to renew the covenant of Ishmael to another 86 years, but he has failed.

1915+86+2001, from 1915 when the building of the Lincoln Memorial began to the events of 09/11/01, it took exactly 86 years, which means that since September 2001, the kingdom of God had begun to shift from America back to Haiti, the Caribbean and the Confederate States of America—Obama was selected to win the war of Afghanistan, the biblical Armageddon to save the American Empire, but he failed—Obama is a loser and a loser cannot win.

1862+110=1972, 1972 was the year Nixon went to China to begin the wholesale transfer of the American wealth to China and the rest of Asia—Nixon went to China because the American presence was already strong in Japan and in South Korea—the history is clear and the numerology does not lie.

1972+40=2012, the year 2012 is supposed to be the year when Obama and Bill Clinton would have completed the transfer of American authority to China by provoking a Civil War in America, but obviously they have failed.

A typical year is divided in Washington D.C. between 196 and 169 days, or 196 and 196 days when 27 more days are added to 365, leading to January 27 of the following year. In the first 100 days, more precisely the first 100 days after January 10 or the first Sabbath (Leviticus 23) or the 110th day of the year or April 20 when human sacrifices are offered to Satan. 110+86=196. 86 days after April 20 lead to July 15 or the Feast of Weeks (Leviticus 23). This is the first half of the calendar year. However, the second half is divided the same way. 110 days from July 15 lead to November 2, around the time of elections in the United States and 86 days later lead to January 27 of the following year, the time for either the inaugural speech for a new administration or the second Inaugural Address by an incumbent president. Hence, the numbers 236 and 244 are found as follows in a typical calendar year; 110 days or April 20 plus 86 days, leading to the 196th day of the year or July 15, the Feasts of Weeks begin and last seven days and human sacrifices are offered in Washington D.C. for the atonement of sins and end on the eight day, according to Leviticus 23. For example, on July 16, 2012, a U.S. Navy boat opened fire on Indian fishermen from the coast of the United Arab Emirates, killing several of them without warning and without provocation—the U.S. offered them as human sacrifices to Satan.

Forty (40) days after July 15, on the 236th day of the year to August 24 or Ramadan, the time when the U.S. Congress goes away on vacation to worship Solomon like the Moslem worship Solomon and Hagar. The U.S. Congress takes the whole month of August off just like the Moslem—this is so because they are quietly worshipping Solomon, but pretend to worship Jesus. Elvis Presley was killed as a human sacrifice on August 15, 1977, the Catholic Day of the Lady of Assumption, during the week of Ramadan by Jimmy Carter. And lastly, 8 days later, the 244th day of the year typically falls on September 1, or on September 2 during the leap year, which is the time of Rosh Hashanah, the Jewish Holiday. The way to know that a nation is worshipping Satan is when they observe holidays whose dates change every year based upon the position of the moon or the sun, not based on historical facts.

110+ 86 = 196 or July 15, the Feasts of Tabernacles, the start of a religious holiday that lasts until July 22 and human sacrifices are offered to Satan (Leviticus 23; 33-35). Bill Clinton offered the women and children of the TWA-800 flight as human sacrifices to Satan on July 17, 1996 by shooting down the plane and on July 16, 1999, Bill Clinton offered John F. Kennedy Jr. and his family as human sacrifices to Satan.

196 + 40 = 236, or August 24, the week of Ramadan

236 + 8 = 244 or September 1; the Jewish holiday of Rosh Hashanah often falls on the week of September 1, depending on the position of the moon.

The Second tranche of 196 days is also divided between 110 and 86, starting from July 15

110 days or the 306th day of the year or November 2; the perfect time for a hunter to offer human sacrifices to Satan because of the alignment of the stars—the day of the dead, the week of Halloween and the time of elections in America where Americans are tricked by politicians in Washington.

From **July 15** to **November 2** = **110** days and from November 2 through **January 27** of the following year = 86 days or 196, the second tranche of 196 days of the calendar year.

Chapter 11

The Three Passovers and the Liturgy of the First 100 Days

According to the dictionary, a liturgy is a rite or body of rites prescribed for public worship. It is also defined as a customary repertoire of ideas, phrases and observances. Consistent with these definitions, the culture of the first-100 day in Washington D.C. amounts to a liturgy, a religious practice. And it was based on these customary repertoires of ideas that Joe Biden guaranteed that Barak Obama would be tested in his first 100 days in office and indeed, Obama was tested with the Somali pirate crisis in which Obama gave his first official order to kill black Africans for the atonement of the sins of the elite. Just as Joe Biden had predicted, the crisis came in early April 2009 and lasted around April 12, 2009 and on April 20, 2009, exactly on the110th day of the year, and precisely 100 days after the first Sabbath, Obama brought a young black Somali pirate to New York, to Babylon for trial as a pirate, a terrorist. Joe Biden was right because he knew about the culture of human sacrifices in the first 100 days of the year after the first Sabbath as stipulated by the biblical book of Leviticus in chapter 23.

The religious murders that have taken place on April 19, 20 and on July10, 15 through 23 and on August 15, 23 and 24 and on June 24 and on September 1 through September 11, based on the position of the sun and the moon are consistent with religious biblical rituals and all the victims are offered as sacrifices for the atonement of sins—as it is written in the biblical book of Hebrews, **"Without the shedding of blood, there is no forgiveness of sins".**

The three Passovers

The American pastors are largely liars; they have conspired with the illuminati to corrupt the truth as written in the Bible by remaining silent as different versions of the Bible are introduced every year. How is it possible for one story to have so many different versions? This happens because each season, as God is prepared to fulfill the prophecies in the Bible, the illuminati change the truth into a lie so that ordinary people cannot see the fulfilment of prophecies, and so that Satan can fulfill the lie, instead of God fulfilling the truth, but in the end, the truth prevails.

The American pastors are the allies of the American government. The IRS made a deal with the Church to allow the Church not to pay taxes, provided that the pastors do not criticize the government while they are preaching on the pulpit. This agreement to turn their eyes away from the crimes of the U.S. government amounts to a complete sell-out of the truth of God by the pastors in America—they have chosen money over the truth and rejected the truth of God. In addition, the pastors are allowed to buy cars, private planes, helicopters and big mansions under the name of their churches to avoid paying personal income taxes. The pastors are also exempt from paying taxes on major purchases like Jewelry and other luxury goods. The U.S. government would not have allowed all these tax breaks for the church, if the pastors were not the servants of the U.S. government. Even the major American Universities are also engaged in the religious lies. While the so called intellectuals from the American Universities pay lip service to the concept of separation of Church and State, in fact most of the universities are built like churches and most of them have churches on their campuses—the University of New Haven actually has a Mosque on its Campus—a church built exclusively for students of Islamic faith, while many pretending to be against the Moslem.

1 the first Passover

A Passover is, in essence, the shedding of blood for the atonement of sins to evade punishment. The pastors have failed to tell the American people that the first Passover occurred when God put a 'Mark' on Cain's forehead with the blood of Abel, after Cain had murdered Abel. This act of mercy established a de facto covenant of human sacrifices—Cain found protection in the blood of his own victim. This is why politicians in Washington murder people as human sacrifices for their protection every Sabbath, Jubilee and super Jubilee. This was what Lincoln did during the American Civil War and this is what Satan elected Obama and Bill Clinton to achieve in this Sabbath, but they will not succeed, this ancient primitive practice of human sacrifices has come to an end in 2012. Cain was brought forth into existence by the will of Satan who impregnated Eve, the wife of Adam. Cain was obviously illegitimate and as such he had no right to exist, unless he could exist at the expense of Abel. So he decided to kill Abel under the inspiration of Satan. By killing Abel, Cain actually made a human blood offering to the living God just as Abel had made an animal blood offering to God. So even though God was angry at Cain, and even though the avenger of blood was angry at Cain, once God put the blood of Abel on Cain's forehead, the avenger of blood was pacified and he did not kill Cain and this became a de facto covenant of human sacrifice, which is still being practiced today in Washington D.C. by people like Barak Obama, Harry Reid, Nancy Pelosi, John Boehner, Bill and Hilary Clinton and others who seek primarily to murder the Haitian, then the black American and then the black African every Sabbath for the atonement of their sins, but this Sabbath the criminals will be punished for their crimes against humanity. The Catholic Church practices human sacrifices. The Catholic Church was first founded in Salem, Massachusetts, and Melchizedek was the first Pope of the Church.

2 The second Passover

This Passover is better known because it involves animal sacrifices, not human sacrifice. It was first used by Abel when he offered a lamb as a sacrifice to God, even though he was righteous, but God was angry at his parents. However, Moses later instituted the animal Passover in Mexico on the night before God killed every first born of Mexico as punishment for enslaving the children of Jacob for 400 years. The first born of every womb usually belongs to Satan in his doctrine of pre-emption, which started when Satan slept with Eve to produce Cain before Adam could father Abel with his wife Eve. Moses was instructed to tell all the Hebrews to kill a lamb and to put its blood on their doorposts and at midnight when the avenger of blood came and saw the blood on the doors, they passed over the houses of the Hebrews, but they killed the first born of the Mexicans. No one should exist at the expense of another human being or even an animal. Whenever one eats the flesh of an animal, like a Cow or a chicken, one partakes in the Passover of Moses—a disciple of Jesus should eat living animals like fish and clean birds, grains and vegetables, he should not eat animal flesh.

Breaking News:

Abel pre-instituted the first animal Passover

The word from the church has always been that God had accepted the animal sacrifice from Abel, but not the first fruits offering from Cain, but the fact is what the Bible meant to convey and actually expressed is that Abel's offering was proper because it was an offering of blood—no one can receive forgiveness without the shedding of blood. But, ultimately, even though Abel's offering was proper, it was not accepted because he failed to find protection from God as Cain was allowed to kill him. Strangely enough, Cain found forgiveness and protection in the blood of Cain. However, the covenant of animal sacrifice was later instituted by Moses and the entire nation of Israel was saved through the blood of the animals they had sacrificed to God.

3 The third and lasting Passover

Finally, the third Passover was pre-instituted in Haiti by Abraham and Melchizedek when Melchizedek gave wine and bread to Abraham after Abraham had defeated a number of kings in battle. However, after Jesus defeated Satan and his spiritual demons, he officially instituted the third Passover on the night of the last Supper, giving bread and wine to his disciples—the bread symbolizes his body and the wine symbolizes his blood. Jesus, unlike Moses and Abel, offered his own blood for the atonement of sins, not the blood of another—he was the lamb that suffered, not an animal, not another human being. The third Passover is significant because as the lamb, the victim was resurrected by the living God, he did not remain among the dead—he lived. Therefore, those who receive salvation from his blood have no guilt and most of all the blood sacrifice Jesus made is eternal, it does not have to be repeated every year.

It is satanic for people not to accept the blood of Jesus for the atonement of their sins. The people in Washington have refused to accept his blood for the atonement of their sins because they have refused to accept the ways of righteousness. But they prefer to find temporary salvation in the Covenant of Cain, the Passover of human sacrifices to placate God's anger and to continue in the path of darkness. However, the covenant of Cain, the Passover of human sacrifices has come to an end. The time for righteousness in the covenant and the Passover of Jesus has fully come. This presentation will continue to show a consistent pattern, a perfect match between the biblical prescription for sacrifices and the crimes committed by actors in Washington, notably, Barak Obama,

Bill Clinton and Hilary Clinton and will conclude that the liturgy of 100 days cannot continue in Washington or anywhere else in the world because it is wrong for one human being to offer another human being as sacrifice for the atonement of his sins—the living God will no longer allow Satan to accept the blood of the innocents for the salvation of criminals like he did with Cain over Abel. The Liturgy of the first 100 days is found in the following events:

- The April 20, 1812 invasion of Russia by Napoleon,
- The April 20, 1861 naval explosion in the first military engagements of the American Civil War,
- The April 19, 1993 Waco fire that followed a 50-day siege that led to the murder of 86 people, including women and children and the unborn by Bill and Hilary Clinton,
- The April 19, 1995 Oklahoma City Bombing that killed 168 people by Bill and Hilary Clinton,
- The April 20, 1999 murder of 13 young people from Columbine High School in Littleton, Colorado,
- The April 20, 2010 oil leak in the Gulf of Mexico engineered by Barak Obama and Hilary Clinton. And among so many other incidents, the fail attempt by Barak Obama and Hilary Clinton to murder Michelle Obama through an airplane 'accident' on April 19, 2011. This pattern is consistent with a religious practice, the practice of human sacrifices in the first 100 days of the year.

Chapter 12

Obama is the Antichrist Prophesied in the Bible: He Came to Provoke a Civil War in America

This part of the presentation will expose Obama as the biblical false prophet as it will show a perfect biblical pattern in the actions and policies of Obama.

Barak Hussein Obama is the biblical antichrist prophesied in the second book of Thessalonians in the second chapter. Barak Hussein Obama is a murderer, a thief, a corrupt Dracula; a foreign born criminal who came to murder innocent American citizens and other citizens of the world for the atonement of the sins of the elite. Like he is doing in Haiti, Afghanistan, Pakistan, Yemen, Libya, Syria, Iran, Sudan, South Africa, Nigeria, Mali and other places in fulfillment of the "Great Tribulation" prophesied in the Bible. The second book of Thessalonians also refers to the rise of the antichrist as an enterprise of lies and deceptions. And indeed the rise of Barak Obama to office is based on total lies and fabrications. Obama was born in Haiti, not in Hawaii, or Kenya—this explains why he cannot show his birth certificate because Haiti and the Haitians have been totally vilified in America. In addition, Obama is a college drop-out, he never attended Columbia University—the New York Department of Education does not have Obama's records from Columbia University and Obama does not have graduation pictures to prove he graduated from Columbia University. Obama is dumb—his dumbness was exposed when he lost all three presidential debates to Mitt Romney, even though Mitt Romney shares Obama's satanic vision and was not looking to really separate himself from Obama. The issues that were debated never addressed the concerns of the American people, but rather the concerns of Jews from the Middle East state called Israel and the concerns of Europeans, Chinese and other people from the eastern hemisphere. Obama is so clueless about the details of the issues a real president has to deal with every day that he became the first president of the United States to be given a full-time teleprompter to manage what he says in public. Obama travels to New York once or twice a month to consult with Bill Clinton who tells him what to say in his teleprompter, prompting some to conclude, **"There is no grown up in the house**." Obama also lies about his health and arrest records as well; the mulatto Dracula is a complete liar.

Barak Obama is in fact the second coming of Barak, son of Zippor, the king of the MOAAB nation that sought to curse the Hebrew nation of Israel while they were in the plain of MOAAB along the Jordan River, after they left Egypt in the Great Exodus (biblical book of Numbers 22), but the living God turned the curse into a blessing. This is very clear; a king named Barak, in some Bible translations, it is spelled Balak, in a place called MOAAB, in some Bible translations it is spelled MOAB; it is spelled MOABA in the Russian Synodal version. King Barak sought to curse the Israelites—this is an historical fact, not an opinion. And the fact that king Barak ruled in a place called MOAAB leads to BARAK of MOAAB or BARAK OBAMA. Everyone in the world must accept this reality as a biblical historical fact that the name of Barak Obama matches perfectly with the name of King Barak who ruled in a place named MOAAB. The nation of MOAAB came from Lot, the nephew of Abraham, the one Satan sent with Abraham when God called Abraham out of Africa to Hai, or Haiti. Satan sent Lot with Abraham to steal the blessing of Abraham and his children. After God destroyed Sodom and Gomorrah, whose ruins created the Grand Canyon in Arizona, the two daughters of Lot, each gave him alcohol and slept with him; the first one had a son named MOAAB or OBAMA and the second one had a son named Ammon, to create the Ammonite nation. Thus, there are three nations of blacks in America; the Hebrew children of Jacob make up the holy nations of the Caribbean, including Judah in Haiti and the Caribbean and the Israel nation of the Confederate States of America, the nations of the south, with the exception of Florida. These black Hebrews were known as "Negroes" in Mexico because they are blacks and black is translated as Negro in Spanish. The evil nation of Moaab existed between Southern Utah, part of Colorado, Wyoming and the southwest of Nebraska—in fact, a small town named Moab with the one (a) spelling, still exists in Utah.

The area of Omaha, Nebraska was also part of ancient Moaab—when the (h) is replaced by a (b), the name Omaha becomes Omaba or Obama, or Moaab, this explains why Warren Buffet, the sage of Omaha is so closed to Obama—Buffet is a white Moaab. This also explains why Obama's Jewish mother originated from the same area, in Kansas, the biblical Midian nation. My version of history makes sense because it is grounded in evidence, not speculation or speeches like the Jewish version. It also matches with today's reality, even after hundreds of years. Today, most of the black Moaabs like Oprah Winfrey and Jesse Jackson live in Chicago, the biblically violent place where the evil blacks conspired with the Romans and the Jews to arrest Jesus without cause. This also explains why the most evil antichrists like Abraham Lincoln, Obama and Hilary Lincolnt or Clinton have roots in Chicago. Meanwhile, the Ammonites, the other nation that descended from the other daughter of Lot are scattered all over the place, many live in the south like Herman Cain and a significant number of them were moved to Philadelphia and the island of Jamaica. This reality exposes the danger of racism and the politics of race because the primary enemies of the black Hebrews, the good American, Jamaican and Haitian blacks are the evil black Semites from the nations of Moaab and Ammonite; hence, the term, "blacks on blacks.". These black Moaabs are criminals; they can be identified by their actions; the life they live and the inferior music they create. A great number of them are allowed to succeed in the evil ways of mainstream America. They are responsible for the worst rap music the world has ever heard—music that are dominated primarily by the vocal sound, not by the true artful and intelligent synchronization of vocals and instruments. Satan used them to denigrate women in their music lyrics, to promote evil and to totally destroy everything that is good and decent in society. These evil blacks, the OBAMAS, or the MOAABITES and the Ammonites engage in criminal gang activities, violence, including murders; they engage in evil drug dealings and all sorts of abominations, they help promote homosexuality, indecencies and filth in American society. Many of them are rich artists and athletes, but the more money they make, the more crimes they commit. Satan use them as the wrong role models to destroy the image of the good American black Hebrews. Race is not a cause because God only cares about righteousness and justice; but it is important to identify the real black and white children of Jacob because salvation comes from them.

Barak Obama returned to life in America in the power of the mulatto Solomon to do to the black and the white American Hebrews what he attempted to do to their forefathers three thousand years ago—his goal is to shed the blood of the American innocents through a Civil War in an operation called "**Bottom Kill**".

Solomon is in fact the antichrist, the builder of the house of Satan, the first Haitian Citadelle. Solomon is the mulatto son of Satan; he was given the power of Cain, the mulatto first born of Satan who was brought forth in a forbidden coupling between the black Eve and the white serpent from the tree of the knowledge of good and evil. Hence, the very first entity who was given birth by a woman, by Eve was Cain, the evil mulatto son of Satan. He was just like Solomon, the mulatto son of the black king David with a foreign white woman, a descendant of Ham, just like Barak Obama is an evil mulatto descended from a black Semite and a white Jewish woman. Obama came in the power, the spirit and the authority of Solomon, the antichrist, the ultimate enemy of the living God.

5 Williams Jefferson Clinton is the beast of this age, the white son of Satan. Williams Jefferson Clinton is the beast, the second coming of Lincoln—the names Lincoln and Clinton are the same (CLINTON or LINCONT), Clinton took the name of his step father in a practical Bar-Mitzvah after he turned 13 years old and in the process, he was given the name and the spirit of Abraham Lincoln with the same mission to help Obama provoke another Civil War in America. The Obama presidency is the third and fourth terms of Bill Clinton—this explains why Obama comes to New York every month, sometime as many as twice and three times a month. Bill Clinton is the beast, Barak Obama is the false prophet and Hilary Clinton is the wife of the beast with the power of Lucifer to whom the authority of the original black Eve was transferred. As Secretary of State, Hilary Clinton is the channel between Bill Clinton and Barak Obama—Hilary Clinton is the second coming of Hitler—the names Hitler and Hilary are the same—they mean shepherd. Bill Clinton has the name of the founders of the two versions of the American nations. He has the name of Jefferson, as in Thomas Jefferson, the writer of the preamble of the U.S. constitution, one of the founders of the American nation, and he also has the name of Abraham Lincoln, the father of the second phase of the American nation, which started in 1862 after Lincoln issued the "Emancipation Proclamation", exactly 86 years from 1776. Bill Clinton has been given the spirit, the understanding and intellectual knowledge of Jefferson and Lincoln. Bill Clinton is also a second coming of Christopher Columbus as well; Clinton received the Democratic nomination for president of the United States in 1992, exactly 500 years after Columbus invaded Haiti in December 1492. And after Clinton became president in 1993, he invaded Haiti in 1994, exactly 502 years after Columbus had invaded Haiti. Clinton came to renew the Columbus era, but the Christopher Columbus era has come to an end. Clinton is like the King, and the mulatto Obama is the priest. He has been given the authority and power of Solomon and Cain—this explains why after Bill Clinton failed to pass the Health Care PPACT, Obama passed it in the power and the authority of Solomon. The Obama-Clinton relationship is like the Moses and Aaron relationship or the same relationship the Pharaoh of Egypt had with Joseph; one had the authority and the other had the knowledge, Bill has the knowledge and Obama has the authority and Hilary Clinton is the channel between them with the authority of Lucifer, Hilary Clinton is the second coming of Hitler, she is extremely evil, the three of them make up the Trinity of Evil.

On February 10, 2007, Obama announced his candidacy for president of the U.S. in Springfield, Illinois at the very same place where Abraham Lincoln gave his **'House Divided'** speech and he invoked Lincoln during his speech. The place was obviously significant to the history of the American Civil War and the date had significance as well; on February 10, 1600, God spoke to Noah, telling him to get on the Ark with his family because he was about to send the waters of the Great Deluge in 7 days, on February 17, 1600. Obama used that very same place to launch his political career in 1997, and he returned to that same place to introduce Joe Biden as his Vice-presidential running mate. Symbolism matters, Obama has engaged in these rituals because he came to duplicate the actions of Lincoln; he came to provoke a Civil War in America just as Lincoln did in 1860 by provoking the southerners to succeed from the Union. The only reason South Carolina seceded from the union was because of the election of Abraham Lincoln—these are facts, not opinions and the angels of God will not apologize for stopping Obama—no one, no nation or nuclear power can stop the imminent judgment of God—God wants Obama out of office—God wants Obama in prison.

On August 28, 2008, 86 years after the building of the Lincoln Memorial and exactly 40 years after the assassination of Martin Luther King in 1968, Obama issued his own "Emancipation Proclamation" in Denver, Colorado by calling on 600, 000 African Americans from Florida to join his campaign. He did so because Lincoln murdered over 600,000, to be exact, 627,000 American soldiers during the American Civil War. Again this is not an opinion, it is a fact. Obama issued an "Emancipation Proclamation" on August 28, 2009. Obama and the Democratic Party actually moved the Democratic convention venue to INVESCO Field, something that has never been done before in the history of American political conventions and they built a replica of the Lincoln Memorial so Obama could assume the position of Lincoln as the next American god.

On the night Obama received the Democratic nomination for president, he stood as the next Joshua, the faithful servant of God who replaced Moses 40 years after the Haitian and the American Hebrews left Mexico. Martin Luther King was the second coming of Moses, so Obama presented himself as the leader who would replace Martin Luther King to lead the people of God to the Promised Land like Joshua led the Hebrews to the Promised Land after Moses wandered in the desert with the Hebrews for 40 years. But, unsuspectingly, Obama is a Jewish demon, a predator, a liar, a deceiver and a murderer who came 86 years after the building of the Lincoln Memorial as the next Lincoln to devour the Hebrew people of God by shedding their blood for the atonement of the elite like Lincoln had murdered their forefathers.

On January 22, 2009, the day after Obama retook the oath of office on January 21, 2009; Alcee Hasting introduced HR645 to the U.S. Congress, a bill that gave FEMA the funding to build at least six concentration camps on military ground to be operated in case of natural disasters or national emergencies. The Bill is called HR645 because Eugene Webb helped provoke the first American national strike, a mini American Civil war in 1894 by creating a new union with 465 chapters. The strike gave the U.S. government the excuse to murder hundreds of thousands of American citizens to satisfy the blood sacrifice that was needed on the fifth Sabbath after the 1862 "Emancipation Proclamation" or 32 years later. Why would such a bill be introduced to Congress the very day after Obama took office? The answer is simple; the bill gave funding to FEMA to build concentration camps to protect the elite in case of 'national emergencies' like riots and race wars if Obama were to prevail; otherwise, the nation should prepare for natural disasters like the Tornadoes that hit Joplin and the Hurricanes that hit the Northeast like Irene and Sandy, if Obama were to lose. And since Obama has lost, the riots and the race wars have not materialized; instead, it has been all earthquakes, tornadoes, hurricanes, but the worst earthquakes and fire from heaven are yet to come. Consistent with HR 645, Obama told Police Departments across the country to expect huge spikes in violence, but the violence never came—God recalled the demons of Obama and sent them to the Middle East. This explains why Obama and Hilary Clinton have been so busy trying to crush the spirit of resistance that has awaken against Satan in Egypt, Libya, in Syria, in Somalia, in Mali, in Congo and other parts of Africa; and in Afghanistan, in Yemen, in Haiti and all over the world. When Obama realized he is a loser, he and his people have started to quietly inform Americans to prepare for natural disasters. Many local and state governments and all major American universities have sent e-mails to students, informing them of what they need to do in case of natural disasters, they call it "Climate Change". But that is not good enough, every American must know that Barak Obama is responsible for the natural disasters that have struck America like hurricane Sandy and the worst is yet to come, including a huge earthquake that will divide America in three and thus dissolve the American alliance forever.

The Noah simulation of destruction

Obama has also been engaged in a number of war simulations, consistent with the Great Deluge of Noah.

To begin with, the Hollywood supporters of Obama are planning to begin filming a movie named Noah next year in 2013—what a coincidence.

Secondly, a number of Acronyms found in the title of some of the key Obama legislations confirm, in Obama's own words, that he is planning a Civil War in America.

Patient

Protection

Affordability

Care

A

C

T

PPACT or PACT as in a PACT of BLOOD with SATAN

In his own words, Obama confessed that his so called Health Care legislation is in fact a PPACCT of blood with Satan to provoke a Civil War in America—this explains why Joe Biden called the passage of the act, a big (...) deal—this also explains why Bill and Hilary Clinton could not pass their version of Health Care—they had to wait for the false prophet of Satan to come.

The following acronyms are found in Obama's stimulus package:

American

Recovery

And

Reinvestment

A

C

T

Ararat and mene

These two words found as acronyms in the title of Obama's stimulus package are found in the Bible in the context of destructions. The word Ararat first emerged when the Ark of Noah came rested on the mountain of Ararat in Haiti on July 17, 1600, exactly 5 months after the flood of Noah started on February 17, 1600. So why has Obama chosen the word Ararat for an acronym in the title of his stimulus? Or is it an accident? The answer to the second question is emphatically no! As the evidence will continue to show, it is not an accident—Obama is willingly and cold bloodedly engaged in war simulations to provoke a Civil War in America.

Moreover, the word MENE is also found in the Bible in the context of destruction. The word MENE was part of the famous Hebrew writing on the Wall in Babylon. God sent a hand to write on the wall of the Babylon Palace the following message to the son of Nebuchadnezzar; **MENE, MENE TEKEL PARSIN,** as a Hebrew, I am very familiar with the word MENE, it is part of my mother's name; **CELIMENE** or **CELI-MENE** and in that message God told the son of Nebuchadnezzar; 'Me Myself or I myself have judged your kingdom' and soon afterward, the Babylon kingdom fell to the Persian Empire, today's Iran (See ARARAT) for an expanded discussion of the concept and translation of MENE. Could these two words have found their way in the title of Obama's stimulus package by accident? The answer is no.

On February 10, 2009, on the day God spoke to Noah, the same day Obama declared his candidacy for the U.S. presidency in 2007, the U.S. Senate voted 61-37 in favor of the stimulus package.

On February 17, 2009 Obama signed the stimulus package into law, the exact date when the deluge of Noah started—all of these precise observances of biblical history and guidance could not have been coincidental.

On March 23, 2009, the same day the King of Persia signed a new edict, giving the Hebrews the power and the authority to defend themselves from a Jewish conspiracy to destroy them and to steal their properties, Obama signed the Health Care Bill, the PACT of blood with Satan to kill the black and the white Americans in an operation called; 'Bottom Kill'.

In addition, Obama found himself on vacation in Maine on top of the Cadillac Mountain in the Northeastern United States exactly on July 17, 2010, the same date when the Ark of Noah came rested on top of Mountain Ararat. What was Obama doing on top of the Cadillac Mountain on July 17? (1532 feet) and why Has Obama called for a Cadillac tax in his Health Care Pact in 2020? The answers to these questions are simple: Obama went to the Cadillac Mountain on July 17, 2010 to simulate that he is the new Noah, the one who would save the Jews of Wall Street from destruction, but Obama is wrong, **Jesus is the only one who can save and I work for him.** Just as Mount Ararat gave rest to Noah, Obama views the Cadillac Mountain in Maine as the new Ararat Mountain and everyone who would have survived his deluge of bloodshed would have been forced to pay a special tax called the 'Cadillac Tax', according to his Health Care Pact with Satan; however, Jesus will not charge those he will save from destruction in his imminent judgment.

The following acronym is found in Obama's jobs bill

These hidden acronyms continue to show that Obama is indeed sending hidden messages that he is planning a Civil War in America.

The

American

Jobs

A

C

T

TAJAT

The word Tajat actually means the crowning of the Queen after her victories. The Queen is in fact the statue of Liberty in New York or Queen Elizabeth or the woman that is worshipped by the

Catholics, the white woman to whom Satan had transferred the authority of the black Eve. The word TaJ by itself means the Queen's crown, but in the Russian synodal, the word Tajat means to melt. This means that Obama intends to totally melt his enemies. It is not possible for so many threatening words to be found hidden in the titles of Obama's legislations by accident. The preponderance of the evidence shows that Obama is indeed planning something very sinister against the American people, but he will not succeed.

On September 8, 2011, Obama addressed a joint session of Congress to talk about the American jobs act, during the speech, Obama proposed a $ 447 billion package to create jobs since the stimulus package never created any jobs. However, a year later, Obama had not created any jobs, the jobs bill was really presented to Congress as part of the simulations of war that Obama is engaged in against the American people.

The true meaning of the number 447, 000 is found in the following:

180.000+447,000=627,000 the number of American soldiers that died in the American Civil War.

The number 447,000 comes from the $447,000,000 that Obama proposed in the Jobs bill, the last 3 '0's are silent—this is spiritually correct, the same way the number 93 stands for 930, the age of Adam when he died because Satan had caused him to sin. The first Emancipation Proclamation of Lincoln was number 93 to symbolize Adam. The reverse of 93, the number 39 also shows the same significance when Martin Luther King Jr. was assassinated at the age of 39, the inverse of 93 or the inverse of 930 because the presence of the '0' is implied, but it is silent. Yes, this presentation is honest and sincere.

Moreover, history is very clear that Lincoln organized the Massachusetts' 57th regiment with a force of 180,000 black soldiers, this number is not in dispute and in the context of the November 6, 2012 presidential election, Mitt Romney and Deval Patrick, the black mulatto are spiritually in charge of the 180,000 black soldiers from Judah and they are leading them to war against the 447, 000 soldiers from Israel and when

180,000 is added to 447,000= 627,000

The exact number of soldiers that died in the American Civil War

The race between Mitt Romney and Barak Obama is a war simulation. The number 180,000 is found in the Bible (1Kings 12:21), when Rehoboam, the son of Solomon mustered a troop of 180, 000 between the tribe of Judah and Benjamin to fight against their own Israelite brothers in a Civil War, but God did not allow the Civil War to come to pass. And the number 447,000 is also found in the Bible, referring to the tribe of Gad and Dan, they are described as men skilled in war—this explains why Obama has spiritually chosen them after he launched a bus tour on August 15, 2011 during Ramadan to promote his Jobs bill, but in reality he was promoting a Civil War.

In his biggest simulation of war, on April 20, 2010, Obama engineered a huge explosion in the Gulf of Mexico to mimic the explosion of Confederate ships in the Gulf of Mexico on April 20, 1861, which really started the American Civil War. The 1861 naval conflict in the Gulf of Mexico lasted exactly 86 days and in July Lincoln addressed a joint session of Congress. Obama did the same thing. He allowed the oil to leak in the Gulf for precisely 86 days because the oil spiritually symbolizes the blood of the victims; it was as if a real fight was going on in the Gulf where the wild lives, especially the fish symbolize the Hebrew soldiers and Obama called it "Good News". Finally, Obama concluded the voodoo ceremony in the Gulf of Mexico with an operation called '**Bottom Kill'** performed around Rosh Hashanah, in September 2010 to signal that the people at the very bottom of American society, the bottom of the pyramid has been murdered in the simulation of war. All of these religious applications and the historical recreation of the actions of Abraham Lincoln in the American Civil War could not have occurred by accident. Barak Obama also used the news created by the oil spill to cover up the crimes of the executives of Goldman's Sachs by engineering their appearance before Congress on April 27, 2010, the same day Lincoln suspended the U.S. Constitution in 1861. This spiritual principle means that on April 27, the law does not exist—this also explains why Obama chose to release a fake copy of his long form birth certificate on April 27, 2011.

On September 11, 2012, Barak Obama, Hilary and Bill Clinton murdered the American Ambassador to Libya to spiritually cover up the real news announced by Ben Bernanke on **September 13, 2012 that the Federal Reserve made an open-ended commitment to the banks and investment firms on Wall Street to buy $86 billion worth of securities, including $40 billion worth of mortgaged backed securities every month.** These securities are the toxic assets held by the banks that lost money in 2008 from the subprime mortgage crisis. In other words, the fed announced the entire looting of the American treasury by giving back to the banks the money they had lost during the financial crisis. The September 13, 2012 announcement was overshadowed by the news of the September 11, 2012 murder of the American Ambassador to Libya. God will not allow Barak Obama to achieve the evil goals of his second term in office—God will stop the primitive practice of human sacrifices in Washington D.C.

On August 7, 1998, two bombs exploded simultaneously at U.S. embassies in Tanzania and Kenya and three days later on August 10, 1998, President Bill Clinton declared a patient bill of rights to amend the Health Care law as it existed at the time. Bill Clinton travelled to Louisville, Kentucky, Lincoln's place of birth where he gave a speech about Patients protection and for the first time he announced a Patient's bill of rights. And 11 years later the words Patients protection will be featured prominently in Obama's health Care Pact, which is titled; "Patient Protection Affordability Care Act, or PPACT as in a Pact with Satan.

The pattern is the same with the events of 09/11/01. Just two days after the events of 09/11/01, the U.S. Congress passed a bill on September 13, 2001 S.J. RES. 23, given the President the authorization to take military actions against nations, organizations and people who were involved in the 09/11/01 attacks. George W. Bush signed the legislation into law on September 18, 2001 on Rosh Hashanah and on October 7, 2001 during the Jewish holiday of Sukkot, which took place between October 2 and October 8 in the year 2001, and then the U.S. invaded Afghanistan. The U.S. Congress also took advantage of the 09/11/01 incident to pass about at least fifty other legislations, including the Patriot Act, which changed America forever, from a nation of some freedom to a Police State. Surely, all these religious precisions could not have taken place by accident.

Moreover, another example of this practice is found when on November 28, 2010, the U.S. government conspired with Julian Assange of Wikileaks to release supposedly classify documents. On that day, Wikileaks announced it will release about three million documents that would embarrass the American government and her allies in the war against terrorism. This news was manufactured by the CIA as a decoy to cover up the crimes of the American government in Haiti where Bill, Hilary Clinton and Barak Obama were hoping to provoke a Civil War through a sham presidential election and the Ivory Coast where the U.S was hoping to provoke a Civil War through a runoff presidential election, on that very day of November 28, 2010.

Fearing that the Wikileaks news decoy may not be enough to cover up the news about Haiti and the Ivory Coast, on November 28, 2012, the U.S. also provoked North Korea by staging a military drill with South Korea in international water. According to reports, North Korea activated surface to surface missiles on launch pad in the yellow Sea and China was encouraged to get the North Koreans to engage in six-party talk; however, soon after November 28, 2010, after God destroyed the presidential election in Haiti, the Korean crisis disappeared like a puff of air, but the U.S. continues to treat Julian Assange, a CIA spy as an enemy in public when in fact, the guy is a spy for the U.S. government.

On November 5, 2009 Obama murdered 14 American citizens, including an unborn child in the Fort Hood shooting to find mystical power to pass the Health Care PACT with Satan. That same week-end, Congress voted at midnight to pass the first leg of the Health Care bill. If anyone wishes to challenge this, he or she must first get the government to release the ballistic report from the Fort Hood shooting; otherwise, they must bow down to this truth and admit that Obama is a mass murderer, a black drakkar or Dracula.

On June 24, 2009, Obama murdered Michael Jackson to use his natural authority and power and to steal his entire fortune, but it will not happen. Michael Jackson was the second coming of John the Baptist, he was killed on the Catholic day of the Feasts of Saint John—his murder was a religious sacrificial offering to Satan. It was the same with Elvis Aaron Presley, obviously a Levite Hebrew from the south; he was murdered on August 15, 1977 on the day of the Catholic 'Lady of Assumption'.

God and the angels of Jesus will make Barak Obama, Bill and Hilary Clinton pay for their crimes against the Haitians, against the American people and against the citizens of the world.

Chapter 13

The Jews are the Priests of Satan

The Jews originated from a black man named Abraham and a Mexican woman named Hagar. Abraham is a descendant of Shem, a Semite who was living with his family in a black community in Chad, Africa. That community did not know the living God and they were living in sins and worshipping other gods. Most of the Semites migrated to Africa sometime after the Great Deluge and after God destroyed the first world Trade Tower of Babel. That tower was being constructed in New York, the biblical Babylon nation. God called Abraham and asked him to leave Africa for Hai, today's Haiti and God changed his name from Abram to Abraham, which means Hebrew of mine or servant of mine, or priest of mine. Abraham listened to God and decided to make the trip. However, because his father Terah wanted to make the voyage to the new land of Haiti with him, God decided to put a break in the whole project and when Abraham and his family, including his wife Sarah, his father Terah, and his nephew Lot, reached West Africa, they settled in Guinea and they remained there and formed a new community until his father Terah died. After the death of his father, Abraham decided to make the trip to Haiti with his wife and his nephew Lot. They sailed from around Cape Verde directly to Haiti, a trip Christopher Columbus would eventually duplicate when Satan called him out of Spain, which is located just below Cape Verde, and like Abraham, Columbus would end up exactly in Haiti, the cradle of civilization, the place where God planted the Garden of Eden.

Satan later sent Hagar, a Mexican woman to secure a seed, Ishmael, from Abraham in the hope to eliminate Isaac, the only legitimate offspring of Abraham. Because Abraham obeyed God by listening to his voice, he became the priest of God, and thus his son Isaac was also the priest of God, but Satan secured Ishmael as his priest from the bloodline of Abraham. All the prophets of the living God descended from Abraham through Isaac, then Jacob, then Joseph and his brothers, the other 11 sons of Jacob. However, all the Jewish philosophers are the priests of Satan; they descended from the lineage of Ishmael. The Jews descended from Ishmael, a mulatto like Barak Obama. As the priests of Satan, the Jews play a crucial role in world affairs to promote the global goal of Satan; the Jews have no loyalty to nations or countries, but only to the broader vision of Satan, which was the original goal of the Tower of Babylon that God destroyed in New York. Hence, Satan sees a world where "all the people come together as one" as "imagined" by John Lennon in his satanic rendition of love and peace and as contemplated by Martin Luther King in his 1963 "I have a Dream" speech. However, the living God does not share that vision. God sees a world where different people of different races and backgrounds live in their own territories and nations, separately to create their own national identities and to promote the diversity of cultures, languages, innovations and glories—each nation with its own economy and tradition.

Ishmael was born when Abraham turned 86 years old and when Abraham turned 99 years old Ishmael turned 13 and on his very birthday—Satan made the covenant of flesh with Abraham—the covenant of circumcision—the very first Bar-Mitzvah. The Bar-Mitzvah is a voodoo ritual in which the Jews seek to assume the blessing of a legitimate child of God by pre-emption—just as Ishmael attempted to assume the blessing of Isaac before he was even born.

Hence, the number 86 symbolizes elimination by pre-emption. To 86 someone is to eliminate or destroy him or her. The number 86 is also the number of transition from one twin to another, one kingdom to another and one era from another. In the history of the

United States, the mystic in the numbers, especially the number 86, confirms that the American experience has been the Jewish experience in the covenant of Ishmael. From 1776 when the U.S was conceived to 1862 when Abraham Lincoln made the "Emancipation Proclamation", it took precisely 86 years. From 1861 when the American Civil War began to 1947 when the Jewish state called Israel was created in the Middle East, it took precisely 86 years. It was also in 1947 that the aliens, the demons of Satan came crashing on earth with Satan, they were overthrown out of heaven. From 1862 when Lincoln made the "Emancipation Proclamation" to 1948 when the Jewish state was officially recognized by the United Nations after Harry Truman secured a second term in office, it took precisely 86 years. From 1922 when the Lincoln Memorial was inaugurated to August 28, 2008 when Barak Obama issued his failed "Emancipation Proclamation's" call when he accepted the Democratic nomination for President of the United States in Denver, Colorado, it took precisely 86 years. And from 1915 when the construction of the Lincoln Memorial began to 2001 when the World Trade Towers collapsed on September 11, it took precisely 86 years, which suggests the end of the American Empire and the end of the Ishmael Covenant. The Jews may have originated from Abraham, but they are the illegitimate offsprings of Ishmael, but salvation comes from the lineage of the black Isaac, the only legitimate son of Abraham.

Lack of spiritual understanding leads to conspiracy theories

The American people understand that the Jews are very influential in American society, but they do not completely understand why. The fact is the American government is a satanic theocracy and the Jews are the priests of Satan which means that all the dispensations of Satan flow from the Jews. However, since it is written that all perfect gifts come from God, the Jews' role is to steal the real spiritual gifts of the black children of Isaac through Bar-Mitzvahs and use them to advance the dark goals of Satan. For example, when a Jew steals a gift of science from a real child of the living God from the lineage of Isaac, that child becomes lost and the Jew gets to use the gift in a satanic manner, not the way prescribed by God. This is why the American leadership has sought to keep the people from gaining any spiritual knowledge since many of them would not accept to be part of the practice of human sacrifices—they are being led by deceptions. But a significant number of Americans, especially those who belong to entry level of freemasonry and those who belong to the clergy of Catholicism, Protestantism, and Mormonism understand that the Jews are the servants of Satan and they help bring financial prosperity to America. The American people are frustrated. They know they are being lied to by politicians who promise one thing and consistently break their promises. And they often wonder why politicians who are supposed to represent them engage in making decisions whose logic they fail to understand, even though they are well informed, well read and well educated. Unfortunately, the politicians must continue to lie to hide the fact that they engage in the practice of human sacrifices and many innocent Americans and other from other parts of the world have to die every year in order to keep America prosperous. The Jews must have first place in American society because they are the priests of Satan and Satan will not accept the sacrifices from anyone else. This was precisely why Barak Obama was selected to be President of the United States—he is a Jewish priest of Satan. His mother was a Jew and the son of a Jewish woman is a Jew. The Jews are leading the leaders of the American nation in the practice of a very ancient cult of human sacrifices through the covenant of Cain and the covenant of Ishmael. The Jews are Satan worshippers and the American confederacy is a satanic theocracy. Sadly, conspiracy theories cannot really help the average American to understand what is really driving actors in Washington. The American people are forced to worship Satan by observing the Jewish un-holidays like Yum Kippur, Rosh Hashanah, and Hanukah among others. And worse, the people who are supposed to help the American public understand what is going on are actually members of this dark culture of human sacrifices; Radio Talk Show hosts like Rush Limbaugh, Sean Hannity and Mark Levin among others are liars, they are actually Satan worshippers disguised as servants of righteousness to deceive the people.

This also explains why the Federal Reserve's decision to spend $86 billion (the number 86 again) every month buying treasuries and mortgaged backed securities have not been challenged, it is because these Radio Talk Show hosts are benefiting from the huge money printing spree that Obama used to buy the Presidential election in 2012—everyone has had his cut.

These deceivers make more money in Radio by selling commercials on the air since Obama took office, than at any time in their lives combined. Just imagine! Rush Limbaugh is reported to make $50 million a year, why would a guy making this much money risk his career by actually telling the truth to the American public? The answer is simple; Rush Limbaugh is a liar and a deceiver whose mission is to help Barak Obama further promotes his evil politics of race and class warfare and to ultimately help him provoke a civil war in the United States, but they will not succeed. Rush Limbaugh was one of the people in the American media who used inflammatory language to incite the 1992 Rodney King riot that killed hundreds and injured thousands of mostly black American citizens. Rush Limbaugh is such a liar that he actually accuses Barak Obama of having a secret agenda for the government to push private insurance out of the health care Insurance business by instituting a single payer health Insurance system in America when in fact he knows very well that is not the case. How do you accuse someone who compels American citizens under threats of financial fines to buy private insurance policies of being anti-insurance companies? The reality is simple; Rush Limbaugh is deceiving his audience by pretending to be against Barak Obama when in fact, he is for Obama and his goal is to help Obama provoke a civil war in America by dividing the people along racial lines like he did in 1992 and like he also attempted to do in the Trayvon Martin case, but there were no riots this time.

This is precisely why Donald Trump has helped bring Arsenio Hall back in the entertainment business. Arsenio Hall was one of the polarizing voices that helped contribute to the division of the races; he fed the black community the venom of darkness and drove them to violence to shed their own blood for the benefit of the Jews, but this time he will not succeed. It is interesting to note that the Arsenio Hall show was cancelled in 1994, the same year Bill Clinton occupied Haiti by returning Jean-Bertrand Aristide to office—Bill Clinton shed the blood of the Haitians in 1994, he also shed the blood of the Africans in 1994 when he helped provoke the Rwanda massacre.

1994 was indeed a very bad year for the children of the living God from Haiti to the United States of America. That year a black son of Satan, the liar and deceiver named Nelson Mandela became President of South Africa to deceive the blacks for the advancement of the cause of the whites.

The Mandela who went to prison was not the same Mandela who came out of prison. Nelson Mandela went to prison supposedly for promoting the cause of righteousness, but upon his release, he recanted, he switched side like in the Stockholm syndrome. It was like the about face John the Baptist made while in prison by expressing doubt that Jesus was really the begotten Son and the Messiah of the living God. The new Mandela sided with his captors upon his release; he told his supporters he forgave his captors and he declared that the war is over because he is being made President, even though injustice and brutal repression continue in South Africa and even though the conditions of the people he pretended to fight for have not improved. He made the fight about him and he totally set aside the plight of the people. He mistakenly thought that because he was freed the rest of the blacks were also freed with him, but that was not the case. Mandela became President of South Africa in 1994, but he has not done anything to improve the lives of the people he claimed he wanted to help, except for the usual 2 percent of the black people and the elite from the ANC or African National Congress.

However, 1994 was a very bad year for the real black children of the living God. It was in 1994 that Michael Jackson was first accused of molesting a Jewish boy; the accusation almost destroyed his career which became irreparably damaged and ultimately, Barak Obama, the Jewish Klan leader would kill Michael Jackson in June 2009 and would allow his Jewish brothers to steal Michael's money by taking control of his entire estate.

It was also in 1994 that O.J. Simpson was accused of double murder and even though he was cleared from the accusations, his life would never be the same and ultimately, 13 years to the day he was acquitted of murder, he would be accused of stealing his own properties and he would be convicted of theft among other charges, he is still in prison to this day. However, times have changed and this Sabbath is unlike other Sabbaths, this is not 1994. This is not 1861 and there is not going to be another Civil War in the United States or in Haiti—period.

Chapter 14

Like Barak Obama, like Bill Clinton, like Abraham Lincoln, like Adolph Hitler and like Harry Truman

Like Hitler, like Obama

Adolph Hitler was a Jewish mass murderer who came to save the Jews during the Sabbath of the Second World War and Obama is a mulatto Jewish mass murderer who came to save the Jews in this Sabbath (2009-2016).

Hitler invaded Europe to collect the Jews and to bring them to the Middle East; he invaded Africa to crush all spirit of resistance and he invaded Russia to collect the Jews from Russia, but he was defeated in Russia in July 1943 like Napoleon was defeated after he had invaded Russia exactly on April 20, 1812, on Hitler's birthday. This explains why the Jews are not as influential in Russia as they are in other western societies—both Hitler and Napoleon failed to subdue Russia. When Hilary Clinton, the second coming of Hitler, said Russia must pay a price—she has overlooked the fact that Russia already paid a price for the freedom of humanity by standing against French's tyranny and by defeating the arrogance of Hitler and his cause of darkness as the shepherd of the Jews.

Europe was Hitler's primary theatre of war, but the Middle East has become the new Europe for Obama. Hitler made it possible for the Jews to have a home in the Middle East, but Obama came to accomplish the rest of Hitler's mission; to bring lasting peace to the Jews and to unite them with the Palestinians in peace as two people living on one land. Barak Obama has significantly escalated the war of Afghanistan because the Afghan war was kept dormant for him to prosecute; it is the war of Armageddon. However, Obama is losing the war decisively and he has been forced to make deals with a number of nations like India to help him in Afghanistan. He wants to crush the spirit of resistance that Jesus has awakened against him; no one can help him. He has invaded Libya, Syria, Yemen, and a number of African nations like Sudan, Somalia just as Hitler did and like Hitler, Obama is now at war against Russia inside Syria.

Hitler was not a German born citizen and Obama is not a U.S. born citizen. It is largely reported that Adolph Hitler was born in Austria and Barak Obama was born in Haiti in 1958—he became a U.S. naturalized citizen in Hawaii in 1961.

Hitler was a Jew like Barak Obama, he cared about the German Jews, but he did not care about the German people and he led them to perdition just as Obama is leading black and white Americans to perdition as he schemes to save his Jewish brothers. However, the people he came to save, the American upper middle class who put their trust in him—the people whose (401k) accounts have been going up since March 2009 after Obama passed the stimulus package, will be severely disappointed because Obama is a loser and a loser cannot win. Many have already been punished through tornadoes, earthquakes, hurricanes, like Irene and Sandy, but the worst is yet to come.

Hitler built concentration camps to preserve the Jewish people he came to save just as Obama built concentration camps for the Jews he came to save. The notion of concentration camps first appeared in the desert of the American Midwest, in Denver Colorado and in the desert of South Dakota, the biblical Mount Sinai where Moses built concentration camps to secure the Hebrew Israelites. The idea of concentration camp is the same spiritual idea of hunter and gatherer that Jesus had expressed when he said he wanted to gather his sheep like a chicken gathers her hens; that was exactly what Adolph Hitler did in Europe for the Jews. He hunted and gathered the Jews from all over Europe and put them in safe concentration camps and later, Harry Truman collected them and took them to Palestine. History is clear; the Jews have been the only winners from World War Two. They emerged from the war more unified as a people than they have ever been. They emerged from World War Two with more power and authority on the world scene than they ever had before and Harry Truman built a state for them for the very first time in their entire history and none of these would have been possible, were it not for the actions of Hitler.

Hitler, in concert with the Polish government, gave a yellow star to the Jewish people to distinguish them from others in anticipation of war. Obama, in concert with Michael Bloomberg, gave special phone registration to Jewish Babylonians in anticipation of a Civil War—this explains why a new Basketball stadium just opened in Brooklyn in November 2012. It would have been used as a safe concentration camp for the Jews and the elite in case of a Civil War; but, instead of a Civil War, Michael Bloomberg and Barak Obama should expect more hurricanes like Sandy and more earthquakes—Obama and Bill Clinton will not succeed in their evil schemes and all foreign troops must leave Haiti at once.

Hitler murdered his girlfriend and Obama, under the advice of Hilary Clinton attempted to murder his wife Michelle on April 19, 2011 by engineering an airplane accident, but he failed—like Hitler, like Barak Obama, like Hilary Clinton, the second coming of Hitler.

Hitler was a homosexual High School drop-out and Obama is a homosexual community college drop-out. Like Solomon, Hitler began his war rampage in his fourth year in office, in 1939; he took power in August 1934. Hitler had some success and his book Mein Kempt enjoyed international success, but Obama's books have not been successful because his mission has failed. Obama will not be able to save the people he came to save and he would have to give back the money he has stolen from the American people.

Chapter 15

The Third and Fourth Terms of Bill and Hilary Clinton

Barak Obama came to complete the agenda of Bill Clinton, but he has been opposed by God. Bill and Hilary Clinton are using the dark authority of Barak Obama, the mulatto son of Satan to accomplish what they could not have accomplished in their own power and authority—they have become more emboldened and more reckless in their evil ways because they are not directly accountable to the American people. The following is a list of events and policies that were first initiated under Bill and Hilary Clinton, but have found resolution under Barak Obama:

The Health Care PPACT with Satan

The passage of the Health Care is the contract with America—meaning the demons of Satan received the green light to provoke a Civil War in America when the Health Care is passed through Congress. This was precisely why Newt Gingrich used the slogan, **"Contract with America"** against Bill Clinton in 1995. The contract called for the Republican Party to be unified against the Democratic Party to provoke a Civil War along party and racial lines after the Health Care is passed. Newt Gingrich was not really against Bill Clinton, he was for him, he needed to show to the public that he opposed Bill Clinton in order to deceive the American people and to divide them along party, race and class lines—it was a dance of deceptions—it takes two to tangle. Bill and Hilary Clinton failed to pass the Health Care PPact, but Barak Obama passed the Health Care PPact in the power of Solomon.

Gays in the military

One of Bill and Hilary Clinton's primary agenda was to allow homosexuals to serve openly in the military, but when they met with significant resistance they settled for "don't ask, don't tell", allowing homosexuals to serve in the military under the cover of anonymity. However, in the power and authority of Solomon Obama repealed "don't ask, don't tell" to allow homosexuals to serve openly in the military. Again, Bill and Hilary Clinton failed, but Barak Obama succeeded in the power of Solomon because Barak Obama was born in Haiti, the true and only biblical Jerusalem—the city of the Great King. The President of Haiti is the most powerful person in the world, he possesses the most natural authority, less he gives that power to someone else, but Barak Obama is not the President of Haiti, the head of the Kingdom, he is the President of Israel, the tail of the Kingdom of the living God. thus, Obama has much less authority than the real anointed Haitian who is the "Faithful Servant" of Jesus Christ.

The 1993 bombing of the North Tower of the World Trade Center occurred under the administration of Bill Clinton as a prelude to the 9/11/01 collapse of the towers of the World Trade Center.

The bombing was first initiated by Bill Clinton to create news to cover up the real crime of Bill Clinton in the Waco affair, which started exactly on February 28, 1993, just two days after the February 26, 1993 bombing of the North Tower. It is important to note that Hitler and his associates used the same spiritual tactic in Germany on about the same date when the Reichstag building exploded on February 27, 1933—Hitler and his associates used the news of the explosion to pass a number of laws, restricting the freedom of the German people and to make a number of deals under the cover of fear and darkness.

The 1993 bombing of the North Tower became the model for Dick Cheney to engineer the events of 09/11/01 to invade Afghanistan, and to trigger the so called war on terror. The war of Afghanistan is the biblical war of Armageddon; which Obama was selected to fight. Obama launched a very strong military surge in Afghanistan by doubling the number of American troops on the ground; he twice replaced military generals in Afghanistan and he also dramatically escalated the cowardly drone attacks on civilians, especially on the border between Afghanistan and Pakistan, but he failed. Obama is a loser and a loser cannot win.

Bill Clinton set the stage for the events of 09/11/01 by giving Dick Cheney the roadmap in the 1993 bombing of the North Tower. Bill Clinton **also** set the stage for the war of Afghanistan by imposing financial sanctions on the Taliban in 1999 for their supposed association with Bin Laden. This whole notion that the United States is fighting Al Qaeda in Afghanistan was wrongly invented by Bill Clinton, the master of deceptions, the convicted liar. In reality, the U.S. is at war with the Taliban, the lawful government of the people of Afghanistan and the Taliban are winning because the living Haitian God is with them, not with Obama or Bill Clinton—this explains why the Afghan war is the longest war the U.S. has ever fought—the longer it goes, the weaker the U.S. becomes.

Bill Clinton also bombed Iraq for 8 years—he found cover in the philosophy of "no boots on the ground"; Obama promised to withdraw American troops from Iraq, but he never did—he kept them there for almost three years before he redeployed them to Jordan and other parts of the Middle East, including Israel—while the sectarian war in Iraq continues.

Bill Clinton's policies helped trigger the 2008 financial crisis. But Obama responded to the crisis by transferring the entire wealth of the American people to criminals on Wall Street through the QE policy of Ben Bernanke and through the Timothy Geithner's scheme to buy Toxic Assets from banks, mortgage companies and investment firms. Bill Clinton repealed the Glass-Steagal Act of 1933 by signing the Grimm-Leach-Bliley Act in 1999. The Act removed the prohibition from banks to act as commercial banks, investment banks and insurance companies all at once—allowing banks to take tremendous risks. Bill Clinton should be in prison, instead he is selling himself as a humanitarian. The policies of Bill Clinton set the stage for bankers to over leverage and make trillions of dollars in risky bets and when they lost their shirts, Obama came to bail them out, so that they would not pay for their crimes and so that they could recover the money they lost through the American treasury by driving every single American into debt like slave. Barak Obama represents the cause of darkness, as long as he is in office, the people responsible for the 2008 financial crisis cannot be punished—he must be removed from office for justice to prevail and he will be removed from office very soon.

Clinton also passed the Community Investment Act (CRA), which encouraged banks to move into minority neighborhoods and to charge subprime rates on mortgages, car loans and other financial products to Blacks, Puerto Ricans, Hispanics and poor Whites, which led to the subprime mortgage crisis. Many middle middle and lower middle class white and black people had thought Bill Clinton was sincerely helping them to buy a new house or a new car, but unsuspectingly, he was setting them up to lose their houses just a few years later. In 2008, Obama posed as the guy who would fix the problem and help those who were losing their houses, but in fact, he never did. The only people who received any help have been upper class Satanists, but the good Americans have been given the 'run-around' by the bankers who usually tell them that their paperwork has been lost. The government now owns a huge number of houses through Freddie Mac, but still, the number of American families who have become homeless has increased, while Obama and Bill Clinton are planning to sell their houses to foreigners from India, China and the rest of the east for pennies.

In 1995, Bill Clinton destroyed Michael Jackson's career by wrongly accusing him of molesting a Jewish boy, but in June 2009, Obama murdered Michael Jackson and he is plotting with his criminal associates to steal Michael's entire fortune, including his fifty percent ownership of Sony.

A June 17, 1994 high speed chase of O.J. Simpson led to his arrest in the murder of his ex-wife and her lover.

Under Bill Clinton, O.J. Simpson was tried and his trial divided Americans along racial lines, but he was found not guilty. However, under Obama, he was accused of stealing his own property, he was tried again and he was convicted and he is now in prison—everything that started under Bill Clinton has found resolution under Obama. And now, in his desperate attempt to provoke a Civil War in America, Obama is considering to retry O.J. Simpson again in 2013—Obama wishes to bring back the same divisive element—another O.J. Simpson trial in American living rooms to provoke a race war, but it will not work—the homosexual Obama is truly evil.

Tiger Woods was targeted by Bill Clinton for destruction

Bill Clinton invited Tiger Woods to join him in honoring Jacky Robinson, the legendary black baseball player, after Tiger Woods had won his first Masters at Augusta Georgia. However, Tiger, not wanting a black image declined the invitation. But in 2009, Obama destroyed Tiger to assume his natural power and authority. Tiger is used like Obama's John the Baptist—Tiger decreased and Obama increased. Tiger Wood's father made a covenant with Satan, which called on Tiger to wear the red shirt and the black pants religiously every Sunday or on every final round of a Golf Tournament.

Tiger won 14 major Golf Tournament every time he had the lead or a share of the lead going into the final round, but the covenant was betrayed in 2009 when he lost to Y.E. Yang in August 2009 and subsequently, Tiger Woods stopped winning major Golf Tournaments since Obama took office because Obama is the mulatto son of the Red and Black god from the Red Maple Tree of the knowledge of good and evil.

In 2000 Bill Clinton failed to intervene in the contested presidential election in the state of Florida between Al Gore and George W. Bush. The contest came close to provoking a Civil War in America, yet Bill Clinton never intervened—the election was decided on December 12, 2000 by the U.S. Supreme Court.

Obama and his associates had schemed to create the same deadlock in the November 6, 2012 presidential election, a dispute that would have ended in violence starting on December 13, 2012, but God destroyed the plan. The supporters of Obama are desperate for Obama to enter his fourth year in office to provoke the Civil War because Solomon began to build his house, the temple on the second day of the second month of his fourth year in office. That would be on Groundhog Day 2013, on February 2, 2013 and on that day, Obama would have begun to win the Civil War, but he will be denied.

Breaking NEWS

What seemed to be a victory for Barak Obama was a defeat for the cause of darkness. Obama stole the presidential election to defeat Mitt Romney on November 6, 2012 to win re-election, but he did not get any closer to provoking a Civil War in America. There was no election dispute like in 2000, there was no Florida dispute, no hanging chads and no vote recounts. Once again, Obama has missed his rendezvous with destiny, he has missed another important deadline but in his desperation, he continues to scheme to provoke bloodshed in Haiti and in the U.S

Lincoln stole the 1864 presidential election by suspending the U.S. Constitution, by crushing all opposition and by jailing all his enemies. And after his election, by February 2, 1865, the Confederate states finally fell and by the end of March and early April the south formally surrendered and Lincoln died on April 15, 1865.

The same thing happened with Harry Truman after he had stolen the 1948 presidential election. Harry Truman needed to be elected for a second term to enter his fourth year to find the mystical power of Solomon to complete the formation of the state of Israel in the Middle East. The United Nations was founded in 1945 under the leadership of Harry Truman after the Second World War to create the state of Israel and to launch the era of globalism in the world. Harry Truman oversaw the complete formation of the Middle East state of Israel and by 1948 the state of Israel was founded and recognized by a number of nations, however, it was not yet recognized by the United Nations until a new application was made in February 1949 with the new power and authority of Solomon, given to Harry Truman after he had entered his fourth year in office. Had Harry Truman not gotten elected in 1948, the state of Israel would not have been formed, or it would have never been officially recognized by the United Nations. Haim Weizmann became the first President of the Jewish Middle East state of Israel on February 17, 1949, in the fourth year, the second term of Harry Truman, on the same day Obama signed the 2009 stimulus package.

From 1776 Declaration of Independence to the Lincoln "Emancipation Proclamation" in 1862, it took exactly 86 years and from 1862 to 1948, it took precisely 86 years to create the nation of Israel. The American experiment is all about the Jews. As the priests of the American nation—the Jews came first and the American government uses American tax dollars to pay for the budget of the state of Israel. The Jews are the descendants of Ishmael, the illegitimate son of Abraham—Abraham was 86 years old when Ishmael was born—the number 86 is a key number in Jewish mysticism.

This explains why Clinton asked for a ceasefire in Syria at the end of October 2012—in the concept of "Entanglement of identical particles". Civil Wars cannot exist in Haiti, or in the U.S, and in Syria at the same time; Clinton needed a brief pause in the fighting to transfer the demons from the Middle East to America or Haiti; he needed to transfer the demons from Syria to Haiti by the end of October 2012, but no one listened to him. And a new cycle started in the contest of good versus evil on November 4, 2012 when Satan turns the clock back one hour and Hilary Clinton demands better cohesion among the groups fighting against Bashar Al Assad to signal that NATO is ready to get directly involved in Syria. The practice of human sacrifices has come to an end.

Chapter 16

The List of Human Sacrificial Offerings on Religious Dates by Bill, Hilary Clinton and Barak Obama

The power dates are the important dates in history when God, the creator, spoke or took action to bring about important changes in the world. A power date is a religious date or a date that marks an important biblical event. It may be a date found in the Festival calendar of the living God, or it may be a date like January 16 when the Great Exodus occurred out of Mexico. Satan seeks to use the same dates to act like God in order to advance the cause of darkness. The leaders of the world have at least some limited knowledge and understanding of the mysticism that is expressed throughout the bible—this is why they are called illuminati—they are illuminated by the light—the knowledge of the gods. To become a world leader one needs to know and understand the mysteries of the universe. This presentation explains, in part, why politicians in Washington pursue policies that appear dumb and against American interests—they are in fact engaged in the pursuit of these policies to satisfy the dark—evil global agenda of Satan.

The following is a list of incidents in which people were murdered consistently on certain biblical religious days while Bill and Hilary Clinton have occupied the White House.

1

The January 8, 2011 Arizona shooting was engineered by Barak Obama during the first Sabbath of the year to satisfy the biblical offering of the Feasts of Unleavened bread and to duplicate and block the prayers o the Haitians on the first anniversary of the January 12, 2010 earthquake. (See "ARARAT").

2

July 20, 2012; the Aurora shooting took place to satisfy the Feasts of Weeks as stipulated by the biblical book of Leviticus.

3

August 5, 2012; the Wisconsin shooting took place to satisfy the sacrificial offerings in the early beginning of Ramadan on the eve of August 6, the day Harry Truman dropped the atomic bomb on Japan.

4

July 22, 2011 The Norway massacre was engineered by the Freemasons to satisfy the Feasts of Weeks—the Aurora shooting was a copycat of the Norway massacre.

5

July 17, 1996; about 280 people, including women and children got killed when a missile struck the TWA-800 flight on its way to France—Bill and Hilary Clinton, in conspiracy with the French government, the old evil Assyrian nation, offered the victims of the flight as human sacrifices to satisfy the Feasts of Weeks, which start on July 15 and last through July 23.

6

July 16, 1999, a missile struck the private plane of John Kennedy Jr. as it approached Martha's Vineyard, Kennedy and his new wife and her sister died. A number of witnesses at first reported seeing a light and then an explosion, but they were forced to recant under threats and pressure. The media helped Bill and Hilary Clinton by vilifying Kennedy, calling him reckless and a dare devil. Ted Kennedy remembered what the Clintons did to his nephew, so in

2008, he decided to endorse Barak Obama over Hilary Clinton for the Democratic nomination for president, but unsuspectingly, he never knew that Barak Obama, Hilary Clinton and Bill Clinton were all one of the same.

The offerings of the first 100 days

7

April 12-20, 2009, As Joe Biden predicted, Obama's first test came in his first 100 days in office. He is credited to have personally given the order to kill Somali pirates in a standoff that took place between April 12 through April 20, 2009 when Obama brought a black teenage Somali pirate to New York as a trophy to showcase to his Jewish brothers his commitment to killing black Semites and black Hebrews for the salvation of the Jews.

8

April 20, 2010, 11 workers died in an explosion in the Gulf of Mexico, which started a massive oil leak that lasted until July 15, 2010, on the day the biblical Feasts of Weeks begin (Leviticus 23). Many friendly nations offered to help stop the oil leak, but Obama turned them down to allow the oil to leak for exactly 86 days, the number of the Jewish Covenant with Abraham. No government in the world should have survived the catastrophe that Obama and Hilary Clinton had created in the Gulf of Mexico by murdering at least 11 people and by destroying millions of wild lives and the livelihood of so many innocent Americans. The living God is fully prepared to put Barak Obama and Bill and Hilary Clinton in prison for their crimes against humanity—they will be punished or the world will cease to exist.

9

April 19, 2011, Obama attempted to murder his own wife Michelle by attempting to engineer a collision between her plane and a military plane that was packed with explosives—Jill Biden, the wife of Joe Biden was also aboard the plane. Obama attempted to kill his wife Michelle so that he and Joe Biden could run for re-election as two grieving widows—they wanted to create a national tragedy, the public execution of Michelle Obama and Jill Biden to invoke the sympathy of the American people, but it did not work. Obama did not win re-election—he stole the 2012 presidential election, but he could not reproduce the 2000 election dispute that would have given him the excuse to start murdering Americans on February 2, 2013—**there is no accident in Washington on April 19.**

10

April 20, 2012, The CIA engineered the murder of 131 people when Pakistani Bhoja Air 737 crashed. The victims were offered as sacrifices to satisfy Obama's first 100 days' offerings for the year 2012.

11

April 19, 2000, Bill Clinton murdered 131 people when Philippine air 541 crashed. The crash had the same character of the TWA crash and the plane crash that killed JFK Jr.; all the planes were either taken off or about to land, putting them in the path of a missile strike.

12

April 19, 1999, Bill and Hilary Clinton murdered 13 young Americans in the Columbine massacre—they were offered as human sacrifices to Satan. The number 13 also surfaced in the Pakistani (131) and the Philippine (131) plane crashes because

Satan asked exactly for 13 animal or human sacrifices in the biblical book of Leviticus in chapter 23; verses 18-19.

13

April 19, 1995, 186 people, including women and children got killed in the Oklahoma City bombing. They were offered as human holocaust to satisfy the first 100-day offerings—the number **86** surfaces in the number **186** to suggest the presence of the Jewish priesthood in the offering.

April 19, 1993, 86 people got killed in Waco, Texas after Bill Clinton gave order to set fire in a compound full of women and children to offer them as human holocaust in order to satisfy the offering of the first 100-day of the first year of his administration. It was a classic offering as Satan asks "a holocaust by fire". The number **86** surfaces again, as it has in the April 19, 1995 Oklahoma City bombing, like it has in the April 20, 2010 explosion in the Gulf of Mexico, which lasted exactly **86** days.

This partial list of human sacrifices in Washington, together with the entire body of evidence, prove beyond any reasonable doubt that Barak Obama, Bill Clinton and Hilary Clinton have murdered a great number of American citizens and other citizens of the world and offered them as human sacrifices to Satan to advance the cause of darkness. I have introduced over 200 units of evidence that shows a direct correlation with the prescriptions for sacrifices offerings found in the Bible and the American reality. This presentation also proves that the landmarks of the American nations are in fact religious expressions; the Lincoln Memorial, the Statue of Liberty, the Pentagon and others.

This evidence has also shown that a number of American presidents who have come on the world scene at certain important Sabbaths have practiced the dark art of human sacrifices to find success in the power of Solomon. And just as Solomon began to build the temple on his fourth year, on the second day of the second month, the American presidents who have typified Solomon, have achieved their main goals in their fourth year, starting on or after February 2 during their second term in office. Lincoln won the Civil War after February 2, 1865 in his second term in office; Harry Truman was able to secure the recognition of the state of Israel by the United Nations on his second term on and after February 2, 1949. And Bill Clinton passed many of his most disturbing legislations; the repeal of the Glass-Steagal Act, the Community Reinvestment Act and others, starting on and after February 2, 1997, in his second term in office; and Ronald Reagan found the power to pass some of his most important satanic legislations after 1985, in his second term and after the bloodshed of the 1983 through the 1986 Haitian Civil War made it possible for the American economy to recover from recession. And Hitler started the war in Europe to lead the Jews to Palestine after 1939, in his fourth year in office. However, Barak Obama, the son of perdition will not be allowed to fulfill his satanic agenda during his second term in office.

Chapter 17

All Men are not Created Equal, but Everyone Should Be Treated Equally in the Eye of the Law

A law that promotes division and discrimination through race and class warfare can bring about violence just as article 4 section 2 of the U.S. Constitution caused the American Civil War

Barak Obama is the unholy spirit in the Evil Trinity of Satan; he is the false prophet, the son of perdition prophesied in the book of Daniel and the book of Revelations. Barak Obama came to provoke a Civil War in the United States by dividing the people through race and class warfare. This strategy is self evident in all the policies and the rhetoric of Barak Obama like it were in the rhetoric of Lincoln as captured in the nation divided speech he gave in 1858. This strategy of class and race warfare is evident in all the major legislations of Barak Obama. They are designed to foster a climate of hate and division and to poison relations among people of different races and different classes. Each one of the major Obama's legislations has a specific clause, a feature that is clearly and intentionally added to provoke division that they had hoped would have eventually led to violence, the same way the issue of slavery implanted in the American Constitution led to the Civil War in 1861, but the living God has intervened to protect the American people, and the punishment of the wicked illuminati is imminent.

Article 4 section 2 of the United States Constitution states:

"No person held to service or labour in one state under the law thereof, escaping into another, shall, in consequence of any law or regulation therein be discharged from such service or labour, but shall be delivered up on claim of the party to whom such service or labour may be due."

This section of the American Constitution promoted and facilitated the practice of slavery in America, giving rise to the culture of racial profiling, which has now become known as "stop and frisk" in New York. The constitution, by law, reduced every black person into slavery because any black man or woman could be stopped and searched on suspicion of being a runaway slave simply by virtue of being black.

This brief chapter takes a look at the evolution of section 2 of article 4 of the U.S. Constitution and shows how the current proposed background check in the gun control debate and the "individual mandate" in the new Health Care legislation could have also provoked widespread violence in America if the living God had not intervened. These two proposed legislations are similar to section 2 of Article 4 of the U.S. Constitution—they keep the law from being applied equally to all without exception. Section 2 of article 4 denies to blacks the free movement throughout the several states as free men and women—accordingly, slavery was no longer a southern institution, but a national institution supported and enforced by the nations of the north. Thus slavery became a conscious partnership between north and south to dominate black people and to restrict their free movement within the several states. This constitutional partnership was to ensure that blacks remain at worst in slavery and at best second class citizens in the United States. The background check in the gun control legislation debate plays the same role as section 2 of article 4, it seeks to deny to some American citizens the legal privilege to exercise the right found in the second clause of the second Amendment to the U.S. Constitution by arguing that some Americans are not responsible enough to enjoy the right to bear arms because of their criminal past, regardless of the nature of the crime they may have committed or because of their mental health. And finally, the individual mandate of the new Health Care Law discriminates against Americans by dividing them along racial and class lines. The new law punishes one group of Americans who can afford to buy health insurance, but chooses not to; it threatens those people with strong financial penalties by forcing them to buy insurance from an exchange—a pool of private insurance companies set up by the states. However, according to analysts, most of the people in this group will remain uninsured because of the soaring cost of insurance premiums. While the new law promises to subsidize those who cannot afford to buy health insurance, the poor blacks, the poor whites, it is increasingly those who belong to the middle class whose insurance policies have been cancelled who are now qualified for Medicaid. Obama promised to give medical insurance coverage to the poor, but instead, he has engaged in a de facto Medicare and Medicaid reform by giving free Medicaid and Medicare to the middle class and to the rich at the expense of the poor. He does this by providing subsidies to those with income well above 133 percent and 138 percent of the poverty level.

The law is supposed to treat everyone equally.

One of the most egregious features of the new health care law is that it specifically disqualifies an estimated 11 million of illegal immigrants from coverage. And worst of all, the new law severely reduces the funding that used to be available for hospitals to provide emergency medical services to illegal immigrants as they were required to.

Contrary to popular American belief, all men are not created equals, it is not self-evident, and it is not true. That notion is obviously absurd, men are males or females: some men are short, some are tall, some are rich and others are poor, some are whites, some are Asians, some are blacks and some are mulattoes—some have special skills and talents, and yet some are extremely talented, while others have no talents at all—some are born to be kings, others are born to be king makers. However, the law should be the unifier of all in a given society, regardless of race, gender, class and social status. All men should be treated equally in the eye of the law. The living God himself said to Moses; **"You and the alien are the same before me in the eye of the law."**

Thus, any time a law fails to extend the same right to all its citizens, regardless of gender, race and class, it risks the peace and stability of that nation because sooner or later the oppressed will revolt and the living God will listen to the cries of the oppressed and take it upon himself to do justice on their behalf.

On February 12, 1793, George Washington signed into law the first fugitive slave Act. The new legislation gave clear guidance about how section 2 of Article 4 should work, especially who should pay for the profiling, the apprehension and the return of the runaway slaves among other details. Over time, the law has caused severe tensions among the citizens of America who became divided between the pro-slavery camp and the anti-slavery camp, regardless of race and this led to a new fugitive Act to be enacted in 1850.

The framers of the United States' Constitution have deposited a cancerous cell of violence and injustice into the document that would ultimately cause events to unfold as it is written. The spirit of the constitutional contract has evolved to perform exactly as conceived and the blacks were treated like slaves, they were profiled along racial line and all free blacks lost their freedom as they were subjugated to the same treatment. Martin Luther King Jr. rightfully observed: "injustice anywhere is a threat to justice everywhere", this means wherever there is injustice, it threatens justice everywhere. A perfect example is the global practice of exploiting workers by paying them low and unlivable wages; this practice is a global threat because workers everywhere are now the victims of this nefarious practice; in this global threat, low wages in China, has a downward impact on wages in the United States.

As the American confederation was looking to expand by integrating the new states from the territories of the Louisiana Purchase, it became necessary to decide whether the new territories will be admitted into the union as free or slave states—American history clearly confirms that slavery was not just a southern institution, but an American institution.

In 1820, the Missouri Compromised was reached to admit the new state of Missouri into the union as a slave state and to ban slavery in the rest of the Louisiana Purchase north of 36*30′. The 1850 fugitive Act was passed to strengthen the institution of slavery by creating tougher enforcement of the law. The Act also threatened to fine law enforcement officials personally if they did not aggressively pursue arrest and eventually return all runaway slaves back to their owners. After Stephen Douglas proposed to let the people decide whether slavery should be admitted in the new territories through "Popular Sovereignty", in 1854 the Nebraska-Kansas Act was passed, which repealed the 1820 Missouri Compromise and a mini civil war known as "bleeding Kansas" ensued as a microcosm of the larger Civil War to come in 1861. In 1857, the U.S. Supreme Court, in deciding the infamous Dred Scott's, case repealed the Missouri Compromise, calling it unconstitutional, declaring that the U.S. Congress had no power to ban slavery in the Louisiana territories. In 1858, Abraham Lincoln exploited the national debate over slavery by giving the "nation divided" speech in which he offered himself as the man who could unify the nation when he said; "a house divided cannot stand", he also said that the issue of slavery must be put to "rest".

During the presidential campaign of 1860 Lincoln continued to espouse the same rhetoric and the southerners took him seriously, threatening to leave the union if Lincoln was elected and immediately after Lincoln's election, by December 1860, South Carolina made good on its promise by seceding from the union and by January 1861, five other states joined South Carolina and by June of 1861 a total of 11 states seceded from the union to form a new nation called; the Confederate States of America.

After Lincoln took office in early 1861, the new crisis that awaited him was no longer the issue of slavery, but rather the issue of secession. The new question was whether the several states that seceded from the union had a legal right to leave the union and Lincoln himself made it clear when he confessed that his struggle was not to abolish slavery, but to preserve the union. Lincoln engaged in the Civil War after he concluded that the union was "perpetual" and no state had the right to leave the union. The issue of slavery caused the division of the secession of the Confederate States, however, the Civil War was fought to preserve the union by force. This idea was clearly expressed in the 'Crittenden Resolution' and it also explains why Lincoln supported the Corwin Amendment to the Constitution, which made the institution of slavery legal and prohibits congress from abolishing or interfering with the institution of slavery.

The Corwin Amendment was passed and is still in the book today; however, because the states became fully engulfed in the Civil War after its passage, it was only ratified by a few states.

America was founded when the several states came together of their own free will as sovereign states and agreed to form a union. However, after the Civil War, America was no longer a free nation; the states of the south were brought back into the union by force, against their own free will. This is a brief history of violence caused by one bad law, which is responsible for the deaths and sufferings of millions of people. The law has produced many decades of injustice, violence and abuse, yet even today, the discrimination against blacks and the unequal treatment of blacks continue, especially in New York, the biblical city of Babylon through an evil policy of 'Stop and Frisk'.

It is interesting to note how this time period mirrors the events of 150 years ago, not only the issues of background checks and individual mandate have some similarities with the fugitive acts, but the issue of homosexual marriage that is being wrongly presented as a civil right issue also looks like the slave issue. The issue of homosexual marriage started just like the issue of black slavery; 150 years ago, only the nations of the south held slaves and the slaves could not freely runaway to another non-slave holding state to live in freedom. Yet, today the homosexuals who are married in one state cannot travel to any other state to live as married people because not all states recognize homosexuality marriage as legal. 150 years ago, the people from the new territories were given to decide through Popular Sovereignty whether slavery should be admitted, today, the people in some states are given to decide through referendum whether homosexual marriage should be made legal and just like the U.S. Supreme Court decided the fate of slavery expansion through the territories in the Dred Scott's case then, today, the U.S. Supreme Court is likely to decide whether homosexual marriage should be legal nationally because every time there is a referendum anywhere, the people have always voted against homosexual marriage.

In addition, the issue of immigration reform also sounds perfectly like the issue of slavery that existed 150 years ago. When Marco Rubio, a U.S. Republican Senator from Florida says that there are about 10 million illegal immigrants in America, it sounds just like the same dilemma that existed 150 years ago regarding the legal status of the blacks that lived in the territories of the Louisiana Purchase, whether they should be considered U.S. citizens and what should be their fate and whether, like the illegal immigrants of today, they should be put to a path of citizenship?

This point is very significant since as late as the early 1900s many in Congress openly questioned whether blacks were citizens of the United States. In many ways, this time period is a complete recreation of the time period that witnessed the American Civil War 150 years ago as if there is an invisible hand that is attempting to orchestrate the same events in order to reproduce the same violence that engulfed America 150 years ago, but 2013 is absolutely not 1861.

Congress should never enact any law that discriminates and divides the American citizens along racial lines. If section 2 of article 4 was not part of the U.S. Constitution, the American Civil War of 1861 would not have occurred.

Today, the **"individual mandate"** invokes the same anger from the American public. The Individual mandate from the health care legislation has already inspired Americans to organize against the law. A group of young activists already vow to oppose the law by refusing to buy health insurance. The law has already been challenged legally, but the Supreme Court upheld it and most alarming of all, just as the 1850 fugitive slave act led to the Civil War after South Carolina seceded from the union, this time South Carolina threatened to oppose the law by wowing not to implement the law in South Carolina as if it never existed.

The concern is real and the syllogism is simple: if the U.S. Supreme Court declared the law constitutional and the state of South Carolina refuses to comply with the law, it amounts to another secession from the union by refusing to abide by federal law—and South Carolina would have become once again the first state to secede from the union by refusing to implement the health care law, but unlike 150 years ago, it will not lead to bloodshed—there is not going to be another Civil War in America.

The individual mandate in the new Health Care legislation:

The word PACT is found hidden as an acronym in the title of the Health care plan that was passed between March 22 and 23, 2010 at midnight and signed into law on March 23. The law is a pact to provoke violence in America.

Patient

Protection

Affordability

Care

A

T

C

The (A) in Act is silent.

The new Health Care law is controversial and unpopular among different groups of Americans, but the most unpopular clause of the new legislation is the individual mandate. The individual mandate essentially compels everyone who can afford to buy health insurance to do so or pay a penalty; the penalty will be assessed on a sliding scale, starting with $95 in 2014, $325 in 2015 and up to $695 in 2016 or 2.5% of income. Most Americans who oppose the law simply argue that the government should not have the power to force them to buy a service or product, even if it is good for them and they should not have to pay a fine or a penalty for not buying that product or service.

There are three fundamental problems with the individual mandates:

Firstly, its compulsory approach is intended to be provocative

The framers of the new law clearly failed to come up with a sensible solution to the problems of medically uninsured Americans, this is so because the individual mandate does not cover or fully subsidize people with an income below the poverty level. This would mean that even if people who can afford to buy Health insurance and choose not to, wanted to fully comply with the individual mandate, they would not be able to afford it because the costs of insurance from the private insurance exchanges have increased tremendously. And many more would still go without insurance coverage simply because they cannot afford it or because Medicaid is too inadequate to cover them. Then the question begs what happens to these people? This is the first fundamental flaw in the reasoning of the individual mandate; it is insufficient to resolve the problem of the non-insured and it divides the non-insured along class based on income—one class of non-insured can afford to pay, but for personal reasons chooses not to, while another class of non-insured simply cannot afford to pay for health insurance.

The issue of class in America has profound racial implications because of institutionalized racism against blacks; thus, most of the uninsured are poor whites from Appalachia, some blacks and many illegal and poor immigrants—many of these people are being deceived—they think the law will give them free health care and it does give some Medicaid coverage to some, but to many others, the law only exempts them from the penalty of the individual mandate. The law does not fully say what will happen to those who cannot afford to buy insurance coverage and are not qualified for Medicaid or Medicare.

Secondly, the individual mandate does not treat everyone equally. The individual mandate fails to resolve the problem of the uninsured because it has exempted a number of groups who will continue to be uninsured and will continue to remain a financial burden on the Health Care system. According to CAHBA; California Health Benefit Advisors, the individual mandate exempts certain groups from paying the penalty if:

- Coverage is unaffordable (exceeds 9.5% of household income)
- They do not meet the filing threshold for the purposes of income tax filing
- They are native Americans
- They have a short lapse in coverage (less than three months since they had minimum essential coverage
- They had suffered a hardship
- They are a dependent or
- They live outside of the United States

Clearly, if all these groups of people are exempted from paying a penalty and are allowed to go without health insurance, then the new health care is not universal and fails in its stated attempt to extend medical coverage to all Americans. And if on the other hand, the government chooses to subsidize medical insurance coverage for some and not others, then the government is engaged in discrimination. The average American consumer has the right to buy a product to satisfy his want or need or the right not to buy a product he does not need. For example, it would be unfair to compel a 30-year old man to buy denture just because his mother and his father wear denture and he himself might lose his teeth some time in the next 25 years, and even though the 30-year old could lose his teeth in an accident anytime in the next 15 weeks, it would not make economic sense for him to buy denture now.

One fundamental assertion in the law of macro and micro economic is that consumers would not make economic decisions that are detrimental to their own interests. A consumer always looks for the very best bargain possible. And when this assertion is coupled with the economic theory of scarcity of resources, it makes sense for a young person without medical challenges to decide not to purchase medical insurance as he seeks to allocate his resources carefully. In a free society, no law should ever dictate to a consumer what product to buy in the marketplace, the consumer should be free to decide what product to buy and at what price in order to satisfy his needs or wants. The government may encourage but should not compel American citizens to wrongly enrich private insurance companies by buying medical insurance they do not need.

Third and finally, the individual mandate is designed to wrongly enrich private insurance companies

One of the basic goals of the new health care law in general, and certainly the individual mandate in particular, is to wrongly enrich the private insurance companies. This is the most extreme outrage in the history of humanity. Consider this simple reality: if the government were to impose a tax on all working Americans to pay for health care, the insurance companies would have suffered because the need to buy medical insurance would have decreased drastically as the government would have paid the service providers directly for their medical services and the cost of health care would have declined significantly. However, Barak Obama did not do that. He ignored the wisdom that the entity with the deepest pocket, the U.S. Federal government should not rely on entities with fewer financial means for insurance coverage; the U.S. government should be self–insured.

By compelling Americans to buy insurance coverage from private companies, the insurance companies enjoy an explosion of new customers and the cost of health care jumped exponentially. In addition, the criminal scheme became obvious when it is revealed that Obama also guaranteed up to 90% of the insurance companies' risk, meaning he pledges that they will not fail. So instead of self-insuring, Obama decided to pay premiums to private insurance companies while promising to cover 90% of their risk.

The individual mandate only helps the insurance companies: the cost of health care remains high, insurance premiums are jumping through the roof as insurance companies' profits soar through new heights, while the poor remain uninsured and the quality of medical services suffers because of the ever growing intrusion of insurance executives between the doctor and his patient.

The individual mandate is not a good legislation because it also threatens people with jail time if they fail to pay the fines the government imposes on them. It is an abuse of authority that has divided the nation along race and class lines because black leaders like Jesse Jackson have convinced black Americans that the new law will help them, when it will not. The provocation in the law has given impetus to certain groups to organize in a national effort to repeal the law.

The Health Care law was supposed to solve the issue of uninsured Americans, but when it is fully scrutinized, it has become increasingly clear that the new law will leave most of the problems unresolved. It does not give health care insurance to those who don't have it, especially those with a pre-existing medical condition; it simply gives them access to medical insurance if they can afford it.

The individual mandate is not scheduled to be implemented until 2014, but already it has inspired fears and anger among the public. The law compels an individual to buy private insurance or pay a fine and it also compels employers to buy "adequate" insurance for their employees or pay a fine. And it compels employers with 50 or more employees to meet certain coverage threshold to cover their employees or pay a fine. However, many employers have decided to pay the fines instead of meeting the new and more expensive government guidelines. And many smaller firms have decided to hire less than 50 employees in order to avoid paying any fine, they are known as the 49ers, while other big employers are avoiding the fines by reducing the number of their full-time employees, leading many to rightfully observe and conclude that the Health Care plan has caused unemployment to remain high and thus has hurt the so called economic recovery.

In addition, the individual mandate is already creating a new class of uninsured as employers downsize the numbers of their employees to avoid paying the fines. It has also caused insurance premiums to go up since insurance companies are mandated to cover people with pre-existing medical conditions and policy holders can now keep their dependents on their coverage up to the age of 26.

It was argued that the individual mandate was necessary to cover at least 30 million Americans, who currently have no health insurance, but the individual mandate does no such thing; it only qualifies some of them to free Medicaid. This false perception wrongly positions one group of Americans against another; and since most of the uninsured Americans are supposedly poor whites, blacks, minorities, legal immigrants in addition to illegal immigrants who are banned from coverage under this new legislation, then the individual mandate has essentially divided the nation among race and class boundaries.

On June 28, 2012, the U.S. Supreme Court released its decision about the Obama's Health Care Law; the Court upheld the individual mandate and Chief Justice John Robert explained his vote and the court's decision to uphold the constitutionality of the mandate by calling it a tax under the Commerce Clause. The decision stunned the partisans of Barak Obama; the elite executives in the media, in academia, on Wall Street and some in the business and the military sectors; they were universally disappointed as they were expecting and hoping that the U.S. Supreme Court would have bailed out Obama and relieved him by default of his promise to extend medical coverage to at least 30 million uninsured Americans. They were hoping that an adverse decision by the U.S. Supreme Court would have surely sparked outraged from black leaders like Jesse Jackson and Al Sharpton who would have encouraged blacks to take to the streets to protest the ruling by accusing Republicans of being against health insurance for blacks and polarizing violence would have ensued, leading into the presidential election of 2012, but none of these scenarios happened; the living God kept Americans safe by defeating the evil plan of the individual mandate.

Justice John Robert has matched the dishonesty in the logic of the framers of the individual mandate by expressing his own intellectual cunning and brilliance in the legal rationale for his decision to uphold the Health Care law by calling it a tax. The decision was the right decision because it undermined and neutralized the consequences of an evil plan; however, Justice Roberts was wrong in his conclusion that the individual mandate, as a tax, was constitutional under the Commerce Clause. The opponents of the individual mandate argued before the court that the government cannot compel an individual to buy a service or a product for their private use because it is good for them. That argument is correct because a private individual should have the right to go into the marketplace to freely engage in the allocation of his finite resources by buying what he feels he needs or wants—a private citizen should make that decision, not the government.

The argument that calls the financial penalty for not buying health insurance a tax is fundamentally flawed since the government cannot tax a product or a service that does not exist. And as a matter of principle, the government can fine people for potentially put their own lives and others' at risk, like in the seatbelt laws, but the government cannot compel an individual to buy a product. A private citizen should never be compelled to buy a service or a product under the threat of jail. What is being proposed in the individual mandate has never been done in the history of humanity—it is a new evil. And since the government is referring to the fine as a tax, then the government needs to provide value to society by extending health care coverage to all Americans. The government simply does not have the constitutional power to force American citizens to enter into a private contract with an insurance company by buying a service they don't believe they need or want. If the government insists that it is for the good of the public at large that all individuals have access to health care, then the government can impose a tax to fund public access to health care—the coverage could no longer be private—it becomes a public product just like Social Security contribution.

Since the government argued before the Supreme Court that the penalty should be considered as a tax under the Commerce Clause and the U.S. Supreme Court agreed, then the government needs to clearly state what it plans to do with the money because the government can only collect taxes to improve the lives of Americans, not to punish Americans: Governments impose taxes to build and repair bridges, to build schools and hospitals, to fight wars, but this administration has not said what it plans to do with the money, it does not say it because it considers it a penalty, a punishment of Americans to enrich private insurance companies, not to improve American' lives.

Recommendation

The only way a government can promote a policy of national wellness is through a tax; which would have changed the health Care Bill into a single tax payer bill; a perfect solution for all Americans. That would have lowered the overall cost of health care, including the high costs of prescription drugs by decreasing the power of the private insurance companies. If the government were to impose a tax on all Americans to pay for health Care for all Americans that would have been constitutional under the Commerce Clause as Justice Roberts has concluded, but he erred in his conclusion because a service or a product that does not exist cannot be taxed—a tax can only be imposed for public good, like the tax that pays for Social Security. The conversion of the current private insurance system to a public single payer system would have given instant financial relief to all Americans. Since most Americans get their health insurance through their employers Their contribution would have been converted from a private contribution to a public contribution and their total contribution would have been significantly reduced since there would not be a need to buy insurance and all American would have been covered, including the poor, the illegal immigrants and those who can now afford to buy health insurance and choose not to.

The new tax would have been deducted from everyone's paycheck just like FICA is and every working American would have been covered, including the poor and the unemployed. In fact, the new health care law takes from Medicare and Medicaid to cover people who are now making up to 138 percent above the poverty level—it is a reverse Robin Hood—it takes from the poor to give to the rich—while pretending to help the poor. The Americans that oppose the individual mandate are not objecting to paying taxes and receiving value as taxpayers, they are rightfully objecting to a government that threatens to fine them for not buying a private service, instead of a government that proposes to tax them to buy the service for them. This is the simple solution of the health care debate—it is not complicated, most of it has been achieved by other nations like Canada, but because of greed and institutionalized racism against the blacks in the United States, it is very difficult to design and implement a government plan that would benefit all Americans equally.

Social Security comes the closest to being a perfect public plan—this explains why Social Security has been under attack from lawmakers—they want to privatize it like they have privatized everything else to enslave the American people by abdicating their responsibilities as public servants. They seek to transfer their responsibility to private hands that cannot be held accountable to the American people for the promotion of public good.

In conclusion, the individual mandate is an evil element designed to provoke division among Americans along race and class lines; it is unconstitutional, and it cannot be considered as a tax since it involves the compulsory purchasing of private and personal insurance accounts that do not yet exist.

This division that has arisen from the individual mandate shares the same racial profiling feature of the 1793 and 1850 fugitive slave Acts that led to the Civil War in 1861, but 2013 is not 1861 and the living God will find a way to keep peace in America, this time evil will be defeated, the blood of the innocents will not be shed through senseless violence and justice will prevail.

Chapter 18

2013 is not 1863: A Time unlike 150 Years Ago

Just as the issue of slavery in the U.S. Constitution promoted division through racial profiling, just as the Individual mandate from the Health Care law is now promoting profound division among different groups of Americans and immigrants, the issue of background checks on gun purchases is now promoting anger and divisions among Americans as well. The gun control debate is supposed to be an attempt to reduce the availability of guns in American society. However, most people agree that the gun reform proposals that have been submitted to Congress would not have prevented most of the mass shootings and the violence that have plagued the nation recently, including the December 14, 2012 Newtown shooting where 26 people died and most certainly, the proposed gun legislation would not have prevented the April 15, 2013 Boston marathon bombing. The issue of gun control, just like the issue of slavery, has its genesis in the U.S. Constitution and the only way to resolve it is to amend the Constitution. The 1820 Missouri Compromise that led to the 1850 fugitive act was a mistake, the U.S. Constitution should have been amended to resolve the issue, but the failure to resolve the issue of slavery from its very genesis led to the Civil War, even though the Civil war was fought to preserve the Union. However, after the American Civil War, which Lincoln fought under the guise of stopping slavery, the Thirteenth Amendment to the Constitution was passed without explicitly repealing Section 2 of Article 4 of the U.S. Constitution or the Corwin Amendment, which renders the Thirteenth Amendment a de facto hoax, a work of deception. The Thirteen Amendment gives a conditional freedom to the blacks who answered the call of the Emancipation Declaration. The text fully implies that slavery and involuntary servitude will continue to exist for anyone who is "duly convicted of a crime". Section 1 of the Thirteenth Amendment states:

"Neither slavery nor involuntary servitude, except as punishment for crime whereof the party shall have been duly convicted, shall exist within the United States, or any place subject to their jurisdiction."

Clearly, this language is not the language of freedom, it is a conditional freedom—it is a contract and a contract can only perform according to its spirit, the spirit of the law is found in the language and the intent of the law as written—the language that is agreed herein.

And per the contract of the Thirteen Amendment, slavery still exists in America and the private prisons have become the new plantations—this explains why Martin Luther King Jr. observed in 1963; **"100 years later, the negro is still not free."**

A national Constitution is a contract through which the citizens of a nation promise to live according to certain principles and ideals. The contract can only perform according to its language, a contract has a spirit; this explains why people use terms like the spirit of the law—this also explains why even what appears to be the most insignificant details of a deceptive contract are included in the language of the contract, even if they are written in fine prints. They are a necessary part of the contract for the spirit of the contract to perform according to its language. The subprime mortgage contracts that led to the 2008 financial crisis for example, contained all the details of the contracts, even if they were in fine prints and in language that was difficult to understand, but the details were still there and the buyers were aware or should have been aware of the terms, regardless of whether they fully understood them.

The framers of the American Constitution have created a lasting conflict in the Second Amendment of the U.S. Constitution. The first clause of the Second Amendment reads as follows;

"A well regulated Militia being necessary to the security of a free state."

This clause is clearly about the defense of the state or the defense of the nation; it is about the National Guard or even the marines where people can own guns in a regulated environment under military and civilian leadership. However, the second clause of the Second Amendment is equally as clear in the following:

"The right of the people to keep and bear arms shall not be infringed"

These are two different and distinct clauses and they should not be read together. The United Constitution does give Americans the right to keep and bear arms and asked Congress not to infringe on this right. So any attempt by the U.S. Congress to take away from the right of the American people to own firearms is unconstitutional and any attempt to divide the nation by taking away the right to keep and bear arm from certain Americans is also unconstitutional.

Like the issue of slavery, which is made constitutional in section 2 of article 4, the American nation has now come into an impasse with the constitutionality in the issue of gun control.

The framers of the U.S. Constitution knowingly and willingly adopted two conflicting clauses in the Second Amendment of the Constitution to create a lasting conflict about gun ownership. The second clause of the Second Amendment to the U.S. Constitution gave to all Americans the right to keep and bear arms; however, the overall availability of guns in American society has created a violent society where many Americans die every year because of gun violence. And now the nation has come to a moment of decision; the nation must decide whether it should move forward with the contract in the language found in the second clause of the Second Amendment, which gives the people the right to keep and bear arm or whether the second clause of the second Amendment should be terminated and transferred to the first clause, which allows the ownership of guns through a well regulated militia for the defense of the country. A decision must be made as no profound and meaningful gun control reform can occur as long as the American citizens continue to enjoy the constitutional right to bear arms—any meaningful reform can only be achieved by amending the U.S. Constitution and the lawmakers understand this.

Lincoln divided the nation by speaking against slavery and a Civil War ensued, millions died and the blacks remain slaves until today. Obama came to do the same. He spoke about reducing the availability of guns, yet his very discussions on gun control have led to an incredible increase of gun sales, not a decrease of guns purchases—this is so because the public does not believe in the sincerity of his heart.

The background checks

It is argued that a criminal background check is needed before the sale of a fire arm to keep guns out of the hands of criminals; however, it is not written in the Constitution that a person with a criminal past should not have the right to defend himself like everybody else. Since "criminal" is not defined, someone who may have been convicted of a non-violent crime where a firearm was not used would be wrongly denied the constitutional right to own a gun. This works perfectly like the racial profiling of the slave issue where the slaves were not permitted to circulate freely in the many different states because of their race—once a background check revealed they were runaway slaves; they were promptly arrested and returned to the south—it is the same with the background check in the gun issue.

Secondly, the background check would also deny people with mental impairment or mental health issue the right to own a gun; it would also deny some people, including those who live in public housing, the right to own guns as well.

The issue of the background checks in the gun legislation debate is the same as the issue of background checks in the fugitive acts debate, the slave issue. In either case, one group of people was qualified to enjoy a right sanctioned by the U.S. Constitutional, while another group was denied that same right. The Thirteen Amendment was written to criminalize the former slave in order to keep him in slavery forever. This explains why once someone is convicted of a felony in the U.S., in many instances he loses the following privileges: the privilege to be appointed to certain jobs, including government jobs and to enjoy a very good income, the privilege and the right to vote, the privilege and the right to own a firearm, the right to live in certain neighborhoods, and the list goes on.

The assertion that the Second Amendment should only apply to a certain group of people in American society is wrong, it complements the conditional racism found in the language of the Thirteenth Amendment, which takes away the freedom of anyone convicted of a crime, any crime. So the spiritual power of the Thirteenth Amendment creates a new class of slaves by virtue of their criminal past and once their criminal past have been revealed through background checks, they lose their freedom instantly and they are forbidden from owning a gun. A black man or woman who has committed a crime is returned to slavery by the contract in the language of the Thirteenth Amendment and thus becomes a criminal who is not qualified to enjoy the right of the second amendment. 150 years ago, a background check would reveal that a black man was a runaway slave and subject to be returned to slavery through the fugitive slave act—his freedom of movement was immediately suspended. Today, when a black man who is contemplating the purchase of a firearm is revealed to have a criminal past through a background check, his right to own a gun is immediately suspended. So the right to bear arm has become a privilege, not a constitutional right: the free has the privilege to exercise his right because he is considered a 'responsible citizen', but those who are returned to slavery, simply by virtue of committing a crime—any crime—are not permitted to exercise their rights to owning a gun.

By law, every American citizen should have the right to own a gun according to the second amendment, even those who have been convicted of a crime involving firearm; if they are out of prisons they should be considered rehabilitated as everyone in society shall be treated equally. In biblical Israel, a man or woman could not be a slave for more than six years, the law demands that all his debts be discharged on the seventh year, the year of the Sabbath when he should be completely rehabilitated without conditions, like the condition found in the Thirteenth Amendment. It is wrong for anyone to argue that only a few should enjoy a certain privilege and to deny that same privilege to others on the basis of race, class or even past criminal behavior. The law should be applied to everyone equally.

In conclusion, the issue of background checks in the gun control debate should be dropped because it only serves to promote more gun ownership and more violence in America. You know a leader is effective in resolving a national issue when what he proposes actually resolves the issue, not making it worst. Abraham Lincoln proposed to put the issue of slavery to rest, but he did not, the issue remains unresolved until today and the millions of people who died through the American Civil War died over the issue of secession, not the issue of abolition of slavery as blacks remain second class citizens and slaves in the United States where the private prisons have become the new plantations and where almost three million of Americans are incarcerated,

This time is different from 1861. This time God will not allow Barak Obama, Bill and Hilary Clinton to use the Individual Mandate in the Health care PPACT, the issue of Background checks in the Gun Control debate, the issue of Immigration Reform and the Stop and Frisk policy in New York to provoke a Civil War in America like Lincoln did in 1861.

Barak Obama is a liar. The Individual Mandate will not extend medical coverage to an additional 30 million of Americans who now have no medical insurance, nor will the proposed gun legislation reduce violence in America—the lies have been exposed, there is not going to be another Civil War in the United States.

The living God has decided that the blood of the innocent will not be shed in this Sabbath, the wrongdoers will be punished and peace will prevail in America.

Chapter 19

HR 645

Natural disasters Versus National Emergencies

The war is between Jesus, the Christ of the living God and Obama, the antichrist of Satan. Obama came to provoke a Civil War in Haiti, the biblical Jerusalem and in the U.S. which controls the real Israel, the Confederate States of America. HR645 was introduced in Congress on January 22, 2009; the day after Barak Obama retook the oath of office to set up the duel between the forces of heavens and the forces of Satan in Washington. The bill directed the director of Homeland Security to set up emergency centers on military ground. The bill contemplated either a number of Natural Disasters like hurricane Sandy, if the forces of God take control of the fight or National Emergencies like the Sandy Hook Elementary School massacre, if Obama were to gain the upper hand against Jesus, but Jesus and his angels gained the upper hand—and the illuminati were forced to admit there is a "Climate Change" in the world. And the punishment of evil is imminent—it will be like the punishment of all the first born of Egypt during the time of Moses.

The forces of heavens sent powerful tornadoes against the people of Moore, Oklahoma on May 20, 2013

On May 20, 2013, in retaliation to all the crimes Barak Obama, Hilary Clinton and Bill Clinton are committing all over the world, especially in Haiti, Afghanistan and in Syria, the living God sent a powerful tornado to punish the people of Moore, Oklahoma. The damages were shocking and extensive and the town of Moore was completely destroyed and thousands of people died. However, Bill Clinton and Hilary Clinton responded quickly by doing the same thing they did in Haiti after the earthquake of January 12, 2010, Bill Clinton took over the Port-au-Prince airport right after the earthquake to keep people from finding out what really happened in Haiti, while he was burying the bodies of the UN soldiers in mass graves at a place called Titanyien.

FEMA was directed to do the same thing by blocking the highway to and from the town of Moore, Oklahoma to keep people from finding out the true extent of the damages in Moore. They moved quickly to downplay the number of dead and injured in the tornado. They did the same thing in Joplin, Mo in 2011 where they kept secret morgues. This is the same strategy they have used in Iraq, in Afghanistan and in other places in the world where they are taking heavy casualties—the kingdom of lies never tells the truth. The Obama administration swiftly deployed the National Guard in Moore, Oklahoma immediately after the tornado hit to cover up the story, allowing only the members of the media who agree to report only what they tell them to report. Interestingly enough, a number of lesbians and homosexuals in the media had the nerve to report that somehow, one hospital that was completely destroyed in the tornado was able to evacuate all the patients in only 16 minutes—the weather service only alerted the residents of Moore just 16 minutes before the tornado hit. The Moore residents had only 16 minutes to react and to take shelter. The hospital in question could not have enough time to evacuate its patients—they all likely perished, especially the very sick—there simply was not enough time to evacuate all the patients in 16 minutes—the wreckage tells the story. In addition, the coverage of the tragedy following the Moore disaster further exposes the members of the media as racist criminals and Barak Obama as the head of the Klu Klux Klan as they have taken care not to show not one dead white body lying down in the trash like they have displayed the dead bodies of the black victims in their coverage of Katrina and like they did in Haiti. Shortly after the January 12, 2010 earthquake struck Haiti, Bill Clinton produced a book in collaboration with Time Magazine, showing the dead bodies of the

Haitian victims, but no such book was produced after the tornadoes hit Joplin, MO and Moore, OK.

The illuminati in the American media are responsible for dehumanizing black people by consistently promoting the images of blacks as criminals, inferiors and sub-humans who deserve to die or imprisoned, while promoting white people as braves and resilient during tragedies, but their desperate strategy will backfire in this Sabbath because the living God will punish evil, regardless of their races, even though this Sabbath is mostly a black Sabbath, which explains why the white Hamites are more affected by the natural disasters than the blacks. The blacks that are affected are mostly Moaabs and Ammonites, not Hebrews. The media expects Obama to retaliate against the living God just as he did after Hurricane Sandy by producing and choreographing Sandy Hook the national emergency, but Obama is about to be caught and put in prison because the living God said; "Thou Shall not kill"; only God has the power to kill, it is always wrong when anyone else kills. To further crystalize this commandment, it is very important to note that whenever someone is moved by the spirit of the living God to kill another, it is in fact the living God who is responsible for the killing, but otherwise, the person is guilty of murder. For example, when King David killed in Israel; it was the living God who actually killed the enemies of Israel through King David. God himself confirmed this when he said to King David in 2 Samuel 7, "I have cut off all your enemies from before you", God took responsibilities for all the killings David did in Judah and Israel. However, when Saul and Solomon killed in Israel, it was Satan that told them to kill and they were wrong, just like Obama is wrong and the living God is about to punish him very soon—Barak Obama is going to prison.

Chapter 20

The Mystics in Some of the Events of 2013 Explained

The mystic in the Jimmy Lee Dykes' affair

As a moaab, Obama continues to offer human sacrifices to Satan to achieve his agenda of darkness. Satan hijacked the mind of Jimmy Lee Dykes, a Vietnam veteran; he was accused of killing a school bus driver and of kidnapping a school boy, which led to a standoff with law enforcement authorities. The government could have ended the standoff very quickly, but decided to prolong it to seven days to fulfill the ceremonial mystic of **February 2,** the day Solomon began to build the temple of blood. Shortly after February 2, 2013, the government moved in and killed Jimmy Lee Dykes to rescue a boy named Ethan. This rescue symbolizes the rescue of the son of Satan through whom all the offsprings of Satan would be saved in this Sabbath, but the voodoo ceremony did not work; Barak Obama was not able to begin to build his house of blood in his second term, on February 2, 2013 on his fourth year in office like Solomon did. The Sabbath in this "climate change" environment belongs to Jesus; and Jesus and our Father in Heaven will decide who live and who die in their imminent judgment.

The Christopher Dorner mystery

Satan hijacked the mind of Christopher Droner in 2008, the year Barak Obama got elected President of the United States. Satan used Dorner as a sacrifice to help Barak Obama provoke a Civil War in America by dividing the nation along racial lines through his satanic writings. Since Barak Obama took office, the American media have been using a number of racial incidents to drive a wedge between blacks and whites, to provoke them to anger and to ultimately lead blacks to fight against whites, but it is not working this time.

His name

Dorner's very name Christopher, suggests that he came to help save the offsprings of darkness; Christopher Dorner had the same spirit of Christopher Columbus who secured 560 years of prosperity for the camp of Satan.

His writings

In 2008, Satan seduced Dorner by introducing trauma in his life after he had been fired from his job as a Police officer in L.A. California. That traumatic episode made it possible for demonic spirits to invade the mind and the spirit of Dorner and put him in a journey of emotional instability, which led him to the torturous path of a dark pilgrimage for Satan. And eventually Dorner would begin to write about his sufferings and how he was wronged by the L.A. Police Department; he claimed he was wrongly fired because he was black. Dorner also started to write about what he perceived to be injustice in the world: he wrote about the Rodney King incident, and many other episodes of injustice in the history of the U.S., in brief, he became the false prophet of Satan.

Satan was hoping that black Americans would rally to his support like they have rallied to support the criminal Rodney King, but they did not. Dorner spoke as if he was anointed by God to write about the truth and against injustice, but he was not, he was the priest of Satan just like Bin Laden and eventually, he would die without advancing the cause of Satan. The priest of the living God is not a vigilante. Moses killed an Egyptian and fled into hiding, but later the living God of Abraham called him and gave him the legitimate mandate to represent heaven, but Dorner never had any official mandate from heaven to do justice and to speak and write against unrighteousness, he spoke on behalf of Satan like Barak Obama is attempting to do and like Lincoln did about slavery.

The sacrifice

After a satanic pilgrimage that started in 2008, just as in the Jimmy Lee Dykes story, after a 7-day manhunt and after a standoff with Police, Satan used the police to murder Christopher Dorner as a sacrifice consumed by a raging fire on the very night, in fact just minutes before Barak Obama was about to give the State of the Union Address on February 12, 2013 to officially enter his fourth year in office. A black man was offered as a sacrifice to Satan just before he spoke to the nation to make his lies believable to the nation and to give him the satanic power to enter his second term in the blood of a black man like the mulatto Cain found satanic power in the blood of the black Abel, but it did not work. Obama is a loser and as a loser, Barak Obama will not be allowed by the living God, Jesus and their angels to shed the blood of 600, 000 innocent Americans.

The sacrifice of Christopher Dorner came exactly one year after Whitney Houston was murdered on February 11, 2012, the day before Lincoln's February 12 birthday and just hours before the Grammy ceremony in which Satan attempted to transfer the natural authority of the black Houston to Adele, a white woman from the eastern hemisphere.

The murder of Christopher Dorner came precisely on February 12, on Lincoln's birthday and like the murder of Whitney, his death came just minutes before a national event took place:

On February 11, 2011, Whitney Houston, a black woman was murdered just hours before a national event; the Grammy and in February 2012 Christopher Dorner, a black man was murdered just minutes before a national event; the State of the Union Address and both came on Lincoln's birthday, the father of the American nation that came to be after the Civil War. These are not coincidences—Barak Obama came to murder black and white Hebrews for the atonement of the Jews like Lincoln did before him.

Memories of Waco

The way the police murdered Christopher Dornan was very similar to the way the U.S. government murdered David Koresh and his supporters in Waco, Texas when the government set fire on the compound, burning everyone alive as a holocaust to Satan on April 19, 1993; like Dorner, David Koresh was also a false prophet whose mind was hijacked by Satan.

The mystic in the Carnival Cruise Ship fire

On April 20, 2010, Barak Obama and Hilary Clinton engineered an explosion in the Gulf of Mexico, the biblical Salt Sea; the explosion killed 11 workers and caused an oil leak that lasted 86 days—a Jewish voodoo ceremony because Ishmael, the father of the Jews was born when Abraham was 86 years old. Barak Obama did this because the Civil War really started when Lincoln ordered a naval engagement in the Gulf of Mexico on April 20, 1861, which created a huge fiery explosion and took the lives of many soldiers. In 2012, Obama shot down a small plane in the Gulf of Mexico on April 20. However, this year, in 2013, Barak Obama engineered a fire in the Carnival cruise in the Gulf of Mexico, exactly on February 10, 2013, the day the living God spoke to Noah, telling him to get in the Ark with his family, 7 days before the Great Deluge started on February 17, the same day Barak Obama signed the stimulus package in 2009.

The cruise ship passengers were dedicated as human sacrifices

The passengers of the Carnival cruise ship have no idea what the living God, the creator of heaven and earth and Jesus his son have done for them, Obama was prepared to murder all of them by offering them as holocaust by fire to Satan. One female passenger captured this miracle when she explained that they were not notified by the ship's management of the fire. When they were awakened in the middle of the night they were told everything was fine and they should go back to bed. Anyone is free to argue and to interpret this statement however he likes, but one thing is for certain; if cruise officials told the passengers that they should go back to bed while the ship was on fire, it can only mean that these officials were involved in a conspiracy to murder them. A huge offering of at least 3000 people would have emboldened Obama and would have made it possible for Obama to offer more Americans as sacrificial holocaust to Satan up to the total destruction of the black and the white children of Jacob, the real Hebrews of Israel who live primarily in the Southern Confederate States of America.

Satan intended to begin to murder the passengers on February 10, 2013, the same day the Living God told Noah to board the Ark with his family before the Great Deluge started on February 17. But the living God did not allow Obama and his associates to murder the passengers of the cruise ship. Consistent with the Civil War, Obama visited Nashville, Tennessee the day after he gave the State of the Union Address because Nashville and Memphis make up the biblical Jericho, the battle of Nashville that took place during the American Civil War was a reenactment of the biblical battle of Jericho.

The symbolism of the ship

The name of the ship—the Carnival is mystically important since this incident occurred exactly on the day the last three days of

Carnival began, leading to Fat Tuesday, the last day of Carnival, which is a satanic celebration. Finally, on Monday May 27, 2013, a fire broke out on the Royal Caribbean's Grandeur of the Seas, but again, no one died, the blood of the innocents was not shed as the Obama plan was defeated.

The mystic in the French Mali invasion

Hilary and Bill Clinton were soundly defeated by the armies of heaven. Bill Clinton as Satan himself has been telling Barak Obama, the false prophet, the son of Satan what to say and what to do and Hilary Clinton, the Lucifer of this age, has been traveling around the entire world to create trouble and political instability to advance the cause of darkness. In one of her last international trips as secretary of State, Hilary Clinton said Algeria should invade Mali, since Algeria was unwilling to act, shortly after she resigned as Secretary of state, the French government decided to invade Mali to set a Waco like voodoo offering through the first 100-day religious doctrine. The French had engaged in the same First 100-day ritual offering that Barak Obama had carried out in 2009 through the Somali pirate episode which ended in the murder of several black Somalis and the arrest of one young black Somali who was brought to New York for trial on April 20, 2009.

The French invaded Mali primarily to set up a 100-day offering that would ultimately end on April 19 or April 20, 2013, but this time the voodoo will not work and Obama will not find any authority under heaven to continue in his path of darkness—Obama will go to prison for war crimes, for thefts and Bill and Hilary Clinton will also go to prison for war crimes and crimes against humanity.

The complicity of the American media

The homosexuals and the Lesbians in the American T.V. media have been attacking everyone who speaks out against Barak Obama; they have even attacked lawmakers and other public officials who defend the cause of righteousness. The media refuse to report the crimes of Hilary Clinton and Barak Obama in Afghanistan where Obama is using drones to murder women and children in a psychological warfare against the Taliban.

The media have remained silent on the huge and incredible losses of human lives that Obama is experiencing in Afghanistan, The media refuse to report the role of Hilary Clinton in transforming the peaceful uprising against Bashar Al Assad into a vicious and violent Civil War, which has quickly transformed into an international conflict involving Syria, Turkey, where NATO has deployed missiles to protect the Syrian rebels, and Israel has also become involved in the war when it officially penetrated Syrian air space in January, 2013 to bomb targets inside Syria in violation of international law. Jordan has also become increasingly involved in the conflict. The state of Jordan is being used as a training ground for American boots on the ground in Syria—Jordan is also overwhelmed with refugees from Syria and Iraq.

Meanwhile the Kurds are also involved in the fighting, mostly against Turkey; however, the living God has put it in the heart of Vladimir Putin of Russia and Ahmadinejad of Iran to help defend the government of Syria to protect Bashar Al Assad. Hilary Clinton has led the U.S. into a war with Russia and Iran inside Syria and the media refuse to report it. Hilary Clinton has set up a fund for Syrian officials who defect from the Bashar al Assad's government and a small number of them has defected, but they have not been able to help Obama overthrow Bashar Al Assad. Hilary Clinton has created a mess in the world, yet the homosexuals in the American media claim she was an effective Secretary of State and she is popular among Americans. If she was so effective why did she quit? The reality is simple; Hilary Clinton was forced to resign from her post because she was not able to achieve her lesbian goals, which included the provocation of civil wars in the U.S. and in Haiti to satisfy the blood liability of this Sabbath. She wanted to use the power of Lucifer to help Obama remove Bashar Al Assad from office to stop the war in Syria so she could transfer the demons from the Middle East to the U.S where they could create mayhem, but she was not able to.

This idea of transferring the dark spirits of war from Syria to the U.S explains why the talk of mental health has been so prevalent in the American discourse today. The freemasons from Washington were expecting a huge number of zombies to invade the minds of Americans and to cause them to act violently and irrationally, but this has not happened.

The mystic of the budget negotiations called sequester and the resignation and the sequester of the Pope

Since Barak Obama received the Democratic nomination for President on August 28, 2008, the illuminati have been engaged in a fierce battle with the forces of heaven for the control of the earth. And a Great Tribulation has ensued in the world because the saints of the living God have revolted against Barak Obama and his demons, as a result, the entire world is now at war. But the American media refuse to report the crimes of Hilary Clinton and Barak Obama in the world. The Washington illuminati use secret codes and secret languages to express their magic art. For example, the average American understands that it is not "normal" for lawmakers to frame a budget negotiation as "sequester", it does not make sense. What does "sequester" really mean?

In this case, "sequester" means that Satan attempted to keep the "Faithful Servant" of Jesus "sequestered so he would remain imprisoned by Satan. And as a prisoner he would not have the power to resist and to fight against Satan, but this voodoo is not working.

Satan also used this voodoo in the doctrine of pre-emption symbolically through the resignation and the sequestration of the Pope. The Pope officially resigned from the Church on the same day "the sequester" went into effect. In the doctrine of pre-emption, this also means that Barak Obama should not be arrested since the Pope has already volunteered to go to prison, to be "sequestered". But the voodoo will not work because Barak Obama is a criminal, a thief, a murderer, a foreign born college drop-out and he will go to prison for his crimes.

The illuminati use this secret code to communicate about many other subjects; the following are a few examples of the secret language of the illuminati:

Sequester: the voluntary resignation and the sequestration of the Pope to symbolize the neutralization of the "Faithful Servant" of Jesus and to prevent the arrest and the sequestration of Barak Obama and Hilary Clinton, but it will not work.

Birth Control: population control, the murder of the innocent people as human sacrifices for the atonement of the Jews and the freemasons

Obamacare: The PPACT of blood legislation passed by Congress on March 23, 2010 to provoke a Civil War in America and to kill at least 600,000 black and white American Hebrews. This PPACT is the same PPACT the Living God made with Moses on January 10 when he told Moses to tell the Hebrew Israelites to select an animal for the Passover dinner. Obama came to kill innocent Americans for the atonement of the freemasons, the Jews, and the Catholics among others—that is not only wrong and immoral, it is illegal—Barak Obama must go to prison.

Gun control legislation: slave reform. America is still a nation of half free and half slaves; the gun control issue is the same as the racial profiling issue that led to the fugitive Act, an Act that ultimately led to the American Civil War

Background check: racial profiling of blacks and some whites—they are the new criminals—with mental health issues.

Repeal of the civil right laws: the reintroduction of measures designed to suppress black votes under the guise of progress and racial equality

Immigration reform: To pave the way for the people of the east, the people from Saudi Arabia, Indonesia, the illegal Mexicans, the cursed Canaanites, the Indians and the Chinese to take the place of real black and white American Hebrews.

Obama came for the people of the east and the part of the legislation that offers jobs and citizenship to foreigners with a special college degree is designed to welcome the Indians and the Chinese who came to the U.S to study.

Entitlement reform: whenever Satan proposes to make any reform, it really means the opposite. This means Barak Obama came to plunder Social Security, Medicare and Medicaid by qualifying the rich and the foreigners of the east for entitlements and disqualifying the black and the white American Hebrews.

The homosexual freemasons of Washington are at war against the real black and white Americans from the Confederate States of America, the biblical nation of Israel and the other children of Isaac and Jacob who live throughout the American kingdom, it is at their expense that everyone in the world seeks to exist and to prosper.

Obama is a thief, he came to steal the wealth of the American people and to transfer it to the Jews on Wall Street to drive Americans to complete poverty, but it will not work.

Climate Change: This is a secret code that means that the Living God is now in full control of the spirits that control natural disasters in the world, including; hurricanes, tornadoes, earthquakes, and fir from heaven. The illuminati said Obama was running from behind after the Living God struck first in Haiti with the powerful January 12, 2010 earthquake that killed the entire United Nations army. And it is just a matter of time before the Living God punishes America. This punishment is likely to come in 2018, 50 years after the murder of Martin Luther King Jr. in 1968. The 50th year is the year of jubilee when the Living God does justice by punishing the wicked and by returning the wealth that was stolen from his children.

Chapter 21

The 2013 Diary of the Syrian Proxy War

The satanic nation known as Israel in the Middle East has attacked Syria on May 4, 2013 and May 5, 2013 without provocation

The Jewish nation of Israel invaded Syria's air space and bombed Syria on May 4, 2013 and again on May 5, 2013 to provoke Syria and Iran to retaliate so that NATO and the U.S can have an excuse to enter the war in Syria. However, in their quest to camouflage Obama's real identity as the antichrist, a war thirsty beast, the illuminati used the nation of Israel to provoke Syria to war. NATO used the same provocative approach in Libya in March 2011 just before NATO began to bomb Libya on March 19, 2011. On that day, Barak Obama was sent to South America with a number of businessmen, apparently on a trip to promote trade between U.S. companies and South American businesses. The strategy was the same in May 2013; Barak Obama found himself away in Central and South America while Israel was bombing Syria by illegally violating the airspace of a sovereign nation without provocation.

By stepping out of Washington while Israel bombed Syria, Barak Obama acted as if he had nothing to do with the action of the Jewish Israel nation, when in fact the actions of the Jewish state of Israel represent a concerted effort between the United States and Israel with the explicit approval of Barak Obama. As an antichrist, Obama must continuously pretend he is the good guy when in fact, he is the son of Satan; a homosexual Dracula; a criminal who was born to lose.

The American media consistently maintain the cover up of Obama as the antichrist by framing all discussions in his favor. For example, after Obama declared that it would be a Red Line if Syria uses chemical weapon against Al Qaeda, the U.S., and other rebel groups backed by the U.S., Obama actually gave chemical weapon to Al Qaeda to use against Syria so that the U.S. would have an excuse to attack Syria by accusing Bashar Al Assad of using chemical weapons against innocent civilians. Barak Obama followed through on his Red Line promise to get involved deeper in the Syrian conflict by arming the rebels and by using Israel as a proxy to bomb Syria on May 4 and again on May 5, 2013, killing a number of Syrian soldiers. But Syria did not fall for the bait, Bashar Al Assad has shown poise and patience and he was rewarded by Russia with a new shipment of anti-ship missiles to defend Syria from Obama's impeding invasion. In fact, according to some analysts, the Israeli attack was also designed to test what kind of missiles Russia had delivered to Syria in order to evaluate Syria's defensive abilities, but Al Assad did not take the bait. By attacking Syria, Israel was hoping that Al Assad would tip his hands by showing the real Syrian military capability and possibly the location of his anti-aircraft defenses, but Al Assad decided not to respond in order to preserve the element of surprise when he defends his country against future aggression from Israel and the United States.

However, the media and many in Congress continue to publically criticize Obama for not following through with his promise to attack Syria, while they know full well that they are lying and that Obama has sent American boots on the ground in Syria to coordinate with the rebels, including Al Qaeda to overthrow Al Assad and Obama has also attacked Syria through Israel. What they really want is for Obama to provide air support to the opposition on the ground in Syria by bombing Syria, but Russia made it clear that such an action would mean war between the U.S. and Russia.

This was the same strategy the Jews had used against Hitler; they continuously criticized Hitler in public to convince the German people that Hitler was against the Jews when in fact Hitler was with the Jews.

Barak Obama is a Jew, a mulatto Jew who was born in Haiti, the biblical Jerusalem like Cain; the first mulatto murderer in the world. Obama was brought forth by a Jewish mother; he was incubated in a Jewish womb for the evil cause of the Jews. If Obama was against Israel why would he pick a cabinet made entirely of Jews, especially in his first term with people like Rham Emanuel, Timothy Geithner, Ben Bernanke and Hilary Clinton among others?

If Barak Obama was really against the Jews, why would he give the entire $800billion from the so called stimulus package to mostly big banks and investment firms like Goldman Sachs that are managed by Jews Sachs? Why?

If Barak Obama was really against Israel why would he allow Ben Bernanke and Timothy Geithner to completely loot the American treasury by printing $86 billion every month to buy mortgage backed securities, the toxic assets of the banks that lost money during the 2008 financial crisis? This also led to a quiet whisper in Washington that the Federal Reserve may never sell the mortgage backed securities it is buying—this is so because they are worthless—the purchase is a giveaway to Jews who have lost money in the 2008 financial crisis. The reality is far from the lies the American media and the European media have been telling the world; Barak Obama is a murderer, a criminal, a thief and a butcher who came to provoke a Civil War in the United States through the policies of division, the politics of race and class warfare, but he is being defeated like a cheap piece of garbage, a piece of basaltic trash from Hawaii, a little homosexual punk who was born to lose.

After Israel bombed Syria for the second day, Israel, the U.S. and the entire European media were shocked that Syria, Iran, Hezbollah and even Russia had not retaliated right away on the face of such extreme and blatant provocation; they wanted to provoke Iran into a war and NATO wanted an excuse to invade Syria, but the Syrian quartet headed by Russia and Iran has remained calm. This Sabbath is being managed by Jesus, the Christ of the living God and the days of bloody riots in the streets of Port-au-Prince, Haiti or in American cities like Detroit, Chicago, Los Angeles, New York, are over and the traditional hot headed moves from Arab dictators vis-à-vis Israel are over.

The living God has taken control of the entire war against Satan. Barak Obama has blood in his underwear as a homosexual, he has blood in his hands as a murderer and he is being defeated everywhere in the world. He is being defeated in Haiti, the real biblical Jerusalem, where the January 12, 2012 earthquake has killed his entire army; he is being defeated in Afghanistan, the biblical Armageddon, where the Taliban have been dealing heavy losses to the U.S and its allies. Barak Obama and his allies are being defeated and humiliated in Pakistan, in Yemen, and throughout Africa where the U.S is also suffering significant losses. The days of emotional responses are over and Syria, Russia, Iran and Hezbollah will respond to the Israeli aggression at a place and a time of their choosing, according to their own battle plan, but they will respond and the U.S and the Middle East evil nation that calls itself Israel will be defeated. No nation can succeed when its leader is a foreign born homosexual college drop-out like Barak Obama, Barak Obama will be defeated. World War III has already started; it is just a matter of time before the U.S. is forced to engage militarily against Russia. Barak Obama has put the world on a nonreversible path of war that would escalate into a nuclear war involving many nations including; Russia and Iran—the Middle East nation of Israel will be destroyed and afterward, the entire world will be at peace for One Thousand years and then forever.

Breaking News:

The May 9, 2013 Benghazi hearings

The illuminati have done everything to convince the American people and the people of the world that Satan does not exist so they can carry on with the work of Satan without being exposed. In 1776, the year the American nation was born, Adam Smith published a book entitled "the Wealth of Nations" in which he referred to Satan as an "invisible hand" who is orchestrating commerce among the people of a nation. However, what Adam Smith failed to explain was that there are two invisible hands; the hand of the living God, the creator of heavens and earth and the hand of Satan who pretends to be god, the adversary of the living God. Satan orchestrates events from behind the scene just as the living God orchestrates events from the invisible world and all human beings react accordingly; those who listen to the living God act according to the guidance of the living God and those who listen to Satan act according to the dictate of Satan.

On May 9, 2013, Satan, sensing that the Benghazi hearings could become a turning point in the eight-month old investigation in the murder of Christopher Stevens, the American ambassador to Libya and three other Americans, decided to engineer two other events in order to pre-empt the news of the Benghazi hearings so that the media would not devote enough time in the coverage of the Benghazi hearings. So just a few days before May 9, 2013, the invisible hand of Satan engineered the escape of three young women who disappeared 10 years ago in Cleveland, Ohio.

The media recognized right away what Satan was doing as the three women symbolize the three women of Egypt or Mexico; three powerful spirits that control the kingdom of Satan. The media wasted little time in sensationalizing the event, covering it almost 24 hours a day, especially on the day of the Benghazi hearings to **'crowd out'** the Benghazi news. But the media did not allow the three women to be questioned and to explain why they have not attempted to leave when they had babies for their kidnapper—they had numerous opportunities to leave, but they have repeatedly chosen not to.

In addition, the very same day of the Benghazi hearing, Satan also engineered the announcement of the verdict in the Jodi Arias murder trial; a criminal woman who savagely murdered her boyfriend in cold blood and attempted to cover it up. The media also jumped on that news as an excuse to not fully cover the Benghazi hearings. Satan is desperately attempting to hide the fact that his son Barak Obama and Lucifer, aka Hilary Clinton murdered Christopher Stevens and three other Americans in Benghazi Libya on September 11, 2012 as human sacrifices, but Satan will not be able to help Obama because the living God, the creator of the heavens and the earth is against him; Barak Obama and Hilary Clinton are going to prison for their crimes against Americans, against the Haitians and against humanity.

This spiritual philosophy is known as the "**spiritual diversion**", the fabrication of a big news story on a date with religious significance, as a decoy to give spiritual cover to an even bigger story. The fact of the matter is, the May 9, 2013 announcement of the Jodi Arias verdict and the continuing coverage of the escape of the three young women from Cleveland, Ohio have no real significance to the nation as the Benghazi hearings; they were simply designed to block the news of the Benghazi hearings and to prevent it from becoming a full story that would ultimately lead to a political scandal that could drive Barak Obama and Hilary Clinton to prison.

Ultimately, the story of the three women that escaped disappeared along with the evidence. The house where the women were supposedly kept in bondage by a man named Castro for many years was bulldozed and Castro was quickly tried, convicted and murdered in prison. The house disappears, the kidnapper is dead and the whole story disappears like a puff of air—the criminals in the American media are liars and deceivers.

Breaking News:

The IRS scandal and the scandal involving the illegal wiretapping of AP reporters' phone conversation do not compare with the gravity of the Benghazi scandal where Barak Obama, Hilary and Bill Clinton actually murdered an American ambassador and three other Americans as human sacrifices to Satan in order to create a diversion to cover up the theft of the entire American treasury, which was announced by Ben Bernanke two days after September 11, 2013 on September 13, 2013.

The Jews and the freemasons in the American media are extremely evil. Their goal is fundamentally against the best interest of the American people—as the priests of Satan, they are only concerned about Satan's global agenda, which calls for China to take control of the Confederate States of America and the Caribbean nations.

The Obama administration has come into an impasse in the Syrian affair because they are being opposed militarily inside Syria by Russia, Iran and Hezbollah and they are being opposed in the United Nations by Russia and China. In addition, the administration is being challenged by the fact that they have not being able to unify the many different factions that are fighting against Al Assad. They have not been able to put a unified coalition together to fight against Bashar Al Assad. Moreover, because they are being opposed by Russia at the UN and because they don't want to risk the exposure of Barak Obama as the antichrist by going it alone in Syria, like George W. Bush did in Iraq, the Obama administration has opted to provoke Syria through an Israeli attack in the hope that Syria would retaliate against Israel, which would have given the U.S. an excuse to openly attack Syria or to attack Syria through Israel.

To this end, the U.S. needs Turkey to work closely with Israel to implement a smoother and a stronger military coalition against Syria; Turkey wants the vacation of Bashar Al Assad from office, but is not comfortable working with Israel because in Turkey's view, the state of Israel is an evil state that has done wrong to the Turkish people and to the Palestinian people. And finally, the administration suffered another setback when a credible UN official confirmed that it was the rebels that used chemical weapons, not the Assad's government. This revelation is enhanced by the admission of John Kerry, the U.S. Secretary of State, that the U.S. gave chemical weapons to the rebels to train them on how to secure chemical weapons sites throughout Syria.

Hence, if Bashar Al Assad has not used chemical weapons, Obama no longer had an excuse to invade Syria and if Barak Obama invades Syria without a credible excuse, Russia, Hezbollah and Iran will become more emboldened in their commitment to help defend the sovereignty of Syria. And Russia and Iran, in particular, would have the moral ground in explaining their actions to their citizens. All of these obstacles put the administration in a precarious position, but the Jews do not care. They want Barak Obama to invade Syria to kill or to remove Bashar Al Assad from office even if it risks war with Russia and Iran, even though they are aware that such a war would risk the lives of millions of Americans and could certainly lead to a nuclear war.

The Jewish illuminati can see that the living God has already stopped the Obama agenda of provoking civil wars in Haiti and in the United States, but in their desperation, they are still hoping to turn events in their favor by provoking a civil war in Haiti by October 2013 through a sham senatorial elections and they are also hoping to provoke violence in the united States by October 2013 for the 2013 war calendar, otherwise Obama would not have any chance of putting his second term evil agenda through Congress.

The Jews also know all the risks inherent in a military confrontation with Russia and Iran and later with Egypt, a nation that will ultimately be forced to side against the U.S. and Israel because of the Palestinian issue, yet, they don't care—they want bloodshed in the streets of the United States and in the streets of Haiti because the righteous blood of the Haitians and the American Hebrews protects every child of righteousness in the world and without weakening the Haitians, Obama has no hope to stop the global resistance against him by removing Bashar Al Assad from office.

To this end, the Jews and the freemasons have created several scandals to put pressure on Barak Obama to act by invading Syria in order to make the scandals go away. However, as soon as Obama succumbs to the pressure and declared that he will supply more arms to the rebels, the media quickly engage in a conspiracy to suppress the reporting of the real scandals, and they decided to create a fake scandal in the Edward Snowden affair.

Breaking News:

Edward Snowden is a CIA agent like Julian Assange—he was chosen to create a fabricated scandal as a decoy to overshadow the Benghazi and the IRS scandals, but it is not going to work.

Snowden is no hero and he has not disclosed any material information that can advance the cause of righteousness. The fact that he has been treated like an ambassador since the story broke makes it obvious that Washington has no interest in arresting him, much like they had no interest in arresting Julian Assange—both Assange and Snowden work for Obama. Furthermore, Snowden is clearly not the messenger of God, the messenger of the living God comes from the biblical Jerusalem, which is located in Haiti, the Garden of Eden, not in hell, in Hawaii, the place of the bottomless pit; the deepest volcano is located in Hawaii.

The American press, including media personalities like Sean Hannity and organizations like Fox News have been pretending to report the news and to expose Barak Obama, but they have been covering up for Barak Obama by suggesting that Obama claimed that the Benghazi attack was provoked spontaneously by an anti Islam video that was aired in Egypt, and that Obama did not want to refer to the incident as a terrorist act perpetrated by Al Qaeda because he did not want the American people to have the idea that Al Qaeda was still a threat after he had killed Bin Laden, especially just two months before the November 6, 2012 presidential election. This criticism is framed to help Obama, not to hurt him, but this time people like Sean Hannity will not be able to help Obama—Barack Obama and Hilary Clinton and Bill Clinton are going to prison. To begin with, Sean Hannity is wrong in his presumption to know what motivated Obama not to respond and to send help to the besieged Americans on September 11, 2013. The media should never assume to know the motive of the Obama administration; the American Congress should ask questions and the investigation should be allowed to run its course in order to reach to the truth. It is well established that Hilary Clinton removed the protection of Ambassador Christopher Stevens, just weeks before September 11, 2012. It has been reported that

Christopher Stevens pleaded with the administration to restore and to beef up his protection, but to no avail. Secondly, it has also been established that on the day of the attacks, the State Department ordered certain units not to intervene on behalf of the besieged Ambassador and Hilary Clinton and Barak Obama also decided not to send any help to them. Clearly, if Obama and Hilary Clinton removed protection from the ambassador just weeks before he was murdered and on the day he was murdered they decided not to send him any help, then the simplest syllogism must lead to the conclusion that Obama and Hilary Clinton wanted him dead. This is clear and the media know it, but they want to cover it up for fear that the culture of human sacrifices, which they are a part of, will be exposed. In addition, the media has not fully explored other aspects of the news on that night. They have not detailed whether the ambassador was actually kidnapped and the facts surrounding his kidnapping. They have not reported in details who kidnapped him if he was indeed kidnapped and the circumstances of his death. They have not really revealed what time he died, and where he died exactly and how his body was recovered. There is so much more to the story that the media and the government have not shared with the American public.

The following questions deserve to be answered: was the ambassador kidnapped? If so, who kidnapped him? Did they make any demand for his release? Who was notified that he was kidnapped? What where the real circumstances surrounding his death? How did he die? Where did he die? Was he killed at the compound or away from the consulate? These are important questions that have yet to be answered—these questions must be explored to really uncover what really happened in Benghazi on September 11, 2013.

Sean Hannity and the rest of the Jewish media are mindful that Ben Bernanke has announced on September 13, 2013 a plan for the

Federal Reserve to buy $86 Billion worth of treasuries and mortgage backed security a month to enrich the criminals on Wall Street, but the media choose to remain silent because they are personally benefiting from the policy of thefts and deceptions. Sean Hannity is a liar and a deceiver, his Radio Show is making millions in selling commercials, while he pretends to fight for the truth. Sean Hannity has made more money in the past 4 and half years of Obama than he made his entire working life combined. He is not really against Barak Obama. Hannity and many others are under the illusion that Obama will save them from the imminent judgment of the living God, but they are sadly mistaken. Obama came to enrich people like Sean Hannity, Rush Limbaugh and Mark Levin, they are all liars and deceivers. If they really wanted to criticize Obama, they would have pointed to the illegal looting of the treasury by Barak Obama, Timothy Geithner and Ben Bernanke and they would have demanded proof that Obama really killed Bin Laden.

A number of lawmakers have already introduced legislation to Congress for the administration to arm the Al Qaeda rebels in Syria with more lethal weapons to fight against Bashar Al Assad, even if this means a direct confrontation with Iran and Russia. These lawmakers are prepared to withdraw their support of the Benghazi investigation against Obama as soon as Obama invades Syria directly or indirectly through Turkey and Israel, but they are delusional because Barak Obama will not succeed when he attacks Syria and this will be made clear when he fails. And the world will know without any doubt that Solomon was not the Messiah, Mohammad was not the Messiah, Lincoln was not the Messiah and certainly, the American Congress will finally understand that the foreign born college drop-out homosexual mulatto named Barak Obama is not the Messiah. Jesus is the Messiah, the son of the living God, the creator of the heavens and the earth; Jesus has been given all power in heavens and on earth and this will be made evident by the end of August through the end of October and through December 2013 when Bashar Al Assad will continue to remain in office in Syria and at that time the U.S. Congress will understand that the homosexual Barak Obama was born to lose and the Jewish illuminati wasted their time by lying to put him in office. Obama will not be able to save them from the wrath of the living God—Barak Obama is done; his second term agenda will not be fulfilled.

If the media wanted to truly expose the crimes of Barak Obama, they would have asked a few simple questions and the Obama administration would have crumbled immediately. For example, the media know that Barak Obama did not kill Bin Laden, if he did he would have produced pictures and videos of the body, like George W. Bush produced the body of Saddam Hussein, but Obama could not do it because he did not have the body of Bin Laden—he did not have the body because he did not kill Bin Laden. The Jewish reporters in the media have also been accomplices in other crimes committed by Barak Obama by deciding to remain silent and by their willingness to report the lies of the administration.

The media made it possible for the homosexual Obama to allow the oil to leak for 86 days in the Gulf of Mexico without questioning the delay because the voodoo was a Jewish religious ceremony performed by the Jewish Obama for the benefit of the Jews. The media remained silent when Barak Obama turned down the help of a dozen countries that offered to help Obama seal the leak. Obama turned down the offers to help just as he and Hilary Clinton turned down repeated requests to help protect and defend Ambassador Christopher Stevens in Benghazi, Libya. Obama failed to act in the Gulf of Mexico because he wanted to wait precisely 86 days, on July 15, 2010 before he could seal the leak, he failed to act in Benghazi, Libya because he wanted Christopher Stevens and three other Americans murdered as human sacrifices to Satan.

Breaking News:

Obama capitulated to the pressure of the American media and declared an escalation of the war against Bashar Al Assad of Syria

Barak Obama and Hilary Clinton have been responsible for the Civil War in Syria from day one. When the real oppressed people of Syria revolted against Bashar Al Assad, Hilary Clinton ignored them, she called Assad a reformer. She and Obama were hoping that Bashar Al Assad would quickly crush the opposition. However, when it became an armed rebellion, they asked Bashar Al Assad to resign so they could quickly replace him with a new evil dictator like they have done in Egypt, replacing Mubarak with Mursi, but when Assad refused to resign, he became their enemy. Notice that Washington did not ask Assad to implement reform to satisfy the demands of the poor, but they asked him to resign so they could continue to oppress the Syrian people through deception by appointing a new evil leader through their traditional sham electoral process in which they give the people of the world the Mark of the beast through the purple ink, which signifies the blood of Abel.

From the onset, Hilary Clinton, as U.S. Secretary of State has put together a coalition of 11 nations, including Saudi Arabia and Jordan to overthrow Bahar Al Assad of Syria—by doing so, she has decided to follow the dark art of Solomon.

The American president is the King of Israel and the King of Israel is supposed to exert power over all other kings of the world, just as all other kings went to Haiti, the real biblical Judah and Israel to offer gifts to Solomon, who became king of Kings after he built the temple, the first Haitian Citadelle. However, whenever the power of the king of Israel is challenged, the king is weakened and if the king cannot crush the opposition, he will be overthrown. This is the spiritual principle that explains why Barak Obama was not able to shed the blood of the innocent Americans through the November 6, 2012 presidential election. And it also explains why Obama has not been able to get his second term agenda, chiefly, his gun reform legislation and his immigration reform legislation through Congress.

Hilary Clinton decided to set up a multi-billion-dollar fund to encourage Syrian officials to betray Bashar Al Assad and to defect to Europe, America, and to Middle East nations like Jordan and Turkey with their families. However, if these traitors were sincere about freedom, they would have not needed money from foreigners to fight for their freedom against Bashar Al Assad—they have defected for money. If there is a Civil War in Syria today it is because and only because Hilary Clinton and Barak Obama have insisted on the resignation of Bashar Al Assad, they never discussed any possibility of economic and political reforms—they are simply engaged in the dark mystical discipline of Solomon, the antichrist.

They have launched a vicious war against Syria; they have murdered tens of thousands of innocent civilians, they have displaced millions more and they have looted almost half of the country. The list of the crimes of Hilary Clinton and Barak Obama is too long to catalog in this presentation—it includes cannibalism where at least one case was documented where a foreign criminal paid by Hilary Clinton and Barak Obama killed a Syrian soldier and took out his heart and ate it on camera, the list also include the use of chemical and biological weapons. The media remain quiet in its Syria reporting as they await the fall of Bashar al Assad, but Assad is sustained by a higher power, the power of the living God who decided to do justice by allowing Assad's resistance to Obama to stand and the living God has also empowered Russia and Iran to support Bashar Al Assad/ In addition, the living God empowered Hezbollah to join the fight on the side of Bashar Al Assad; and as a result, the Syrian Army was able to begin to gain the upper hands by repelling the rebel forces of Barak Obama from different parts of the country, notably in Qusair, in Aleppo in Homs and other suburbs of Damascus.

So when Barak Obama realized he was defeated, and sensing the momentum was shifting in favor of Bashar Al Assad and not wanting to miss the opportunity to overthrow Al Assad in the power of Solomon in the coming month of Ramadan in August 2013, especially between august 15 through August 22, 2013, in June, 2013, Obama declared that Assad used chemical weapons and that the United States would officially get involved in the war by arming the rebels with lethal weapons and by proposing the imposition of a no-fly zone in part of Syria.

The media embraced the news. The Jews were finally relieved because they don't care about the American people; they only care about the global agenda of Satan. At the June, 2013 G-8 meeting, Obama once again, in his desperation, attempted to convince Vladimir Putin of Russia to back down from supporting Bashar Al Assad, but Putin flatly rejected his homosexual advances, Putin made it clear to Barak Obama that there was no evidence that Bashar Al Assad used chemical or biological weapons and that it will be a mistake for NATO or the U.S. to attempt to impose an illegal no-fly zone inside Syria and Putin also made it clear to the homosexual that Russia will continue to honor its contractual obligations to Syria by selling arms to Syria, including S300 and S400 weapons.

By June 24, 2013, on the Feast of Saint John, or the day Satan murdered John the Baptist or the day Barak Obama murdered Michael Jackson in 2009, there were clashes all over the nation of Syria; in Damascus, in Aleppo, in Homs and even in Lebanon, the war was being fought everywhere and several car bombs were detonated in Damascus, a sign of more destructions to come to fulfill the prophecy of Isaiah when he wrote:

"Damascus will cease to be a city, but will become a heap of ruin".

(Isaiah 17:1 NIV)

So like Saul, Obama is on his way to Damascus to bomb Syria back to the Stone Age even worse than he did Libya, but it will be too late for Obama to shift the demons from the Middle East to provoke civil wars in Haiti and in the U.S.

Barak Obama has come to the end of his deceptions; he will soon find himself at a dead-end where impeachment and prison await him and his associates, including Bill and Hilary Clinton.

Chapter 22

The July 2013 Journal of the Great Tribulation

Breaking News:

The month of July 2013 started with human sacrifice offerings in Arizona where 19 firefighters were killed overnight in a wildfire

They were offered as human sacrifices to Satan to satisfy the feast of trumpet from the biblical book of Leviticus, in chapter 23.

July is the American New Year, the Jewish New year, the Canadian New Year, and the illuminati New Year. The American fiscal year begins on July 1st. On July 1, 2013 Barak Obama found himself under great pressure in Salaam, Tanzania, Africa, the last stop on an African tour that included South Africa. Obama went to Africa to beg African nations to help him in his war against the saints of the living God. The homosexual Obama has invaded a great many African nations where he has been taken a lot of casualties, but the Jews in the American media have decided not to report the number of American and UN soldiers that have been dying all over Africa—they are hoping that in time, Obama will be able to turn the tides of war in his favor, but Barak Obama is running out of time. And perhaps, the most egregious aspect of this entire trip was the presence of former President George W. Bush who came along on the trip to help convince African leaders to help Barak Obama by committing military troops to his campaign against the innocent people of the living God. Barak Obama decided to ask George W. Bush for help because George W. Bush has had better relations with African leaders because he has had a much better record with them than Barak Obama who only paid lip service to their concerns. George W. Bush committed significant financial resources to Africa in the fight against the spread of AIDS and HIV, among other undertakings. During a speech in South Africa, Obama attempted to take credit for what George W. Bush has done, the same way the mulatto Solomon has taken credit for everything King David has done before him, so he could pass for good, like King David. Obama wanted to find favor from the African leaders by reminding them of the U.S. commitment to help fight the spread of HIV and AIDS in Africa.

George W. Bush should not have consented to help Barak Obama—if he feels the nation is in trouble he should just allow the impeachment and the subsequent arrest of Barak Obama, but he should not have accepted to go to Africa and ask African leaders to help Obama in any way.

Furthermore, Obama's troubles were not just in Africa. Obama is in trouble everywhere in the world, including in Afghanistan, the biblical Armageddon, Pakistan, Mali, Libya, Iraq, Yemen and Syria among other places. In the meantime, events in Middle East Egypt has taken a turn for the worst where huge numbers of Egyptians gathered in Cairo on 6/30/2013, on the one-year anniversary of Mohammad Mursi's rise to the presidency through an American engineered election to demand Mursi's resignation. And on July 1st, 2013, the Egyptian army issued a 48-hour ultimatum to Mursi and to the opposition to reach an agreement. The army warned Mursi that they intend to take over control of the situation to prevent the nation from falling into the abyss of a Civil War.

Barak Obama is in trouble—his hope to provoke a Civil War in the United States and in Haiti by bringing calm to the Middle East through the overthrow or the killing of Bashar Al Assad is rapidly fading. Not only Assad is still in control of Syria, but the violence of civil wars is threatening to engulf other places like Turkey and Egypt.

Breaking News:

As a sign that Barak Obama is in trouble, on July 3, 2013 the White House announced the delay of the Employer Mandate part of the Health Care PPACT Obama signed with the devil to shed the blood of innocent Americans; the part that requires employer to provide adequate coverage to their employees.

That part of the law was supposed to begin to be implemented in 2014, but now it won't happen until 2015. Just imagine this: a homosexual mulatto rose to power in the United States, a mostly white racist nation and begin to pass laws that are completely archaic and uncivilized, yet everyone is happy to comply with the dictate of Barak Obama because the United States is an uncivilized homosexual nation. Obama came to help the Jewish illuminati, the freemasons, the Catholic Illuminati on Wall Street and to pay financial restitution to homosexuals, but his plan to shed the blood of the black and the white Hebrews for the atonement of sinners will not work.

Breaking News:

Barak Obama, Bill, Hilary Clinton urged the Egyptian military to force Mohammad Mursi out of power to avoid another Civil War in the Middle East

Jesus has commissioned me to write many books to expose the secrets of Satan so that the children of the truth may believe and so that they may be saved. The truth has arrived and there is no longer a need for anyone to engage in conspiracy theories.

Satan seeks to enslave everyone—even his own offprings—that is his nature—he is a negative force—the disobedient woman, Eve is his servant—she is the negative pole of the battery. Jesus the son of the living God is the positive pole and the living God himself is the alternator—the source of all energy that powers the universe and he is sovereign above the negative and the positive poles.

For example, The United Constitution gave the U.S. citizens a Bill of Rights with Ten Amendments. These Amendments tell the U.S. citizens what rights they have, but these so called rights have been taken away from them over time to enslave them.

However, God gave Moses Ten Commandments, which tell the Hebrew Israelis what not to do, otherwise they are free to live in complete freedom. God does not tell his children what right they have because his children are free—he only tells them what not to do in order to avoid death and destruction. God started the journey of life with men by giving Adam only one Commandment, one law: Thou shall not eat from the tree of the knowledge of good and evil, the day you eat of it you should surely die—except for that one tree, Adam was free to eat from any other tree from the Garden.

Since Washington practices a satanic theocracy, the actors in Washington always support dictators that oppress their own people—keeping them on a tight leash so they would not revolt. Thus, Washington is pleased when a leader is strong enough to keep his own people in bondage by ruling over them through deceptions. For example, leaders like Fidel Castro, Hugo Chavez have been the quiet friends of Washington, the actors from Washington pretend to criticize them in public, but privately Washington was very pleased with Hugo Chavez, but Chavez only paid lip service to the plight of his people. The Venezuelan masses remained in poverty until today while Chavez made a name for himself as a progressive who cared about his people, but the evidence betray him, the same goes for Fidel Castro, whom Washington quietly adores, but again, the evidence show that Fidel Castro has totally abused his people, driving them into a desperate poverty, yet the American media have helped him built a legacy of a true revolutionary, when in fact, Fidel Castro is one of the most corrupt criminal that the world has ever seen.

The philosophy of Satan is to dominate over others, even his servants. In order to achieve this, Satan uses world dictators to subdue their own people by deception and to keep the underclass in quiet poverty until the people wake up and the dictator's shield of deceptions is pierced. Dictators like Fidel Castro and Hugo Chavez rule over the people by deceptions, but the minute their shield of deceptions is pierced and they are uncovered by their people and the people started to revolt against them by demanding change, Washington often acts quickly by replacing the dictator to keep the people from achieving a true revolution by choosing their own leader who would take care of them and help them build a society with prosperity and justice for all. For example, The U.S. had great relations with Iran while the Shaw was in power in Iran, ruling over the people by deceptions by doing the homosexual will of the west; however, when the Iranian people revolted and staged the 1979 revolution by rejecting the homosexual values of the west, the Iranian people became the enemies of America.

The same thing happened in Syria. When Bashar Al Assad took office after the death of his father, the west, notably the U.S., praised him as a reformer and for a long time, he ruled over his people in a quiet bondage, but the U.S. never questioned him, Washington was pleased with him. And as late as 2011 Hilary Clinton called Bashar Al Assad a reformer in the early days of the revolt against him. So when Washington finally realized that his shield of deceptions was pierced and that the opposition against him was not going away, they asked him to resign so they could replace him with another dictator with a fresh mandate of darkness, but Al Assad refused to resign. In order to deny the people of Syria the opportunity to achieve freedom in their revolution, the U.S. quickly decided to send foreign criminals affiliated with Al Qaida to invade Syria in the hope to remove Al Assad from power in order to pre-empt the real people of Syria, but it is not working—the living God is allowing the Assad defiance to stand long enough to deny Obama the opportunity to stop the violence in the Middle East and to bring the demons here in America to cause mayhem and riots in the streets.

This is exactly what happened in Egypt in the early days of the January 2011 revolution against Hosni Mubarak. When the revolution began, at first, Washington demanded Hosni Mubarak to crack down on the protesters and killed them, like animals, and for a brief moment Mubarak attempted to do just that. However, the make-up of the Egyptian nation is different from that of the American nation. Egypt is largely a homogeneous nation with few sectarian divides compare to America where there exist significant and pronounced racial and ethnic divides and as such, it is much easier for a group of white Chicago policemen to shoot at a crowd of largely black people.

So after some in the Egyptian military refused to kill the protestors, Mubarak was urged to resign by Washington, this way they could pre-empt the revolution of the people by giving them Mohammad Mursi through a sham electoral process. This is how Washington keeps the people of the world in bondage. They form secret pacts with evil and criminal leaders throughout the world to oppress their own people and they pretend to criticize some of these leaders in public to pay lip service to the idea of justice and to deceive the people of the world. And whenever a people revolt against an evil leader, the U.S. becomes the first to take the lead in asking that leader to resign so they could replace him with a new criminal; this way the new liar has a fresh mandate of deceptions.

As usual, Jimmy Carter was in Egypt as an observer to elect Mursi and after the election the people of Egypt cried foul, but Jimmy Carter defended the election by conceding there may have been irregularities, but not enough to affect the integrity of the elections—he declared that Mohammad Mursi was legitimately elected and that the will of the people should be respected.

After Mursi took office, he began to consolidate power right away; he attempted to give himself unchecked power, he undertook the writing of a new constitution, an Islamist constitution, according to the perverted views of the Muslim brotherhood, and he completely ignored the will and the needs of every day Egyptian. Meanwhile, the U.S. supported him wholeheartedly and the U.S. continued to fund the Egyptian military, giving them money and military equipments. When the protests slowly started against Mursi, the U.S. Ambassador to Egypt discouraged the protests by reminding the Egyptian people that Mursi was legitimately elected. However, when it becomes clear that the people was not going to back down and the movement against Mursi was real and significant, Washington quickly conspired with the military to remove Mursi from office to avoid another Civil War in the Middle East, but it is too late, the seeds of a Civil War have been sown in Egypt because the military seeks to do the will of Washington, not the will of the people of Egypt and in time the people will realize this. The events that are unfolding in the Middle East and other parts of the world make up the 'Great Tribulation' that was prophesied by Jesus himself. The Great Tribulation is a global movement of resistance against the rule of Satan. This resistance is unlike any other that the world has ever seen. It is a movement where no one is willing to compromise or negotiate with Satan—they are willing to give up their lives so that the will of the living God may be done on earth, not the will of Satan. This is precisely why the people of Egypt and other people of the world will continue to struggle for justice and for righteousness until they prevail in the power of Jesus, not Mohammad.

Breaking News:

On July 3, 2013, under the direction of Barak Obama, General El Sissi overthrew Mohammad Mursi from power in the bloodiest coup in modern history

On the eve of the 4th of July, on the day Barak Obama is scheduled to return from Africa to America, symbolically as the new Mandela, the new Joseph who just got out of prison to become President, Mohammad Mursi was removed from power in Egypt, but the Obama voodoo is not going to work and what happened in Egypt on July 3, 2013 is not the end of Obama's trouble, but the beginning of his troubles. In fact, a number of Egyptians who demanded the resignation of Mursi became very upset when they heard of the plan for the military to take over control of the nation. They understand that the Egyptian military has been bought and paid for by Americans, after Egypt signed the peace accord with Israel. The Egyptian military is the enemy of the Egyptian people, but the friend of America and Israel and the only way out for the people of Egypt is for the military to become divided and for the nation to dissolve the accord with Israel.

Breaking News:

Consistent with the guidance from the books of Leviticus, human offerings were made to Satan from a number of suspicious incidents that occurred around the world, staring on July 7, 2013

In the United States, an Asiana airliner went down in California, killing a number of people, but only two people have been reported to have died, that is absurd. On Saturday July 6, 2013, Asiana airlines Boeing 777 crashed down in flames at the San Francisco International Airport. A number of inconsistencies in the reporting of the incident have triggered suspicions and lead me to easily conclude that the incident was not an accident, but a very deliberate sabotage to attempt to offer the victims of the incident as human offerings to Satan just before July 10, 2013, the Day of Atonement of sins. To begin with, it is reported that the pilot saw a blinding light just seconds before the plane went down and among a number of other details, it was also reported that once the plane was on the ground, the survivors were not sent any help for over an hour. The people repeatedly called 911, but no one came to help them; the ambulances did not show up to rescue them. The officials attempted to defend the delay by arguing that it was too risky to send anyone to the scene for fear that the plane might explode, but that is not an excuse—ambulances are sent all the time to rescue the victims of plane accidents.

Breaking News:

A train derailment in Canada caused a massive fire that triggered incredible damages to an entire neighborhood and killed over 13 people

The Canadian train derailment was also suspicious because it happened about the same time of the plane crash described above and a number of questions remain unanswered to this day about the cause of the train derailment. The evidence shows that it was done to offer human sacrifices to Satan. Around the same time period, a number of other incidents occurred around the world, including the explosion of an Ethiopian airliner in England—the plane caught fire after it had landed, but no one was reported to have died.

Breaking News:

On July 10, 2013, the Day of Atonement, Dzhokhar Tsarnaev was brought to court as a scapegoat to save the offsprings of Satan, but it is not going to work. The fact that Dzhokhar was brought to court on the Day of Atonement further proves that the illuminati are following the guidelines of Satan.

I must remind the reader that this presentation is primarily concerned with the explanation of religious and spiritual concepts—it is a dissertation on the mystery of religious principles and how the illuminati are openly practicing an evil and archaic practice of human sacrifices wide in the open by deceiving the American people and by murdering innocent Americans to atone for their sins. This presentation further proves the assertions I have made in all my other books about the practices of human sacrifices in Washington D.C. I have shown a very clear and consistent pattern of violence on all the dates where Satan demands animal sacrifices in the Bible. I have also explained that there are three Passovers: The Passover of Cain, which is built on human sacrifice through the blood of Abel; the Passover of Moses, which is built upon the animal sacrifice; and the Passover of Jesus, which is founded on the final and voluntary sacrifice of Jesus who offered his own life and blood as a one-time sacrifice for the remission of the sins of those who believe in righteousness. And since without the shedding of blood there is no forgiveness of sins, those who don't belong to the nation of Israel and belong to the covenant of Cain offer human sacrifices instead of animal sacrifices for the atonement of their sins, and they must do so every year. Thus, when the bible gives guidance to offer animal sacrifices, for the offsprings of Satan, it always means human sacrifices.

Breaking News:

Like the Tsarnaev brothers, George Zimmerman and Trayvon Martion were chosen as the two goats and Zimmerman became the scapegoat

"He shall then slaughter the goat for the sin offering for the people and take its blood behind the curtain and do with it as he did with the bull's blood: He shall sprinkle it on the atonement cover and in front of it. In this way he will make atonement for the Most Holy

Place because of the uncleanness and rebellion of the Israelites, whatever their sins have been."

(Leviticus 16:15-16NIV)

In an interview with Sean Hannity, George Zimmerman stated that it was the will of God that he murdered Trayvon Martin, he was wrong because Satan is not God. Satan did not create the world and he is not the ultimate decision maker as to who shall live and who shall die. There is no question that Satan told George Zimmerman to kill Trayvon Martin as a human sacrifice to provoke riots throughout the United States of America in order to shed enough blood for the atonement of the sins of the Jews. They need the blood of the black and the white Hebrews to be shed for their atonement or else, the angels of the living God will come soon to punish them through earthquakes, fire from heaven, tornadoes, tsunamis and many other disasters. America is about to be punished and many places will no longer be recognizable and some areas will completely disappear.

The freemasons in Washington and those in the media know this and they are growing more and more desperate to provoke violence among the blacks and the white Hebrews to shed their blood in Haiti and in the U.S., but it is not working. The Living God has shifted all the violence to the Middle East where division is needed to bring about real and fundamental changes that would lead to the freedom of the great masses that have been kept for generations under the thumbs of dictators who have conspired with Washington to enslave them, from Egypt, to Algeria, to Libya, to Syria, to Lebanon, to Jordan, to Yemen, to Saudi Arabia and everywhere in the Middle East and Africa.

Consider this brief chronology of events: on about the same day Tsarnaev was brought to court in Boston. The defense on the George Zimmerman case rested on the very Day of Atonement, on the 10th of July 2013 and between Thursday July 11and Friday July 12, 2013, both sides made closing arguments and turned the case to a jury of six women; and on Saturday the 13th of July they have pronounced a verdict of not guilty, making George Zimmerman an official scapegoat according to this entry from Leviticus 16.

"When Aaron has finished making atonement for the Most Holy Place, the tent of meeting and the altar, he shall bring forward the live goat. He is to lay both hands on the head of the live goat and confess over it all the wickedness and rebellion of the Israelites—all their sins—and put them on the goat's head. He shall send the goat away into the wilderness in the care of someone appointed for the task. The goat will carry on itself all their sins to **a remote place**; and the man shall release it in the wilderness."

(Leviticus 16:20-22 NIV)

As it is written above, the live goat will carry on itself all their sins to a remote place. This is precisely the case with George Zimmerman who was led to a remote place after the verdict was read, an undisclosed location for fear of his life to fulfill the guidelines found above. The Jews in the media knew right away that George Zimmerman was sent as a scapegoat for their salvation that is why they defended Zimmerman from day one. They were hoping that violence would have erupted that very night of the 13 of July, but it did not. Barak Obama, the chief priest of the Jews jumped in front of the story by making a statement after the verdict was read in which he said that America is a nation of laws. By this, he meant that he was prepared to clamp down on those who violate the law by rioting in the streets. Obama made this statement to reassure the Jews that he was firmly prepared to shed the blood of the black and the white Hebrews who would engage in riots, but the violence Obama anticipated never came; instead, it was in Egypt that the news headlines showed that 7 people got killed and hundreds of others were injured by the Egyptian military to further solidify a coup against the 'freely and legally' elected Mohammad Mursi, a coup that Obama himself supported and strongly encouraged in the hope to stop bloodshed, but Obama is not strong enough to stop the Civil War that is coming to Egypt.

The people of Egypt will have to fight to be freed from the yoke of the Peace Accord through which they have been enslaved by their own military in concert with Washington and Israel.

Three days after the George Zimmerman verdict was announced, when Washington realized that there were no riots in the United States, they panicked and decided to send politicians to make inflammatory statements to provoke anger in the American national consciousness. And so one by one, some of the most powerful politicians started to come out to criticize the verdict. Harry Reid commented on the verdict, hinting that the case may not be over, Hilary Clinton—Lucifer herself came out and criticized the verdict, she too hinted that the case may not be over—she is the most desperate of them all because she is the most evil of them all. And among many others, Eric Holder, the U.S. Attorney General made an appearance at a NAACP conference in Orlando, Florida to make a speech in which he promised that the Justice Department will review the evidence in the case to decide whether federal charges could be brought against George Zimmerman. They are desperate because the George Zimmerman case is their last best hope to provoke a race war in America in this Sabbath.

And since the verdict did not trigger any violence, they are scheming to find a way to produce a second round of the George Zimmerman saga, perhaps a federal trial in the hope to provoke bloodshed in America along racial lines. However, the creator of heaven and earth will not allow the blood of the black and the white Hebrews to be shed for the atonement of the wicked. Barak Obama, the head of the Klu Klux Klan, the false prophet of Satan has failed once again. God will do justice in the Zimmerman case by taking the offsprings of Satan in their own trap.

Breaking News:

On July 14, 2013, Obama sent a team to Egypt to help the Egyptian army manage the transition from the July 3, coup

Obama panicked and sent a team to Egypt to ease the violence, but his envoys were met with more violence; on July 15, 2013 over 7 people were killed in Egypt and many others were injured. Obama was hoping that these deaths would have taken place here in the U.S through the Zimmerman protests, but unfortunately for him, the demons have been transferred to Syria, to Egypt, to Turkey, to Libya, to Iraq and other places in the Middle East—Obama is done—there is not going to be another Civil War in America.

Chapter 23

The Year of the Jubilee

Why did Barak Obama comment on the George Zimmerman's verdict on July 19, 2013?

The answer is twofold:

Firstly, Obama made the comments to fabricate a news story spiritually designed to block out another even more significant news story; the news that the city of Detroit filed for bankruptcy on July 18, 2013. The bankruptcy filing was a way for the city of Detroit to rob American investors of their invested money by putting Revenue bond holders ahead of those who own General Obligation bonds, which are backed by the full faith and credit of the city of Detroit. This is significant because, according to the contract agreement, as long as the city of Detroit has taxing power, it is obligated to honor the General Obligation bonds ahead of any other claim. But Obama decided to ignore the law once again. Those who invested in Detroit's municipal bonds are about to be paid pennies on the dollars. Secondly, the Detroit bankruptcy is also designed to seek serious concessions from the pension plans of retirees and current employees including; firemen, policemen, and others. And finally, the bankruptcy also demands that the city of Detroit cuts cost by further reducing the services it provides to its citizens. This was huge news since the city of Detroit is the biggest city to have filed for bankruptcy in the history of the United States and worse yet, the concessions that the filing is seeking may set the wrong precedent by encouraging other cities with the same problems to also declare bankruptcies by making the same reverse Robin Hood demands

The Religious aspect of the bankruptcy

"At the end of every seventh year you are to cancel the debts of those who owe you money. This is how it is to be done. Each of you who have lent money to any Israelite is to cancel the debt; you must not try to collect the money; the LORD himself has declared the debt canceled.

(Deuteronomy 15: 2 GNT)

According to the above entry from the biblical book of Deuteronomy, at the end of each Sabbath or every seventh year there must be a forgiveness of debt throughout the land. This is the biblical concept that established the bankruptcy laws in America, especially the concept of chapter 7. And since America does not follow the laws of the living God; it does the reverse; a reverse Robin Hood where the rich asked that their debts be forgiven by the poor and the middle class. Essentially, the rich simply refuse to pay their debts and instead of cancelling the debts of the poor, the poor end up with even more debts and more misery—a complete travesty. This explains why the number of bankruptcy filing has skyrocketed under Obama, especially from major American companies like GM, Chrysler, American Airlines and others—these companies buy goods and services from smaller firms and simply refuse to pay them—they enrich themselves at their expense. This dark reality is a classic reconciliation with the biblical guidelines. The poor was supposed to be bailed out in this Sabbath, instead the rich demand that they get bailed out and Obama did just that because, as the antichrist, he came for them. The college students' loans were supposed to be forgiven, instead, Obama and Congress shifted the issue from the exorbitant debt to the interest rate the students are supposed to pay, meaning the rate of interest becomes the issue, not the debt itself. The people who lost their houses were supposed to get their houses back, but instead, the Wall Street bankers who held toxic assets from the subprime mortgage crisis got bailed out when Ben Bernanke announced on September 13, 2013 the purchase the toxic assets by buying $86 billion of mortgage backed securities every month.

This is precisely one of the reasons why Barak Obama has commented on the George Zimmerman verdict on July 19, 2013—the comments were made to draw the attention of the American people away from the Detroit's bankruptcy filing and to keep it from exploding into a real national scandal.

In addition, the following entries provide even more details about the timing of the Detroit's bankruptcy filing:

"Count seven times seven years, a total of forty-nine years. Then, on the **tenth day of the seventh month, the Day of Atonement,** send someone to blow a trumpet throughout the whole land. In this way you shall set the fiftieth year apart and proclaim freedom to all the inhabitants of the land. During this year all property that has been sold shall be restored to the original owner or the descendants, and any who have been sold as slaves shall return to their families."

(Leviticus 25: 8-10GNT)

"In this year all property that has been sold shall be restored to its original owner."

(Leviticus 25: 13 GNT)

This above biblical entry explains the concept of Jubilee, the year after the seventh Sabbath, or the 50th year. In that year the Living God promises not only to return people's properties, but he also promises to punish the evil doers by liberating those who are in captivity. It would be exactly 50 years in 2018 since Martin Luther King Jr. was murdered in 1868; 2018 will be the year of Jubilee—a great judgment will come upon America in 2018.

The timing of the filing on July 18, 2013 also satisfies the biblical guidelines in the satanic theocracy of Satan, which the U.S. adheres to. July 10 is the Day of Atonement, but the bankruptcy was filed on July 18, 2013 to coincide with the birthday of Nelson Mandela, who has been the priest of the kingdom of Satan since 1994, the year after Bill Clinton, the beast who came in the spirit of Lincoln (Lincoln and Clinton mean the same thing, it is the same set of letters) became President of the United States.

The second reason Obama made the announcement on July 19, 2013 was to use the dark art of secret coded messages to transfer anger to the black community so they would express anger and to riot on July 20, 2013, the same date Obama himself killed a number of innocent Americans in a movie theatre in Aurora, Colorado in 2012. Consider this: Obama said; "This could have been me", supposedly referring to the murdered Trayvon Martin; however, this short statement is not the proper language of a statesman who is commenting on a murder trial that captivated the attention of the entire nation. That statement does not elevate the nation and does not inspire black people to look forward to the future with a sense of optimism, instead, it fosters the despair of blacks because if a guy who is supposedly a black president could not do justice or could not inspire a jury to make the right and the just decision, then black Americans do not have any other reason to hope. If a black President cannot help them, then all they have left is despair and thus their only recourse is to express their anger through violence by engaging in riots and mayhem. However, the living God has put a real and legitimate hope in the hearts of all Americans to convince them that justice will be done soon in America and that the angels of heaven are on their way right now to punish those who are conspiring with Barak Obama, Bill and Hilary Clinton to murder innocent Americans.

When Barak Obama talks about white people locking their cars when they see a black American, that kind of discourse does not elevate the nation, it reduces the nation to the primitive state found in the old language of darkness that divides Americans; that language is only designed to drive Americans into the darkest and the deepest abyss of despair that ultimately leads to a cult-de-sac of violence and deaths, but this time it will be different.

From the night of July 13, 2013, when the verdict in the George Zimmerman trial was first announced, up to July 19, 2013, when it became clear that the verdict had failed to provoke riots throughout American cities from angry and disappointed blacks and other Americans, Barak Obama panicked and decided to make the comments in the hope that the marches that Al Sharpton had scheduled for July 20, 2013 through at least 100 or 101 American cities would finally provoke riots and shed the blood that he needed to continue to dominate the children of Jacob, but it did not happen. Al Sharpton was not able to help Barak Obama shed the blood of the innocents, instead, violence exploded in the east; in Egypt, in Syria and massive riots exploded in Australia. Barak Obama the false prophet, Bill Clinton, the beast and Hilary Clinton, Lucifer are finished like the dinosaurs that they are—their criminal deeds have been exposed and soon they will go to prison for their crimes against the Haitians, the innocent Americans, and against humanity.

Breaking News:

On July 23, 2013 the violence continues in Cairo, Egypt between the Muslim Brotherhood and those who oppose Mohammad Mursi

Barak Obama was hoping to help avoid a Civil War in Egypt by removing Mursi from office, but instead he moved Egypt closer to the brink of a Civil War much quicker than anyone could have anticipated.

By removing Mursi from office, Obama violated the foundation of the core principle of democracy; the notion of free and fair election through which the people of a nation freely and democratically participate in a process to elect the leader of their nation and it was through that process that Mohammad Mursi came to power and he was celebrated by Washington as a freely elected leader. Therefore, his forceful and violent removal from office by the Egyptian military has betrayed the notion of democracy and has further exposed the hypocrisy of Washington. The military coup against Mohammad Mursi was bloody; many people died and thousands of others have been arrested and Mursi himself has remained in prison 20 days after his removal from office on July 3, 2013.

Washington has done this before; they had engineered the same coup in Haiti against Jean-Bertrand Aristide in 1991. The coup was led by General Cedras who looks almost like the brother of General Al Sissi, the one who led the coup against Mursi of Egypt. The Haitian coup was as bloody, even bloodier and it appears that Mursi is following the same script Aristide adopted by refusing to resign and by demanding he be returned to office as the legitimate, freely and democratically elected leader of Egypt. Aristide was ultimately returned to office because as Haitian, his God is superior to the God of Bill Clinton, but the will of the Haitian God remains to be seen in Egypt. And since the people of Egypt are crying for justice and since the Egyptian military has been hijacked by Israel and the United States, every Egyptian who believes in freedom will have to fight against the military for his freedom, which makes a Civil War inevitable in Egypt. The people of Egypt could never be free unless they are willing to engage in an honest Civil War to destroy the corrupt elements of the military that has been bought and paid for by Washington and the Jewish state of Israel, and then freedom will ring in Egypt.

Breaking News:

On July 24, 2013, consistent with the Feast of Tabernacles, a huge train derailment in Santiago, Spain has killed over 80 people and injured hundreds of others

The incident was not an accident; it was a deliberate action from the Spanish government to offer the victims as human sacrifices to Satan, consistent with the guidelines from the Feast of Tabernacles:

"The LORD said to Moses, "Say to the Israelites: 'On the **fifteenth day of the seventh month** the LORD's Festival of Tabernacles begins, and it lasts for seven days. The first day is a sacred assembly; do no regular work. **For seven days' present food offerings to the LORD and on the eighth day** hold a sacred assembly and present a food offering to the LORD. It is the closing special assembly; do no regular work."

(Leviticus 23: 33-36NIV)

It is clearly stated above that the Feast of Tabernacle starts on July 15 and lasts for seven days where human offerings would be presented until July 22 and on the eighth day, on July 23, additional offerings are to be presented. Again, the global reality throughout the NATO nations matched perfectly with these guidelines in the month of July 2013, from train derailments in France and Canada that killed score of innocent citizens, to a plane crash in California, USA that killed a number of people, to the Santiago, Spain disaster on July 24, 2013. The leaders of the world from Washington to the rest of the NATO allies have been murdering their own citizens to offer them as human sacrifices in the dark practice of human sacrifices from the de facto Cain Passover.

This archaic practice of human sacrifices is responsible for the most egregious events that have unfolded in the world; from the 1861 explosion in the Gulf of Mexico, to the 1933 Reichstag fire that brought Hitler to power in Germany, to the events of September 11, 2001 that started the current Great Tribulation with the invasion of Afghanistan, to the events of Waco, the Oklahoma City Bombing, and many more.

When eyewitnesses reported that they heard a big explosion just before the train's derailment, the Spanish government was quick to deny that the incident was caused by terrorism. This denial was suspicious because the only way to know it was not terrorism before a real investigation is conducted is if the government itself was involved in the commission of the tragedy and it was—the Spanish government murdered its own people and offered them as human sacrifices to Satan to comply with the biblical guidelines from the book of Leviticus.

Breaking News:

On Saturday July 27, 2013, days after general Al Sissi of Egypt urged the supporters of the July 3, 2013 bloody coup against Mursi to take to the streets of Cairo in a show of support for the military, the Egyptian army massacred a huge number of innocent civilians who engaged in the peaceful protest of the coup by demanding the restoration of Mursi to office

According to news reports, over 165 people have been killed and thousands have been injured. Witnesses reported that men dressed in black from the military shot teargas in the crowd and then shot live ammunition in the middle of the panic; however, the crowd did not disperse as the military had hoped and they vowed to continue to gather peacefully to demand the restoration of Mursi as the legitimate leader of Egypt.

Here it is! Barak Obama is completely mismanaging the world. The homosexual college drop-out has created a Great Tribulation in the world by invading most of the African continent directly or through the United Nations, by continuing to wage war in Afghanistan, by continuing to bomb Yemen indiscriminately, killing women and children and the innocents, by continuing to wage war in Iraq. The situation in Iraq is worst that ever, in fact, the violence in Iraq is as great as, perhaps even greater than the violence in Syria, because of the policy of Barak Obama. Barak Obama and Hilary Clinton and Bill Clinton and Susan Rice, the aggressive lesbian, continue to oppress the Haitians. The United Nations' occupying force is still in Haiti and Bill Clinton, in collaboration with Jean-Claude Duvalier, Michel Martelly and Laurent Lamothe, are still scheming to provoke a Civil War in Haiti to defeat the Haitians and to take over Haiti—but they are delusional—they will be defeated very soon—they will be forced out of Haiti in tears.

Barak Obama and his team of advisors, including Susan Rice and Hilary Clinton and Bill Clinton spoke to Mursi, urging him to leave office just hours before the bloody coup. They promised him a safe passage to a number of foreign nations, but Mursi refused and in desperation to keep "peace" in Egypt, they gave General Al Sissi the go-ahead to overthrow Mursi and to murder his supporters like they did in Haiti back in 1991 with the overthrow of Aristide.

With this latest episode of violence, General Al Sissi has lost all credibility and Barak Obama and the politicians in Washington have lost all moral authority to even pass judgment on people like Bashar Al Assad of Syria since they have refused to condemn the coup and to cut off financial and military aid to the Egyptian military.

Obama is not powerful enough to bring "peace" in the world. What does peace means? Peace is the absence of conflicts, a state of calm, tranquility, and serenity among people in society and among nations of the world. This state can only happen if there is justice in the world and if everyone in the world adheres to the same beliefs and ideals. The only way to bring everyone to accept the same ideal is for one side of the spectrum to convert some of those who resist their ideology and to destroy those who refuse to conform by force through war. And since Satan is not military strong enough, its homosexual ideology can never prevail in the world.

Obama and Hilary Clinton murdered Qaddafi in the street of Libya in the hope to bring peace, yet the situation in Libya is even worse now than it was during the last days of Qaddafi, the same thing happened in Syria. Obama and Hilary Clinton have created this mess in Syria by arming criminals and homosexual thugs from the Middle East, yet the supporters of Barak Obama, writers from Reuters, people like Phil Stewart, Mark Hosenball, Lesley Wroughton, Alistaire Bell, Claudia Parsons, Matt Spetalnick and Warren Strobel are attempting to cover for him by writing lies, suggesting that Obama never wanted to arm the rebels and to intervene militarily in Syria—this is absurd. Obama and Hilary Clinton provoked the civil war in Syria simply because they want Bashar Al Assad out of power. They have set up a fund to encourage top Syrian officials to defect, they have armed rebels from all over the Middle East to fight against Al Assad from the very beginning, they have moved patriot missiles to Turkey, they have moved American troops to Syria through Jordan and by early 2013, the rebels came close to controlling almost half of Syria, until Hezbollah decided to lend support to Bashar Al Assad. The trained fighters from Hezbollah have helped turn the tide of war by retaking strategic towns like Qusair and now the government of Syria is making a push to recapture some of the territories it had lost in the past year and half.

By overthrowing Mursi from office, Obama, Susan Rice, Bill and Hilary Clinton have put Egypt in a path to a Civil War. John Kerry has practically admitted that Washington was behind the removal of Mursi from office by arguing that they have acted to avoid a Civil War, but he is about to find out that he was dead wrong and that the actions of Barak Obama did not help Egypt avoid a Civil War, but in fact, his actions on July 3, 2013 helped cause a Civil War in Egypt.

The Great Tribulation continues, as Obama and Bill and Hilary Clinton battle against the saints by invading the entire African continent, by engaging in wars throughout the Middle East; notably in Libya, in Egypt, in Yemen, in Iraq, and in Syria. And by continuing to fight the war of Afghanistan, which is the biblical Armageddon. However, the forces of heavens have also responded by punishing people through earthquakes during the month of July in China, in Oklahoma, in Columbia, in Alaska, in Papua New Guinea, in New Zealand and in many other places to fulfill what is written in scripture about the coming of Jesus, the son and the only messiah of the living God, the one who is prophesied to come and to destroy the antichrist with his breath, the words of his mouth. Barak Obama, the homosexual college drop-out antichrist will soon be overthrown from office—Obama is going to prison.

Breaking News:

On July 30, 2013, European Union foreign policy chief, Katherine Ashton was allowed to meet with Muhammad Mursi to discuss a way out of the current political crisis

Barak Obama and his team of advisors, chiefly, Hilary, Bill Clinton and Susan Rice are completely mismanaging the world—they are making a lot of mistakes. After they engineered a coup to remove Mursi out of office on July 3, 2013 in the hope to avoid another civil war that could further complicate the equation of instability in the Middle East, Obama met with some unexpectedly strong resistance from the Muslim brotherhood and the supporters of Mohammad Mursi who refuse to accept the coup and insist that Mursi be restored to office as the legitimate leader of Egypt. The Egyptian military, under the urging of Barak Obama, massacred a huge number of Mursi's supporters during most of the month of July, but the people did not back down, they have found the power and the resolve to resist and to fight in the nobility of their cause. So now, as the month of July comes to an end, Obama, Bill and Hilary Clinton are quietly looking for a way to ease the situation. The fact that they decided to allow Katherine Ashton to visit Mursi in prison signals a strong possibility that Washington is looking for a way out of the mess they have created. However, it is already too late and Egypt has already descended into the abyss of a Civil War.

If Mursi is returned to office by agreeing to a coalition government until new presidential elections are held, he and General Al Sissi would not be able to co-exist. Al Sissi would have to go into exile and if Mursi agrees to co-exist with Al Sissi, he will certainly break that pledge once he is returned to office just as Jean Bertrand Aristide reneged on a number of promises he made to Bill Clinton after he was returned to office in 1994. Obama has opened a window that has put Egypt into a path of no return to a Civil War.

Chapter 24

The August 2013 Journal of the Great Tribulation

The month of August 2012 started with the orchestration of a Passover meal at Chick-Fil-A on August 1 when Americans ate chicken sandwiches to honor the cow; the Golden Cow Aaron built in the valley of Sinai to lead the Israeli people in the way of Satan in disobedience to the living God. It was the same statue Nebuchadnezzar built in Babylon, the modern city of New York. That same Golden Cow is being worshipped on Wall Street today to symbolize the bull market. Accordingly, a bull market is defined as a time of prosperity for the offsprings of Satan at the expense of the children of the living God, their prosperity is symbolized by the original bull Aaron has built. A bull is viewed mystically as representing a human sacrifice; it is written in the biblical book of Isaiah, "to sacrifice a bull is to sacrifice a man".

However, the month of August 2013 started with the deception of the 'three women of Egypt', the matriarchs of the kingdom of Satan. These three spirits are being represented by the three women who were supposedly the victims of Ariel Castro. That very day, Ariel Castro was sentenced to life in prison plus One Thousand Years. The spiritual symbolism of this sentencing should be a little easier for those who seek spiritual knowledge to grasp since this current struggle of good versus evil is for the control of the next 1000 years. And since the kingdom of Satan is the kingdom of the woman. The trinity of the women at the foundation of the kingdom of Satan includes; Eve, the mother of the mulatto Cain, the son of Satan; her power was later transferred to Lucy, a white woman who became the true embodiment of Satan. The word Lucifer came from the name Luce or Lucy, which means light, in reference to the light of the moon. Thus, Lucifer means the bearer of light; that bearer of light is a woman; she is depicted as a huge statue with a torch of fire in her hands in New York City where she is known as the Lady of Liberty, a woman of license who promotes homosexuality, lesbianism, murder, thefts and injustices in the world. Lucifer is a woman criminal like Hilary Clinton who has no respect for the law, a woman of license who does as she pleases, but this time, the living God is totally against her and the punishment of Babylon is near.

In addition to Lucifer, the one who bears the light, Bathsheba, the mother of Solomon and the daughter of the Pharaoh of Egypt, the wife of Solomon represent the other two women. Thus, the three victims of Ariel Castro represent these three women and now they are free by supposedly defeating Ariel Castro who would be imprisoned for One Thousand years, but I, Harry Francois, in the power of Jesus Christ declare this voodoo null and void because it is written that it is the false prophet, Barak Hussein Obama, the Beast, Bill Clinton and Lucifer Hilary Clinton who will go to prison for One Thousand years. This voodoo is performed to open the contest of the month of August 2013 because Solomon was able to finish the construction of his palace during the month of August, the month of Bul, on August 15 to be precise, in the power of Lucifer. This is precisely why the Catholic Church celebrates August 15 as the Day of the Lady of Assumption, meaning the woman who assumed the kingdom from Adam; she defeated Adam by sleeping with him after she had slept with an animal, the beast, the serpent from the tree of the knowledge of good and evil that metamorphosed into a man. But Jesus took the kingdom back from her by doing the perfect will of his Father, the creator of heaven and earth.

In early August 2013 Obama also announced the closure of a number of American embassies around the world because the State Department received specific terrorist threats from Al Qaeda, led by Ayman Zawahiri, the CIA employee who pretends to be against

Barak Obama, but is for him. This is done because Obama expects to engage in a real desperate struggle during the month of August 2013—Obama is planning to offer more human sacrifices throughout the month of Bul (August) by engineering terrorist acts in the U.S. and abroad, he also hopes to regain the upper hand in the Syrian war against Al Assad, especially between August 15 and August 29.

The warnings were also issued as a cover for Barak Obama to invade Yemen with American boots on the ground. On August 6, 2013, the day Harry Truman dropped the atomic bombs on Japan, the BBC reported that the United States deployed Special operations forces to Yemen to help Yemeni troops in their struggle against the saints who have been making very strong gains against the corrupt government of Yemen. The American media have conspired not to report on the conflicts that Obama is engaged in around the world to buy Obama time to crush the spirit of resistance that Jesus has kindled against him. The world is in the midst of the Great Tribulation that has been prophesied in the biblical book of Revelations, as Barak Hussein Obama has invaded dozens of nations around the world, including: Haiti, the holiest of all the nations of the world, the biblical Judah, the home of the biblical Jerusalem. Obama reinvaded Haiti under the advice of Bill and Hilary Clinton in January 2010 after the January 12, 2010 earthquake killed the entire United Nations force that was oppressing the Haitians. Barak Obama and the other homosexuals in Washington know that Haiti is the Garden of the Lord and the living God is willing and prepared to destroy America over Haiti, yet they have reinvaded Haiti anyway in their delusion that Barak Obama, the homosexual college drop-out could lead them to victory in their eschatological struggle against the saints of the living God just because Obama was born in Haiti, but they are severely mistaken—a loser cannot win.

Barak Obama has invaded Yemen, Libya, Syria, Sudan, Somalia, Ethiopia, Pakistan, Central Africa, Mali, Ivory Coast, Liberia, Congo, and Darfur among other places where the CIA is conducting special operations including Iran, Lebanon, Russia, Tunisia, Egypt and more. America is at war everywhere in the world with the majority of its forces in Afghanistan, the biblical Armageddon, but the American and the European media refuse to report it in order to conceal the fact that Barak Obama is the evil antichrist who came not to save, but to kill and destroy. Obama is worst than Hitler, he has invaded more nations than Hitler ever could. Europe and Africa were the center of the Second World War followed with the big conflict with Russia, but now, the Middle East and Africa are at the center of Obama's rampage, which will eventually lead with a direct conflict with Russia, but first, Obama will be defeated in Haiti where every homosexual troop from the United Nations will be made to leave by force—everyone will understand then, that Haiti is the holiest place on earth, the biblical Jerusalem—the richest and the most beautiful land on planet earth. The same thing happened to Napoleon, the French criminal who invaded Haiti in the late 1700s. The Haitians led by the mighty Jean Jacques Dessalines, defeated Napoleon in December, 1803 and Napoleon was forced to sell the land of Louisiana in 1804 to the young American nation, a nation that would become the next nemesis of Haiti. And on April 20, 1812, Napoleon invaded Russia where he was soundly defeated again by the Haitian Living God who empowered Russia to a shocking victory. The same thing is already happening to America under Barak Hussein Obama.

Barak Obama, sensing defeat and not wanting to see a third official Civil War in the Middle East, has decided to send Senators Lindsey Graham and John McCain to Egypt to mediate a peaceful agreement between the Egyptian military and the Muslim Brotherhood, the supporters of Mohammad Mursi who was overthrown by the military on July 3, 2013. However, on August 7, 2013, the Egyptian military declared that the talk failed and that the military was prepared to use force to disperse the supporters of Mursi who have been gathering in several places in Cairo to protest the coup by demanding Mursi be restored to office as the legitimate president of Egypt. In his desperate attempt to keep the people of Egypt under the brutal oppression of the Egyptian military through the appearance of peaceful mediation, Obama repeated the same steps he had made back in January 2011 when the Egyptian revolution began. On January 30, 2011, just five days after the Egyptian people took to the streets of Cairo in massive number against Hosni Mubarak, Hilary Clinton, the then U.S. Secretary of State went to Haiti to put pressure on the Haitian government to go ahead with the second tour of a corrupt presidential election. She did this because it is in the power and the authority of the Haitians that the United States find her authority in the world. Whenever the Haitian saints assume their authority by walking in the way of righteousness, the U.S. is weakened; however, when the Haitians are coerced to give up their authority by doing the homosexual will of Washington, the U.S. is emboldened in her evil ways. For example, in 1974 Haiti became the first black nation to participate in the Soccer World Cup in Munich, Germany, it was a rare moment on the world stage for Haiti, and the spotlight was on the Haitian nation. However, that very same year, the American nation was mourning the resignation of Richard Nixon; America was in political and economic darkness. This is the law of the universe. As long as the U.S. continues to worship Satan through Lucifer, she will always be the enemy of Haiti because the kingdom of the living God belongs to the Haitians. When the Haitians live in sins, they decrease, and the U.S. increases, however, when the Haitians live in righteousness, they increase and the U.S. decreases.

Senators Lindsey Graham and John McCain were sent to Egypt to try to ease the political tension, Senator Ben Nelson of Florida was sent to Haiti at the same time to put pressure on the Martelly Government to organize parliamentary elections later this year as the elections would give Washington a final opportunity to provoke a Civil War in Haiti in 2013, but they will not succeed, just as they have failed to provoke a Civil War in Zimbabwe where Robert Mugabe won after telling the world and the people of Zimbabwe that homosexuality is not a civil right—no individual has the right to engage in sins and provoke the anger of the living God, the creator against an entire nation.

In reality, Graham and McCain did not go to Egypt to mediate any peaceful resolution of the conflict, they went to Egypt to tell the Muslim Brotherhood to abandon the idea that Mursi will be returned to office; they went to advise the Muslim Brotherhood to accept "reconciliation" like Nelson Mandela did in South Africa and to abandon the street protests, the same way they told Martin Luther king Jr. to stop marching before they killed him in 1968. It was reported that Lindsey Graham and John McCain did not even bother to meet with Mursi; they made no real attempt to engage in any meaningful discussions with the Muslim Brotherhood that could address the concerns of all the parties and to negotiate a mutual solution that could lead to peace. They did not do so because that is not part of their calculus. They are the offsprings of Abraham Lincoln, a beast who unleashed four years of terror on the confederate States of America. The nations of the south were brought into the union by force, against their will after they lost the Civil war—America is not a free nation—it is a nation where half of the citizens are living under occupation. Can a nation that only knows the language of war ever make peace? The answer is no! America cannot make peace because peace can only come out of the equation of righteousness, which leads to the satisfaction and freedom of all parties; but whenever a party seeks to dominate and oppress another, it produces injustice and without justice there cannot be peace.

Graham and McCain left Egypt with an understanding that violence is about to explode, but they hope that the military will crush descent swiftly and organize elections in nine months and the crisis will be defused, but they are severely mistaken. The people of Egypt, including a great many that protested against Mursi are now against the military coup. They know that the coup came from Obama, Hilary and Bill Clinton—they believe the military betrayed the cause of the people of Egypt by siding with Israel and Washington. The supporters of Mursi also believe their cause is right and they are prepared to give up their lives to fight for freedom. This new movement they are calling the Arab Spring is different from other movements like the Mandela movement that accepted emancipation and reconciliation. This is the Jesus movement. This generation of protesters; from the Occupied Wall Street movement in New York, to other protests against police brutality in other American cities, to the Haitian resistance against the Martelly administration, to the cries of freedom throughout the Middle East is protesting in the power and the spirit of Jesus. Jesus promised to bring the sword of division, not the Kool-Aid of reconciliation. Those who believe in true freedom are the disciples of Jesus, therefore they do not compromise and if they are not willing to compromise, it must mean they are prepared to fight and to die for the cause of freedom. Even though many in Egypt think Muhammad is their savior, it is in the power of Jesus alone they can find freedom. Muhammad enslaved them for a long time after their military sold the nation to Israel and Washington for money—and millions of Egyptians have been forced to live in utter poverty and humiliation for decades to satisfy the illusion of Israel in their zeal to create a satanic version of Israel in the Middle East.

However, those who believe in Jesus are about to find freedom, and the ones who gave their lives for the cause of righteousness will be brought back to life. The fact is the real nation of biblical Israel is found in the Confederate States of America. Just imagine this! For the satanic nation of Israel to continue to exist in the Middle East, millions of people have to die and tens of millions more must live in extreme poverty. This evil cannot continue to stand and God and Jesus have now empowered the people of the Middle East, including groups like Hezbollah and nations like Russia and Iran to fight and to end this evil forever. War is good. It advances the cause of righteousness and ultimately leads to freedom from the spirit of darkness. The people of Egypt have no choice but to engage in a holy war against the corrupt leadership of the Egyptian military. (Entry: 8/7/2013)

The mystic in the Alex Rodriguez's Suspension

I continue to remind the reader that the world is primarily managed by the spirits from the invisible realm, jointly with human beings from the visible world. As spiritual beings, everyone is pre-wired to receive commands from the spiritual entities; however, some humans are more illuminated than others. To be a world leader one has to understand the world, this is why I was given the understanding to share with those who seek spiritual understanding. The world of the spirit influences our world every day. The unseen entities that influence our world every day are more powerful than the visible entities. The world of the spirit requires faith because it is unseen and the way to communicate with the spirit is mainly through signs and symbols.

It is in this backdrop that I have decided to explain to the reader the signs and symbols behind the mysticism of the Alex Rodriguez suspension—it is mysticism 101. As a general rule, whenever the American media engage in extreme coverage of a story that seems somewhat bizarre to most Americans, there is always the probability that they are engaging in a very important voodoo ritual to advance their cause—the cause of darkness. Most of the members of the American media belong to secret underground societies that worship Satan through Solomon. Many of them are CIA spies in the service of the U.S. government. The notion of the freedom of the press has been long gone in America as the media receive their talking points from the Middle East state that calls itself Israel and from Washington. Most of the American News channels have been converted from News stations to talk shows where homosexuals and lesbians give their own opinions to the American people to push them further into the precipice of ignorance. All the cable news channels, including CNN, Fox, MSNBC and others have moved away from reporting the news, they are now in the business of shaping and influencing opinions by expressing their own views on national and world events.

Consider the signs and the symbols in this story. After weeks of announcing that Alex R might be suspended, finally, on August 5, 2013 (power date: Harry Truman dropped Atomic bombs on Japan on August 6) it was officially announced that Alex R and 12 other players have been suspended. It was also announced that the other 12 players accepted their suspensions, but Alex R. decided that he will appeal his suspension and that same day, Alex travelled with the Yankees to play in Chicago.

Before I explain the rationale behind this voodoo operation, I invite the reader to go through the basic elements of the story step by step.

13 players got suspended; 12 plus Alex Rodriguez. In this voodoo design, Obama features Alex Rodriguez as his version of Jesus and the other 12 players as his disciples. According to the biblical story, after Jesus was arrested, his 12 disciples got disbanded and fled,

but Jesus fought on until his death and resurrection. So far this interpretation is coherent; 13 baseball players who belong to the same league and take performance enhancement drugs are disciples; they share the same passion, the passion for the game, they also belong to a subgroup that shares a desire to succeed by almost any means. This is the first set of signs and symbols. The story is enhanced when Alex Rodriguez, the Jesus version of Barak Obama, travelled to Chicago as Chicago was the very place Jesus was actually and historically arrested. The version of the Gospel that is being preached today is corrupt—it is the version of lies—and it does not fit. It is written in the book of Matthew in chapter 24 that before the coming of Jesus the truth will finally break through and "this Good News of the Kingdom will be preached throughout the whole world and then the end will come." This very book is part of the Gospel that is prophesied in the book of Matthew. The city of Chicago is the windy city where Jesus was arrested and beaten by white and black Moaabs, including Judas. The Bible makes it very clear that it was so cold on that evening when they brought Jesus before Caiaphas that Peter was outside trying to warm up among some people who recognized him because of his southern accent as one of the 12, one of the disciples of Jesus. In addition, there are other symbols in the numerology of the story. For example, Alex Rodriguez is supposed to receive a 211-game suspension through 2015. The number 211 is significant since Adam, the black man the living God created in Haiti was defeated by Eve, his black wife at the age of 56 and since Jesus is the second Adam; 56*2=112 and 112 is the inverse of 211. My evidence fits and if the evidence fits you must believe. It must be noted as well that A-Rod is expected to collect his full salary even if his suspension is upheld after the appeal. This means the entire story about the A-Rod's suspension is a fraud—he is still playing while he is appealing his suspension. And he expects to collect his full salary regardless of the outcome of the appeal, he is not expected to pay any price at all for violating the league rule on banned substance. Moreover, A-Rod is injured, he is about to turn forty years old and his game has been on the decline, that is partly why he has been chosen by the illuminati for this voodoo ritual.

Obama and Bill Clinton have designed the voodoo operation the same way they have designed the deception in the Snowden affair. Obama was in trouble with the Benghazi affair and the CIA affairs, so Satan decided to create his own version of scandal to give to the world. And as long as the world continues to pursue the fake scandal, Obama will find temporary immunity from the real scandals. Snowden is a CIA agent who was given to deceive the American people and world leaders, like Vladimir Putin of Russia, by releasing information that the world already knows—he is not a hero.

It is the same with the Alex Rodriguez voodoo operation, Obama has created his own version of Jesus and as long as he could control his version of Jesus, the real Jesus, he hopes, would be weakened; it is just like when a voodoo doll is used to represent an individual, whatever is done to the doll is supposed to affect the real individual.

In this case, if the voodoo doll that symbolizes Jesus in the person of Alex Rodriguez is under suspension through 2014 until 2015, then the real Jesus will not be able to contest against Barak Obama in 2014 and 2015, two of the last three years of the 7-year Sabbatical contest between God and Satan, which started in 2009 and will last until 2016. Obama hopes to win the contest by engineering civil wars in Haiti and in the United States of America, but he is delusional—he is completely mistaken. Alex Rodriguez is not Jesus and Jesus could never be under suspension—Obama is the one who is under complete suspension and humiliation UNTIL HE IS ARRESTED AND PUT IN PRISON.

Breaking News:

On August 8, 2013, the day Alex Rodriguez's suspension officially began; Barak Obama attempted to assassinate Bashar Al Assad

If Barak Obama came in the power of Solomon, as I have asserted, clearly, the only one with legal authority to challenge him is Jesus, the legitimate son of God. Solomon is the Christ of Satan and Jesus is the son and the Christ of the living God. And if Bashar Al Assad has been able to defy Obama for two years, he could only do so in the power and the authority of Jesus and for Obama to kill Assad, Jesus would have to remove his authority from Assad or Obama would have to subdue Jesus and the suspension of Alex Rodriguez was designed to do just that, but it did not work. Jesus is using Russia, Iran, and Hezbollah to protect Assad until he decides to remove his authority from Assad and that will come when a new Civil War starts in Egypt and or in other nations in the Middle East to free millions from the bondage of the Camp David Peace Accord with Israel.

Breaking News:

In anticipation of Al Assad's assassination, Barak Obama scheduled a Press Conference on August 9, 2013 to react to the news, but he was sadly mistaken

Obama scheduled a Press Conference on August 9, 2013, but no one knows why Obama scheduled the conference as nothing new was announced. The press conference was long, boring and exposed Obama as a cretin, someone who cannot speak without prepared remarks from his teleprompter. But what most people failed to realize was the reason for the Press Conference was for Obama to look good and to sound tough when he would have been asked to react to the news that Bashar Al Assad was assassinated, but unfortunately, as a loser, Obama was denied again as Bashar Al Assad survived the assassination attempt and Obama's authority is still contested. This is not the first time Obama scheduled events to coincide with the timing of his murderous rampage on Americans and citizens of the world. In November 2009, in anticipation of the Fort Hood shooting, Obama was scheduled to give a speech and he was in the middle of taking questions when he was told about the Fort Hood shooting and he proceeded to make a public comment about the incident—this was one of a series of events where Obama just happened to be given a speech in public when a tragedy involving the deaths of innocent Americans had occurred. This trend shows that it is not an accident—it has been all planned—Obama is a vampire—he is the mulatto Dracula—the antichrist who came to kill and to destroy—but his authority has been taken away.

Obama is so weak that the U.S. Congress had to convene a special session to lower the bar for him to get some of his nominations through the U.S. Congress. They lowered the requirement from a 60 super majority to a simple majority of 51; otherwise, Obama could not even muster enough authority to put a full cabinet in place. And as to immigration reforms and other ambitions Obama may have had, he can forget it—Obama is finished.

Breaking News:

Barak Obama gave the Egyptian military the go-ahead on August 14, 2013 to commit a huge massacre against the unarmed supporters of Mursi

As expected, in the early hours of August 14, 2013, one day before the Catholic Day of the 'Lady of Assumption', the Egyptian military assaulted the camps of the supporters of Mohammad Mursi, killing unarmed men, women and children—there was bloodshed everywhere in Egypt, including Cairo and Alexandria.

The American media refuse to report the shocking number of casualties, but Euronews reported that more than 300 supporters of Mursi were massacred in Cairo alone in the first hour of the operation and there were more casualties in other cities like Alexandria. A conservative estimate should put the number of those that are killed and injured in the thousands. Obama is a criminal. He gave direct order to General Al Sissi to massacre his own people for money, under the advice of Hilary and Bill Clinton and Susan Rice. The Egyptian military used snipers to shoot people in the head, they fired tear gas at women and children, choking them like roaches. The entire capital was blanketed by black smoke. The Egyptian military actually used low grade chemical weapon against its own people right before the eyes of the international community, and still, Washington expects people like Vladimir Putin to negotiate with them in good faith about the war in Syria and other important issues.

By 10:00 A.M. EST, the international community started to react to the massacre. It was reported that Iran expressed concerns that the situation in Egypt was quickly degenerated into a Civil War. Turkey's Prime Minister Tayyip Erdogan appealed to the UN Security Council to stop the massacre. Erdogan has been one of the few world leaders who have been on the right side of history vis-à-vis the July 3, 2013 military coup that overthrew Mursi from office. From the very beginning he has called it a coup and urged the restoration of Mursi. Like Mursi, Erdogan was on the wrong path—they both were friends of Barak Obama and Erdogan collaborated with Barak Obama to attempt to overthrow Bashar Al Assad from power in Syria. However, now, Erdogan and certainly Mohammad Mursi in his jail cell have come to realize that Barak Obama is Satan himself, a little homosexual punk who has no regard for life and whose mission is to advance the cause of darkness in the world at any price. Erdogan must now choose if he wants to remain friend with Satan or if he wants to see justice done in the world.

The people of Egypt did not back down in the face of tanks and machine guns. The supporters of Mursi fought back with rocks and they have set fire to a number of buildings throughout Egypt and they have also stormed through Police Stations around the country, setting them on fire and in some cases, they have taken over some weapons. If Obama, John McCain and Lindsey Graham thought the Egyptian military could just clear the camps and disperse the people by intimidating them with bullets, they were severely mistaken. It is written in the bible that the people who came out of the 'Great Tribulation', "do not care about their lives' meaning they are prepared to sacrifice their lives to see justice done in the world. The people of Egypt are now emboldened by this round of bloodshed—their cause has been strengthened by the blood of the martyrs and they are ready to go all the way until justice is done in Egypt and criminals like Al-Sissi are put in prison. From this day of August 14, 2013 forward, neither Barak Obama, Bill Clinton, Hilary Clinton, Lindsey Graham, John McCain, nor the rest of the U.S. Congress have any more credibility in the world. They exposed themselves as Satanists who engage in human sacrifices to advance the cause of injustice in the world. The time for talk is over—they have engaged in massacres in Egypt, in Syria, in Somalia, in Mali, in Haiti, in Afghanistan, in Yemen, in Libya, in Iraq and all over the rest of Africa and they must now wait for the punishment that is coming for them. They will be punished by the armies of heaven who have been deployed against them, it is just a matter of time—the judgment is near and America as it is known today will be severely punished because of its crimes against the saints of the living God.

Breaking News:

The world reacts to the massacre in Egypt on August 15, 2013, the day of the Lady of Assumption

It is official. The entire world now knows and admits that General Al Sissi, the commander of the Egyptian military that overthrew Mohammad Mursi on July 3, 2013 has committed a massacre on August 14, 2013 by murdering unarmed men, women, and children who were protesting the July 3, 2013 military coup and demanding the restoration of Mursi to office. The death toll has been so significant that even the Egyptian military conceded that over 525 people have been killed, which means at least over 3000 civilians have been murdered in cold blood by the military. A spokesman for the Muslim Brotherhood said the death toll is at least 4 times the official number. In addition, dozens of bodies that have not been previously accounted for have been discovered in a mosque wrapped in blankets—it has been a profuse shedding of blood—a real carnage—the killing has been indiscriminate as even reporters and the elderly have been killed.

The coup will fail

When the West realized that their ploy has been uncovered and that the coup has not worked just the way they had planned. Western leaders were forced to come out on the 15 of August to make public statements, seemingly to condemn the massacre, but they have chosen their words very carefully because the Egyptian military was acting on the advice of Barak Obama. Francois Hollande of France, the biblical evil nation of Assyria reacted by appearing to condemn the massacre, but he took no action against the Egyptian military. A world leader cannot afford to just pay lip service to such a massacre. Meanwhile, Barak Obama, in a follow up to the statement the U.S. Secretary of State John Kerry made, in which he called the actions of the Egyptian military; "deplorable' also used the same word in this following statement, which is obviously written by Bill CLINTON, the second coming of LINCOLN;

"The United States strongly condemns the **steps** that have been taken by Egypt's interim government and security forces," before he added:

"We **deplore** violence against civilians. We support universal rights essential to human dignity, including the right to peaceful protest."

Notice the cleverness of evil. Obama said the U.S. strongly condemns the **steps** taken by the government, but made no references to the massacre—that is deception, which suggests that the United States is behind the Egyptian military massacre of its own people. And notice also that Obama has used the word "deplore", the same word used by John Kerry. "We deplore violence against civilians" he said, but he does not specifically reference the Egyptian military massacre of its own people on August 14, 2013. Obama has also attempted to deceive the world by pretending to take actions against the military of Egypt, by cancelling a scheduled joint conference between the United States and Egypt's military. However, that is not a punitive action. Obama is a liar—he is caught in a lie and everything he has done has backfired. He and John Kerry used General Al Sissi to pre-empt the people's revolution against Mursi by staging the July 3, 2013 coup, but the coup has backfired because the people of Egypt continue to cry for justice well after a month since the coup—Obama is finished.

When Qaddafi defied the authority of Barak Obama, Obama invaded Libya and killed Qaddafi in the hope to crush descent and to transfer the spirit of war and bloodshed to America where Obama came to provoke a Civil War. Later in 2011, Bashar Al Assad of Syria defied Obama by refusing to resign from office in the face of national protests against him, but for two years Obama has been unable to remove Al Assad from office and the longer Assad stays in office, the weaker Obama has gotten. However, Barak Obama has calculated that if he is not able to remove Bashar Al Assad from office before new elections that are scheduled in Syria for 2014, more likely Al Assad will not run for re-election and certainly, Russia could encourage Al Assad not to run for another term, this way, the defiance would have stopped and Obama could be free to transfer the bloodshed from the eastern hemisphere to the western hemisphere sometime in 2014, provided no new civil wars explode anywhere else in the Middle East. But now the situation in Egypt is quickly degenerated into a new Civil War. And this time, it is the reverse of the two previous cases. This time Obama is facing the ghost of a man who is still alive—Mohammad Mursi whom he had removed from office to prevent a Civil War. The calculus in this new equation is not easy to solve, especially for a beast who only knows the way of violence. If Obama restores Mursi to office, again as I have observed earlier in this presentation, Mursi could never co-exist with Al Sissi who has committed crimes against humanity since the coup by murdering thousands of innocent civilians. However, since Mursi did attempt to impose an Islamist agenda on the people of Egypt while he was in office, a significant sector of the population will continue to view him with suspicion. And finally, the west and Israel will not really trust Mursi to keep any promises he may be forced to make in order to be returned to office, especially in the light of what Mursi had done to Israel by preventing Israel from invading Gaza to shed the blood of innocent Palestinians and to offer them as human sacrifices to Satan in December 2012 just before Barak Obama took office in January 2013 for a second term. This was the only good thing Mohammad Mursi did as President of Egypt and this is really why Obama and the west have turned against him. Israel and the American illuminati, including Hilary Clinton who was

Secretary of State at the time still believe that things have not been working for Obamà in 2013 because the invasion of Gaza did not take place to offer the human sacrifices as they did in December 2008 just before Obama took office the first time in January 2009. And they will never forgive Mursi for interfering in that operation because, as it is written in the biblical book of Hebrews, **"Without the shedding of blood there is no forgiveness of sins".** The shedding of blood is a way of life for the offsprings of Satan; innocent people must be murdered like animals and offered as sacrifices for their sins.

The blood of the Palestinian is shed in the east for the benefit of the Jew and the blood of the Haitians and the black and white Hebrews are shed in the west for the benefit of the Jews.

Moreover, the fact that Mursi never agreed to resign his position as the legitimate President of Egypt makes it easier for the people who are protesting the coup to be precise and direct about their demand—the restoration of Mohammad Mursi to office. When Americans protested against Barak Obama in 2011 through the Occupy Wall Street Movement, the opponents of the movement criticized the protesters—arguing that they had no specific demand, but this is not the case in Egypt. The people of Egypt has one simple demand; the restoration of democracy in Egypt through the return of Mohammad Mursi to office.

Finally, in this calculus, some have and are still considering the murder of Mohammad Mursi, but that option is not going to help Obama as it could only strengthen the movement for democracy in Egypt by making Mohammad Mursi a martyr for the cause of democracy. Jesus is not a college drop-out like Barak Obama, he has made his move and he is waiting for Barak Obama and Bill and Hilary Clinton to make their next move in Egypt in their hopeless and audacious quest to stop a Civil War—Obama is going to prison soon.

The homosexual Barak Obama has endorsed the massacre of thousands of Egyptians because he is an antichrist criminal like Abraham Lincoln. It is very easy for the world to see that Obama is behind the August 14, 2013 massacre that took place in Egypt because the United States of America has a very clear history of using force to kill its own civilians, starting with the 1861 Civil War which was provoked by Abraham Lincoln. Lincoln destroyed the American Constitution, after he has ignored the law by invading the newly formed nations of the south—the Confederate States of the South. In reality, the 1861 war was not really a Civil War; it was an aggression, an invasion of a free and independent nation. The Confederate States of America came together as one nation when a number of states decided on their own free will to come together as one nation after they had withdrawn from the northern states. However, Lincoln refused to obey the law and to recognize the states of the south as free, independent, and sovereign states, he called the original union supreme and eternal; therefore, no state had the right to leave. Clearly, Lincoln was wrong. It is not written in the U.S. Constitution that the union was perpetual as expressed in the Articles of Confederation.

After the American Civil War, a new nation had come into existence with the evil and criminal spirit of Lincoln, the guy who does not respect the law, the lawless one. In 1894, the Pullman strike became the first national strike in America and the American government used force to stop the strike by murdering thousands, even hundreds of thousands of civilians from all over the nation and especially in Chicago, Illinois where the strike had originated. In the 1920s the U.S. government deployed the military against the American people and murdered civilians to crush descent, notably in the battle of Blair Mountain, and in the Tulsa, Oklahoma race riot of 1923. Even as recently as 1992, the L.A. National guard was deployed to break the Rodney King's riots. The National Guard murdered score of American civilians, mostly blacks, but the Jews in the media always downplay the number of deaths, just like they are doing today in Cairo. Every time people die, it is always for the benefits of the Jews and the Freemasons. And now the Jews are claiming that the people of Egypt cannot be free because the Egyptian military has a Peace-treaty with Israel, meaning, that the military is not the military of the people of Egypt, but it is an organization of sicaires, or paid criminals employed by the west to keep the people subdued into poverty of soul and spirit, but the time for freedom has come to Egypt.

I, Harry Francois declare today, in the power and in the authority of Jesus, the only begotten son of the living God, the Christ of the living God, the creator who has given him authority in the heavens and the earth he has created, that the military coup that Barak Obama orchestrated in Egypt on July 3, 2013 will fail and I further declare in the name of Jesus that freedom will ring in Egypt after the Egyptians of the Middle East, who are sincerely seeking freedom, take up their crosses and fight a real war against Al Sissi and the corrupt leaders of the Egyptian military. Satan will no longer be allowed to do as he pleases in the world—Barak Obama, Bill, Hilary Clinton, John Kerry, Susan Rice will be contested everywhere in the world and they will be defeated.

I hereby declare today, in the authority and power of Jesus that Barak Obama will be defeated in Afghanistan, the biblical Armageddon, in Pakistan, in Yemen, in Syria, in Libya, everywhere in Africa. And certainly, the homosexual will be defeated in Haiti where the Garden of the Lord will be restored and every homosexual invading troop will be made to leave Haiti by force. The agenda of Satan has been defeated.

August 16, 2013

On Friday August 16, 2013, the day after the official day of the Lady of Assumption, the people of Egypt returned to the streets of Cairo, Alexandria, Dumyat where at least 8 people were reported killed, and other cities of Egypt to protest and to demand the restoration of Mursi to office and the resignation and arrest of General Al Sissi. The leaders of the Muslim Brotherhood vowed never to compromise with the criminals involved in the orchestration of the coup and promised their people that they will not rest until justice is done in Egypt. They urged their followers to march and to defy the curfew orders imposed by the military. Meanwhile, the military continues its carnage against the people, killing dozens of civilians throughout Egypt. It is clear that a Civil War has officially started in Egypt as all windows of opportunities for a peaceful settlement of the current crisis seem to have closed. In many ways this is good because the world has now entered a new phase—it is the phase of freedom and justice and these cannot be negotiated.

The Egyptian military wants to oppress the people of Egypt so they could continue to subject them to a life of poverty and shame under the thumbs of the Jews and their Washington brethren, but the Muslim Brotherhood who has been wrong on so many issues, including their belief in a false prophet named Mohammad, have now found themselves on the right side of history as they fight for a narrow principle of democracy, which is preached by the hypocrite nations of the west, including the United States.

The Muslim brotherhood wants the restoration of Mohammad Mursi to office as the legitimate leader of Egypt before they would agree to negotiate any other issues that are important to all the people of Egypt. They have now realized that they have made some serious mistakes and they will be willing to address the failures of Mursi before the coup, but the restoration of Mursi to office is not negotiable—it is the only way to bring peace to Egypt.

Meanwhile, the Great Tribulation and the prophecies from the Bible regarding these last days before the return of Jesus, the Christ of the living God, continues. A sectarian war, a Civil war is being waged in Iraq where the violence has been fierce and consistent since 2011. The struggle continues in Tunisia, Algeria, Libya, where the violence has been fierce, and all throughout Africa, especially in Sudan, Nigeria, Somalia where the NGO organization named Doctors without borders has announced that they will suspend their operation in the country because of violence and threats of violence against them. The war is also being waged in Mali, Angola, Senegal, Uganda and other parts of Central Africa. In Afghanistan, the Taliban continues to fight and to resist Satan and Obama is on the defensive because he knows he is about to be defeated.

Obama has also launched a new offensive in Syria, which includes a new mission from the United Nations charged to investigate the use of chemical weapons in Syria. The new team is scheduled to arrive in Syria on Sunday August 18, 2013, however the mission has two goals: firstly, it is a mission of espionage. The U.S. hopes to use the UN inspectors to locate the areas where the Syrian government has stored key chemical and biological weapons facilities and the inspectors hope to establish a better coordination and communication protocol between the Obama rebels and NATO for future air operations. Secondly, Obama is hoping that the mission will conclude that Bashar Al Assad used chemical weapon and this time, Obama intends to use that report as a legitimate reason for the U.S. and NATO to attack Syria and to establish a no-fly zone in parts of Syria.

On August 16, 2013, violence was reported in Lebanon where a car bomb detonated and killed more than 22 people.

National Emergencies or Natural Disasters

The Great Tribulation continues in its expression of the National Emergencies and Natural Disasters as contemplated in HR 645. The natural disasters continue, while the frequency of apparent accidents also continues. The small plane crash in East Haven Connecticut, the crash of a UPS Cargo plane in Alabama that killed the pilots on August 15,2013 and on August 16, 2013 a Ferry carrying over 700 people sink after colliding with a Cargo ship. Could all of these events be accidents when they occur exactly on Catholic Feast days, while the U.S. Congress is on vacation, worshipping the Catholic woman, the Statue of Liberty also known as Lucifer? The answer is no. This explains why the illuminati want Hilary Clinton, a murderer as the next President of the United States—they wish to complete the Trinity of Evil—from Bill Clinton to Barak Obama and to Hilary Clinton.

On August 16, 2013, several earthquakes were also reported, notably in New Zealand where an earthquake of magnitude 6.9 was felt.

August 17, 2013

The violence continues on August 17, 2013 all over Egypt, particularly in the Sinai area where a number of Egyptians and other Arabs are battling against the Egyptian military because of its support for Israel. The attacks on military personnel have increased in recent days with boldness and a passion that did not exist before the coup. Egypt is officially in a Civil war. The coup is one of the bloodiest military coups in world history; certainly, the coup is the most cowardly coup in the history of humanity; never before has a military murdered so many unarmed civilians, its own people in such a short period of time. Since July 3, 2013, the Egyptian military has killed well over 5000 unarmed civilians; they have murdered women, children and the elderly. The coup has the coward signatures of Bill Clinton, Hilary Clinton and Barak Obama, the same people who reinvaded Haiti in the aftermath of the January 12, 2010 earthquake. What kind of animals would invade a people while their nation was traumatized from a natural disaster? The answer is simple: Dinosaurs disguised in human clothing, Obama is a coward, a murderer, an animal. He gave the order to Al Sissi to murder his own people and then he sent a number of liars from the American and the European media to defend a military that has no defense. The criminals have now argued that the U.S. does not have any leverage on the Egyptian military because the other nations of the Gulf have increased their financial support to Egypt. However, that argument is false. Any real and significant money from the Arab nations actually comes from the U.S. if the U.S. stops buying oil from Saudi Arabia and other Arab nations, they will go broke overnight. Yes, the U.S. does have leverage and calls the shot in Egypt from behind the scene.

On August 17, 2013, the Egyptian military murdered an additional 1500 Civilians and the carnage continues.

August 19, 2013

The Great Tribulation continues with a train fire that killed over 50 people in India—the high and unusual incidence of train, plane and automobile accidents continue.

And the bloodshed continues in Egypt, while the UN begins a new mission to find out whether Bashar Al Assad used chemical weapons in the Syrian war.

It was reported on August 18, 2013 that the Egyptian military massacred close to 40 protesters who have been taken to prison—

they were murdered while in custody of local authorities—the carnage continues. Meanwhile, the Obama administration has become more emboldened in its lies. They know that the crimes of the Egyptian military cannot be defended and they also know that the military is about to release Hosni Mubarak from prison to reverse the January 2011 revolution, so they have orchestrated a rumor that the Obama administration has decided to cut some aids to the Egyptian military, but they deny the report in public. This strategy of lies would allow them to further the deception in the minds of some, given them the impression that they have taken meaningful actions against the bad guys from the Egyptian military when in fact, they have not. The report that the Obama administration has cut some aids to Egypt is totally false. Barak Obama totally supports the actions of the Egyptian military vis-à-vis its own citizens. Barak Obama and Bill and Hilary Clinton gave the order to the military to remove Mursi from office and to release Hosni Mubarak from prison, but their actions have backfired—the coup will ultimately fail and violence will continue to escalate in Egypt until justice is done. Obama and John Kerry thought the coup could have prevented a civil war, but it has only assured a civil war in Egypt.

Breaking News:

August 20, 2013

The Egyptian military arrested Mohammad Badie, the Muslim Brotherhood spiritual leader for inciting violence in the wake of the July 3, 2013 military coup that removed Mursi from office. The military continues its purge of the Muslim Brotherhood in the hope to silence the voice of resistance and to intimidate the people of Egypt. However, the Muslim Brotherhood reacted quickly by naming Mahmoud Ezzad the new spiritual leader of the Brotherhood.

Elsewhere in Pakistan, it has been reported that former Pakistani President, Pervez Musharraf has been indicted for the 2007 murder of former Prime Minister Benazir Bhutto. Bhutto was gunned down shortly after revealing to a BBC reporter during a live interview that Bin Laden had been killed.

Meanwhile in Hollywood, Lee Thompson Young, a 29-year old black actor was found dead at his North Hollywood home by Police who was alerted by his co-workers from the TNT cable drama series; "Rizzoli and Isles" when he failed to show up for work. The Police concluded that he committed suicide, but that does not make sense. Moreover, it is a little suspicious that his co-workers would call the Police so quickly before any of his co workers would personally check on him. Usually when someone fails to show up for work for just one day or one morning people don't think of the worse and rush to call the Police, they would wait after they had made several attempts to contact the person before they notify the police.

Barak Obama has been murdering Americans and accused them of committing suicides; this latest murder is reminiscent of the August 15, 1977 murder of Elvis Presley by Jimmy Carter who conspired with a dentist to poison him.

August 24, 2013

By August 24, 2013, a number of important developments worthy of recording have occurred: Barak Obama engineered the release of Hosni Mubarak from prison to totally reverse the 2011 revolution that had yet to yield any concrete and significant gains since Mohammad Mursi was not fully committed to the cause of the people. Egypt has effectively returned to the era of oppressive military dictatorship. However, in order not to completely incite the anger of the people, the military announced that Mubarak will be kept under house arrest, but that is a lie—the military has a secret plan to release the former dictator to do as he pleases. Obama used the same tactic in Haiti after he returned his blood cousin, Jean-Claude Duvalier, the former Haitian dictator to Haiti in January 2011 after 25 years of exile to France, Obama claims that he is under house arrest, he was even paraded before judges on several occasions, but everyone in Haiti knows that Jean-Claude Duvalier is free to do as he pleases, including attending important national events as the special official guest of Bill and Hilary Clinton and Michel Martelly.

Obama released Mubarak from prison because his very presence as a free man in Egypt, not only symbolizes the return of the military to power, but it gives a spiritual advantage to the cause of darkness as the spirits that formerly walked with Mubarak are now free to return to the scene to impact the Egyptian reality from behind the scene, but they could only contribute to a Civil War since the equation in Egypt has already brought the nation to the brink of a civil war. The military continues to assault the people of Egypt and the Muslim Brotherhood. In addition to high ranking Muslim Brotherhood leaders like Badie, hundreds of mid-level brotherhood members have been arrested and thousands of others civilians have also been arrested and murdered.

Elsewhere in Syria, Obama has further exposed himself as a liar and a deceiver, a desperate antichrist who is on his way to prison. Just days after a UN team of inspectors arrived in Syria on August 18, 2013 to investigate a previously reported possible use of chemical weapons, it was widely reported that a major chemical attack took place in Damascus on the night of August 22, 2013, which killed over 1300 people, including women and children. The rebels who are fighting against Al Assad quickly blamed Assad for the attack and they released a video that appear to show people foaming at the mouth, including children who have been affected by the nerve agents. However, some question the authenticity of the video, suggesting the people in the video may be paid actors. The NATO allies have seized the opportunity to call for the use of force against Syria, but others, including Russia and China have urged against a rush to judgment and they have remained opposed to the use of force against Syria. In addition, many political observers have expressed serious doubt that Al Assad would use chemical weapons the very same week when the UN weapons' inspectors arrived in Syria, it would not make sense. It is clear that the rebels and the NATO allies who are desperate to overthrow Al Assad from power would be the only ones to benefit from the use of chemical weapons, not Assad, as such action would give NATO an excuse to officially intervene militarily in Syria. As I observed before in my book titled, "ARRAT", published in 2011, Obama will attempt to intervene in Syria militarily to remove Assad from office—as long as Assad remains in power, Obama will not be able to get anything done. He will not be able to get his second term agenda through the U.S. Congress and he will not be able to transfer the demons that cause wars and mayhem from the Middle East to provoke a Civil War in America and in Haiti to fulfill his Health Care PPACT with Satan and to satisfy the Jewish blood liability for this Sabbath—the defiance of Al Assad has neutralized the authority of Barak Obama.

Meanwhile, the Great Tribulation continues: major floods have hit China, Russia, and the Philippines. A 6.9 earthquake has hit Mexico and other places in the world.

By August 26, 2013, the American and the European media have concluded that Barak Obama and the NATO allies, including England and France will attack Syria. They argue that even though Syria has allowed the UN weapons' inspectors into Damascus to visit the site where the alleged chemical attack took place, it was too little too late because five days after the attack, the evidence has been compromised. Imagine this. A team of inspectors arrived in Syria on August 18, 2013 to investigate chemical attacks that had occurred about three to six months ago, has now declared that after five days, the evidence may be compromised, even though they felt they could confidently investigate evidence that are six months old—this is beyond hypocrisy—it has reached the summit of deceptions—these lies are simply Clintonite and Obamanite.

Finally, the fact that the UN team of inspectors is made up of 20 people suggests that it is a mission of betrayal—they have already decided to give a report that is beneficial to Barak Obama and Hilary Clinton by ignoring the evidence. The number 20 is spiritually broken down as 19 plus 1, the leader. King David was betrayed by 20 soldiers, 19 plus the leader. The 09/11/01 betrayal of America was led by Dick Cheney plus 19 other traitors; this is why they claimed that 19 Muslim hijackers were responsible for the events of 09/11/01 in addition to the Bin Laden the leader, which brings the number to 20. And just as the events of 09/11/01 took place exactly and precisely 7 days before the September 18, 2001 Rosh Hashanah, the Jewish un-holiday, last year in 2012, Christopher Stevens, the American ambassador to Libya and three other Americans were murdered in Benghazi on 09/11/12, precisely 7 days before the September 18, 2013 Rosh Hashanah.

Based on this tradition of evil, Barak Obama is more likely to attack Syria on Wednesday August 30, 2013, exactly 7 days before the September 4, 2013 Rosh Hashanah, however, to capture the spirit of September 11, Obama and his Jewish brothers are planning to attack Syria on 09/11/13, precisely 7 days after the September 4, 2013 Rosh Hashanah, 12 years after 09/11/01 and one year after Benghazi.

Breaking News:

Obama delayed the strike on Syria to capture the Jewish religious voodoo in the September 11 date, not to give Congress a real opportunity to vote for a war resolution

Barak Obama has already decided to officially invade Syria and he intends to do so whether the U.S. Congress votes to give him official authorization to go to war. However, Obama took the risk to bring Congress into the conversation to buy time until September 11, 2013, 7 days after Rosh Hashanah to strike Syria, believing that a military strike on that day will be more potent because of its spiritual significance and that the entire venture will be more likely to succeed. But he is about to be tragically disappointed. In addition, Barak Obama has also miscalculated by inviting the U.S. Congress to vote for the authorization of the war against Syria, in that, if the U.S. Congress votes no and Obama still invades and the war goes badly, which it will, the case for impeaching Obama will be made much easier and Obama would have hastened the reservation of his prison cell.

Obama and his team of liars from the media have been very cautious in defining the mission by stressing that the goal of any strike on Syria is not to remove Bashar Al Assad from power, which it is, but they underlined that the goal is to punish Assad and to send a message that chemical weapons should not be used.

Barak Obama and the Freemasons have decided to take this timid approach because it is written in the biblical book of prophecies that the antichrist will subdue three kings. And as the antichrist, Obama has already subdued three kings in the power of the first beast, in fulfillment of his dark destiny. Obama has also subdued another king in his own power in concert with Lucifer or Hilary Clinton when he removed President Manuel Zelaya of Honduras from office on June 28, 2009; just four days after Obama had murdered Michael Jackson on June 24, 2009. The CIA orchestrated the coup by directing the Honduran military to take Zelaya to exile in Costa Rica. After Jean-Claude Duvalier was returned to Haiti in January 2011 Barak Obama found the power to subdue three kings: in 2011, Obama, in concert with Hilary Clinton murdered Muammar Qaddafi of Libya and overthrew his government and killed his children; on July 3, 2013, Barak Obama overthrew the democratically elected government of the Middle East Egypt in the most violent military coup in modern history and removed Mohammad Mursi from office as President of the country; Mursi is in prison to this very day without any trial and without any formal charges brought against him. Obama is looking to fulfil his destiny as the antichrist by killing or removing a third king from office. In the power of Jean-Claude Duvalier, the first beast. But he is not allowed by the forces of heaven to remove Bashar Al Assad from power by overthrowing the government of Syria.

The living God has put it in the hearts of Vladimir Putin and the leadership of Iran and the leadership of Hezbollah to protect Syria and Bashar Al Assad from Obama and his Jewish brethren from NATO and Israel and there will be serious consequences for the United States, France, England and the little nation that calls itself Israel in the Middle East if they attack Syria under the pretext that Assad had used chemical weapons. The United States is in no position to pass moral judgment on any nation as it relates to the use of dangerous weapons; the U.S. gave chemical and biological weapons to Saddam Hussein in the 1980s to fight a proxy war against Iran. And Saddam used the weapons against Iran and later against his own people. The U.S used Agent Orange in Vietnam against civilians to destroy their food supplies; Bill Clinton and Barak Obama used Agent Orange to poison the waters of Haiti in late October 2010 to kill Haitians so they could steal their land, Bill and Hilary Clinton and Janet Reno used poison gas against American women and children during the Waco massacre, and among many other atrocities, the U.S. remains the only nation in history to have used the Atomic bomb—Harry Truman dropped atomic bombs on Japan during World War Two.

However, this is a very different time. The United States will no longer be allowed to do as it pleases in the world; the U.S. will be confronted everywhere in the world and defeated by the saints of the living God. The U.S. is losing in Haiti; all the attempts to provoke a Civil War among the Haitians have so far failed and it is just a matter of time before the UN occupying force of homosexuals are driven from Haiti by force. The U.S. is losing in Afghanistan and it is just a matter of time before the Karzai government leaves office; the U.S. is losing in Yemen, the homosexual Ali was driven out of office and it is just a matter of time before this current regime of evil supported by the U.S. is defeated; the U.S. is losing in Egypt as the Egyptian military has been forced to expose itself as evil and detestable by engaging in the carnage of unarmed women and children on behalf of Washington and Israel. Obama is certainly losing in Syria, which explains why the U.S. and its allies are now seeking to intervene because the army that Hilary Clinton has put together to overthrow Assad has failed. Hilary Clinton has said that Russia must pay a price for using its veto power at the UN to oppose a NATO invasion of Syria, but it is the U.S. and Israel that will pay a dear price if they decide to invade Syria.

August 28, 2013

On August 28, 2008, exactly five years ago, Barak Obama accepted the Democratic nomination for President of the United States of America. On that day, Obama issued an "Emancipation Proclamation" by calling 600, 000 blacks registered voters from Florida, USA to join his campaign. That call was the call to slaughter 600, 000 blacks through a new Civil War just as Lincoln slaughtered over 600, 000 black soldiers from the 54th Massachusetts regiment during the American Civil War.

Obama came to provoke a Civil War in America to satisfy the blood liability of this Sabbath, but his plan has failed as the case of George Zimmerman and other cases like the Casey Anthony case failed to provoke riots in Florida. On the night of August 28, 2008, the Jews in the American media promoted the events as the commemoration of the 45th anniversary of Martin Luther King's "I have a dream speech", but in reality it was the commemoration of the 86th year since the inauguration of the Lincoln Memorial. The era of Abraham Lincoln was officially over after 86 years, just as the era of George Washington was over after 86 years, from 1776 to 1862, when Lincoln made his own "Emancipation Proclamation's" call to blacks. George Washington passed the baton to Abraham Lincoln after 86 years and Lincoln was supposed to pass the baton to Barack Obama in 2008 after 86 years, but Obama has been denied. And now the homosexual, in his desperation, is attempting to issue a new "Emancipation Proclamation" call to blacks, hoping to shed their blood to satisfy the liability of this Sabbath, but Barak Obama is five years too late, his time has passed and judgment will soon come upon him and those who support him—the liars who embrace the cause of darkness and injustice in the world.

Obama pretends to commemorate and honor Martin Luther King because King made a terrible mistake when he gave the "I have a dream speech". He was not supposed to say he had a dream because he did not create the world. Like Jesus, Martin Luther King was supposed to say, "**It is written**" as the living God already has a plan, a vision for humanity. The speech was completely satanic. When Martin said "It is a dream deeply rooted in the American dream" he was wrong and there is absolutely no evidence that the American dream included fair treatment of blacks; that promise was never made as George Washington, the first president of the United States signed the Fugitive Slave Act in 1793 to enforce the constitutional agreement that blacks would not have freedom of movement throughout the states. When Martin said, well, when he echoed Thomas Jefferson by saying "We hold these truths to be self-evident that every man is created equal", he was wrong again because Thomas Jefferson, as a liar, was always wrong, everyone is not created equal, but everyone should be treated equally. There is a formula for black freedom and prosperity; that formula is to serve the living God in perfection as written in the Bible. But to do this, the black and the white Hebrews must reject the lies of the Jews by recognizing and embracing the true fact that they are the real children of the living God—and obey his laws and his statutes—this is the only way for them to reclaim their lost possessions. The black Hebrews are the children of the living God, they live on the most beautiful and richest land in the world and they have ultimate authority in the world, they possess the perfect gifts of God and therefore, every perfect innovation from medicine to arts and to sports comes from them and most of all, salvation comes from them. However, in order for the black Hebrews to come into their full power they must know who they are and they must know whose they are and they must serve God exactly as he has commanded them through his son Jesus who gave his disciples the Great Commission from the Stone Mountain of Georgia. Otherwise, the blacks and other children of God will remain in the wilderness of injustice. Martin Luther King did recover from his terrible speech to oppose the war of Vietnam very firmly and as a consequence, he was killed. And now Bill Clinton and Barak Obama want to deceive the world by pretending they love Martin when their forefathers actually killed Martin—however the deception will not work.

August 29, 2013

In the power of Jesus, the only begotten son of the living God the creator I, Harry Francois declare null and void the Voodoo ceremony that Bill Clinton, Jimmy Carter and Barak Obama conducted at the Lincoln Memorial on August 28, 2013 as a new "Emancipation Proclamation" call to blacks in order to slaughter at least 600, 000 of them to satisfy the blood liability of the Jews for this Sabbath. The living God has decided that there is not going to be another race war in America and Barak Obama, Bill Clinton and Hilary Clinton will go to prison for their crimes against humanity and certainly, for their crimes against the Haitians, the black and the white American Hebrews, the children of Abraham, Isaac and Jacob—Justice will be done.

Chapter 25

What is the real reason behind Obama's invasion of Syria?

Spiritual understanding is not easy to grasp. The spirit is the ultimate teacher, understanding comes from the spirit. There are a number of very important spiritual principles involved in understanding why Obama is so obsessed on overthrowing Bashar Al Assad out of power. Even though I have explained some of these principles above, in earlier chapters, I find it necessary to escalate the understanding here, in this chapter, as current events are unfolding in Syria and around the world in order to further crystalize the concept for the reader.

The Pyramid

The Pyramid is the standard scheme of Satan. In his ultimate vision class and race are important. Satan places the elite at the very top of the Pyramid and the very poor at the very bottom of the pyramid, and in between, he created several other subdivisions that decide people's fate within the pyramid based on their races and their talents. In this pyramid the leader, usually a dictator, dominates the people and compels the masses to live in quiet poverty under harsh conditions that are enforced by fear; and the threat of force is ever present to crush any descent. Accordingly, the United States as a satanic theocracy is quietly pleased with strong dictators, as long as the dictator himself is a friend of the U.S. and does not really interfere with U.S. interests. These dictators often engage in public and overt criticism of the United States in order to further deceive their people and convince the world that the U.S. is their enemy when in fact the U.S. is pleased with them. And even when the United Nations issues a condemning Human Right Report about a dictator, the U.S. is quick to overtly criticize the leader of that nation for public consumption, but the U.S. does not really care. Fidel and Raoul Castro are two examples of dictators that the U.S. is extremely pleased with, but pretend to criticize them for public consumption.

The biblical concept of King of kings

Beyond the notion of the Pyramid, there is also a matter of spiritual principle that says, according to the bible, that the King of Jerusalem is the greatest King in the world—he is King of kings and whosoever should disobey him and fail to bring him gifts should be punished. Solomon was the first King in Jerusalem to truly receive such honor and all kings around the world went to Jerusalem to pay him respect and to bring gifts to him. And now since the United States control the Kingdom and dominate Haiti, the biblical Jerusalem, the President of the United States is considered to be the President of biblical unified Judah and Israel, the leader of the world. Thus, the leader of every nation should respect the President of the United States and bring gifts to him. And the fact that Bashar Al Assad refuses to obey the President of the United States by resigning from office as he has been commanded to do amounts to disobedience and represents a grave threat to the power of the President. And as long as the disobedience continues, the President of the United States will continue to be weakened practically and spiritually.

Entanglement of Identical Particles

The concept of "American Exceptionalism" is rooted in the biblical understanding that I explain above, and consistent to this avenue of mystical understanding, whenever the power of an American president is challenged by any king, it weakens the president who finds himself unable to get things done at home and abroad.

Finally, the last mystical principle is expressed in the concept of "Entanglement of Identical Particles"

Obama invaded Libya on March 19, 2011 because he was scheming to provoke bloodshed in Haiti to atone for the sins of the Jews and the Freemasons through the March 20, 2011 presidential run-off but he was not able to because the principle of "Entanglement of Identical Particles" had triggered a resistance against him in Libya—much like it did against Ronald Reagan in 1986 when Reagan successfully compel Qaddafi to back down by bombing Libya, but 2011 is not 1986—this Sabbath is different.

The concept of "Entanglement of Identical Particles" is best explained in the duel that exists between God and Satan through the Western and Eastern hemispheres. The living God exerts the greater control over the western Hemisphere because his kingdom is found in the west, even though the entire world belongs to him, but Satan exerts the greater control over the Eastern Hemisphere because his kingdom is found in the east, even though Satan himself lives in Babylon, the modern city of New York.

The earth is in fact one giant particle that is divided in two identical properties; the western hemisphere, which represents the man and the eastern hemisphere, which represents the woman. However, even in separation, whatever affects one particle also affects the other. In this view, Qaddafi became defiant to the U.S. when he decided not to resign. Qaddafi refused to resign because he did not believe that the opposition had a legitimate case against him and his government. And indeed he was correct as the core of the armed resistance against him was made up of foreign paid criminals with no real legitimate claim on Libya.

The Concept of Spiritual Demons of War

Finally, it is important that I explain the notion of the spiritual demons of war. Again, it is important that I remind the reader that this presentation is primarily a course on mysticism. Ordinary human beings act and react to a secular and physical reality they can see, feel and understand. However, that understanding is very limited because the reality of existence makes up the seen and the unseen universe. This means other entities that are unseen in our realm of existence influence our world and dictate our actions every day. The unseen world includes the world above, the realm of the saints of the living God in the heavens, and the world below, as in below the earth and the sea where the demons exist. There are rules and laws that govern the actions of the angels of the living God, as they relate to their communications with human beings on the earth and the same rules and laws also bind the demons in their quest to influence events on earth. In fact, the bible makes it clear to human beings not to make any representation of any entity from below the earth or above in heaven. The representations include paintings, sculptures and the likes. Thus, when an artist paints a picture of a mermaid, he or she does so in violation of the law of the living God. The Living God is Supreme above all the creatures in heaven, in earth, and below the earth and the sea. Thus, in times of war he is able to command demonic spirits to travel to a certain nation to possess people in mass and to compel them to engage in war like activities. Satan also has the power to command these evil spirits, in fact, they are his disciples, but the Living God has the greater power. In addition, the Living God is able to command his angels to go against any evil spirit and to defeat him—the angel is more powerful than the demon. Consistent with this explanation, and in anticipation of a civil war in the U.S., Obama and the media started a campaign to alert American of the reality of "Mental Health", meaning that as illuminati, they were expecting the demons to come to America and to possess the minds of Americans to lead them to commit heinous crimes against one another and ultimately to engage in a civil war, but the Living God stopped the demons of war from coming to America by driving them to the Middle East.

Once Qaddafi, as a king, expressed resistance against the will of Obama, it became automatically difficult and almost impossible for Barak Obama to succeed in his evil endeavors. And therefore, Barak Obama, Bill and Hilary Clinton were not able to provoke civil wars in Haiti and the United States. In consequence, Barak Obama was forced to invade Libya and to kill Qaddafi, but by the time Qaddafi was murdered around October 22, 2011, it was too late because by then, the October deadline had passed for Bill Clinton to provoke a civil war in Haiti (see ARARAT). And by then a new spirit of resistance had arisen against Barak Hussein Obama in Syria where Bashar Al Assad refused to resign and where another civil war had already started.

Obama is running out of time. Clearly, this explanation, which is true and trustworthy, is very different from what is being advanced and theorized in the American media.

However, as it is for any major move of Satan, Obama is still plotting to use a strike in Syria to cover up something scandalous like the 09/11/12 Benghazi attack was used to cover up the 09/13/12 Fed announcement that it would start buying $86 billion worth of securities every month indefinitely.

The move could be used to mask the fact that the Fed will decide to continue the policy of buying $86 Billion worth of securities every month, over a trillion dollars a year even though it has promised to reduce the purchasing activities—it is very wrong for the Federal Reserve, a private company to be allowed to print over a trillion dollars a year to give to the class of investors at the expense of everybody else in society. The notion that the fed policy is designed to improve the economy is false. The policy has not improved the economy—it has not created any jobs—it only helped bankers like Jamie Diamond who use tax payers' money to make heavy bets in the artificial space of derivatives. Moreover, Obama is concerned about the roll-out of the Individual Mandate in his Health Care plan, which is supposed to be launched on October 1, 2013 and since the U.S. Supreme Court had refused to bail Obama out of the Individual Mandate by declaring it constitutional and since Obama has already delayed the Employer Mandate, Obama might take opportunity of all the noises from the war in Syria to quietly delay the Individual Mandate—these are among some other issues that can find cover through the Syrian war.

A pretext to attack Iran

Finally, just as the 09/11/01 gave the U.S. the excuse to invade Afghanistan, the Syria war will give Israel an excuse to attack Iran.

(Journal entry September 7, 2013)

Breaking News:

The living God and Jesus have stopped Obama, John McCain and Lindsey Graham along with Israel from invading Syria, for now

Since God has given me the mind to understand the way of Satan, I have been able to make all the right analysis and predictions about Obama's next move, except in cases when God is doing something new. In this case, my analysis has been perfect, but thankfully, the living God and Jesus have not allowed Obama to invade Syria at this time. This happened for two basic reasons: as I noted in the earlier chapter, Obama took a big risk when he delayed the attack on Syria under the pretext that he was seeking Congressional approval when in fact the reason for the delay was to find the perfect mystical alignment in the date of September 11 to seek satanic power to make the attack successful. Secondly, Russia and Iran made it clear to Obama and the United States that an attack on Syria will be an attack on Russia and Iran and that they were prepared to fight to protect the government of Syria for humanitarian reasons and to protect their own personal interests in Syria. Not only Vladimir Putin warned Obama, but he also took prompt, decisive and concrete actions to back up his rhetoric by moving a number of warships and heavy military equipments to the region to send a clear message to Obama and Israel that they should prepare for a war with Russia if they attack Syria. In addition, Vladimir Putin took constitutional steps at home by going to the Russian Congress to seek a vote that supports his actions in Syria and the Russian Congress voted overwhelmingly to support the position of Vladimir Putin by declaring that any attack on Syria by the United States and Israel will amount to a serious crime against humanity, given that the Syrian people have been suffering for more than two years of a Civil War engineered and promoted by Hilary Clinton. The Russian Congress also referred to the crimes of the United States in Libya where the United States and NATO bombed indiscriminately, killing women and children and completely destroyed the nation's infrastructure, as criminal. The Russian Congress voted to give Putin the authority to do whatever he needs to do to prevent the same thing from repeating in Syria. That resolution was passed just short of a war declaration, but they leave the possibility of updating the resolution to declare war against any nation over Syria, including the United States if it becomes necessary.

So Barak Obama was looking at the official start of World War Three right in the face and when it became clear to him and his supporters that neither the American Senate, nor the House was about to vote to give him the authority to invade Syria under the false pretext that Bashar Al Assad used chemical weapons against his own people, Obama decided to withdraw his threat of war and settled for a temporary pause for diplomacy until the next opportune time.

Obama has been completely weakened; his tactical moves in the war of Syria have not worked, and his authority for getting anything through the U.S. Congress has been totally taken away.

Breaking News:

Obama engineered the Navy Yard shooting as a plan B to replace the invasion of Syria, but the bloodshed is not nearly strong enough

Just five days after September 11, 2013, two days after Yom Kippur, another Jewish un-holiday, on September 16, 2013, the Navy Yard shooting occurred. The shooting incident features the same classic characters; 13 people, including the supposed shooter died, the same number of deaths in the Fort Hood shooting in addition to the fetus of a pregnant woman; it was precisely the same number 13 times two, the number 26 people that died in the Sandy Hook Elementary shooting in Connecticut. In addition, just as Congress moved to vote for the Obama Health Care PPACT exactly two days after the Fort Hood shooting, just two days after the Navy Yard shooting, the Federal Reserve announced on September 18, 2013 that it will continue to buy $86 billion worth of securities every month. It is very important for the reader to note that the pattern of introducing a new policy or making a new announcement two days after a national tragedy has been so long that it cannot be an accident, it has become a science. For example, just after Hilary Clinton and Barak Obama murdered four Americans in Benghazi, Libya, including Christopher Stevens, the U.S. ambassador to Libya on September 11, 2012, the Federal Reserve announced two days later on September 13, 2012 that it would start buying $86 billion worth of securities every month. Two days after the August 7, 1998 attacks on the U.S. Embassies in Kenya and Tanzania Africa, on August 9, 1998, Bill Clinton announced a patient Bill of rights in his Health Care plan, the same policy is found in the Obama Health Care PPACT. Two days after the February 26, 1993 bombing of the North Tower of the World Trade Center, the siege of Waco began in Waco, Texas on February 28, 1993, leading to the explosion of the building on April 19, 1993, killing a total of 86 people, including women and children.

These events show a clear pattern that politicians in Washington are behind the most notorious cases of violence in America and throughout the world, as they engage in the archaic practice of human sacrifices to advance the satanic cause of darkness.

As soon as the Navy Yard shooting occurred, Barak Obama and Joe Biden rushed to introduce legislations of darkness against gun control. The question begs, why does Obama seek political gains from the bloodshed of American citizens? And if Obama stands to gain by advancing legislations of darkness whenever innocent Americans died, then Obama is the one who is behind all the recent mass shootings in America. Unlike, Adam Lanza, the accused in the Sandy Hook Elementary School shooting in Newtown, Connecticut, Obama has the motive to commit the murders: to create a national urgency to pass gun reform legislation. The accused in the Navy Yard shooting did not have a motive to kill the people he has been accused of killing, but Obama does. The story that is told about the Navy Yard shooting is highly suspect and it is simply not true. The accused would not be able to enter such a secure location with his guns, as it is alleged, unless he was allowed to. And he would not need to use other weapons as it is alleged. The reality is simple: more than one weapon was used during the shooting because more than one shooter was involved. Just as more than one shooter was involved in the Aurora shooting, in the Fort Hood shooting and in the Sandy Hook Elementary School shooting—the pattern is the same because all of these crimes have been committed by Obama against the American people.

The situation in Syria will continue to unfold and when it comes time for Bill Clinton, Hilary Clinton and Barak Obama to attempt to provoke a civil war in Haiti through parliamentary elections later this year, around late October and all the way to mid-November as the date of the elections have not been set yet, Obama will seek a cease-fire in the Syrian war in order to weaken the resistance against him, but it will not work. Kofi Annan, the former UN General failed to secure a peace deal in Syria, he was not even able to secure a cease-fire in Syria and he was forced to resign as a UN special envoy for the Syrian affair. And his successor, Lakhdar Brahimi, also failed to secure a cease-fire in Syria in October of 2012—Obama is finished—the resistance will continue against him until he is impeached and put in prison.

Chapter 26

The October 2013 Surprise

After Barak Obama and his Jewish brothers were forced to engage in a diplomatic deal that called for the destruction of chemical weapons in Syria, Obama was also forced to engage in diplomatic talk with Iran about their nuclear program. However, the violence continues in Egypt to the point where Obama has announced that he would withhold some aid to the government of Egypt. This is so because the perpetrators of the military coup against Mohammad Mursi has used such brute force against the unarmed civilians that it is no longer possible to ignore such level of carnage, but still, the resistance has not faded, Egypt is already engaged in a civil war. And the only reason that the civil war in Egypt is not as brutal as the one in Syria is because the resistance does not have international backing for arms and military equipment.

Meanwhile, the many groups that make up the opposition against Bashar Al Assad in Syria continue to fight and the criminals supported by Washington do not have the decisive upper hands that they had hoped. This means when change comes to Syria after the departure of Al Assad, Obama will not be able to use cannibals to hijack the revolution of the Syrian people; the Syrian people will see a positive change—they will not be dominated by a new criminal dictator as Washington had done to the Egyptian people with the election of Mohammad Mursi. Thankfully, Mursi went rogue on them by keeping Israel from invading the Gaza strip to shed the blood of the Palestinians in December 2012. The state of Israel had hoped to use the Palestinians as human sacrifices to help Barak Obama like they did when they invaded Gaza and murdered thousands of Palestinians in January 2009, just before Obama took office, and just as they are planning to do in January 2014 if they fail to provoke a civil war in Haiti.

Meanwhile, the Great Tribulation continues. In addition to major earthquakes in Mexico, Philippines were hundreds died in a 7. 2 magnitude earthquake, shocking weather came upon South Dakota and large sections of the state was blanketed with snow, and violent tornadoes struck the American Midwest. These events went largely unreported by the media whose role is to help Obama deceive the American Middle Class. They are misled into thinking that Obama can make them safe and prosperous because the values of their (401k) have increased over 1000 percent since Obama took office, but in fact, they are neither safe, nor prosperous. The American people is unaware that Obama is plotting to lead America into a nuclear confrontation with Russia; the people is unaware that the Living God has already given the order to his angels to punish Obama and Bill Clinton and Hilary Clinton for their crimes against his children in Haiti, in the U.S. and throughout the world. Unfortunately, the American people, especially the middle class, have no idea that Wall Street has become a Ponzi Scheme and the elite are planning to take their profit first and leave the rest of the people holding bags of worthless paper—the next economic crisis will be worse than the 2008 economic crisis.

However, the biggest surprise of October 2013 is that the U.S. government was shut down for 17 days during the month of October from October 1 through October 17, 2013. This is ominous because everything that occurred under Bill Clinton has thus far happened under Obama; the government was shut down twice under Bill Clinton.

Obama will continue to attack Syria in 2014 and beyond

Since Obama cannot succeed unless he can provoke a bloodshed in Haiti, which in turn would make it possible for the blood of the black and white American Hebrews to be shed through race riots and civil wars, then Obama is prepared to take extreme measures in 2014 in a last desperate attempt to shed the blood of the children of Isaac and Jacob in Haiti and in the U.S.

This means that the 2014 calendar will look a lot like the 2011 calendar for the Obama administration. In 2011, Barak Obama, Bill and Hilary Clinton plotted to provoke a civil war in Haiti through the November 28, 2010 presidential election, but the fraudulent election failed to provoke a civil war in Haiti, even though some violence was recorded and a second tour was needed to decide the election, which was scheduled for March 20, 2011. In order to give himself the maximum opportunity to succeed in shedding the blood of the Haitians on March 20, 2011, Obama returned his blood cousin, Jean Claude Duvalier to Haiti on January 16, 2011, the day the Hebrews tasted freedom from Egypt (Mexico). And then, on January 30, 2011, Obama sent Hilary Clinton to Haiti to provoke the Haitians by demanding that Jude Celestin, a presidential candidate who came in second to withdraw from the runoff and to allow Michel Martelly, a candidate who finished third to move up in the runoff against a woman named Mirlande Manigat. However, Obama was not done yet, he decided to engineer the return of Jean Bertrand Aristide to Haiti from South Africa by issuing him a passport exactly on February 7, 2011, and Aristide would ultimately arrive in Haiti on March 18, 2011, exactly two days before the March 20, 2011 presidential runoff election. This was done to recreate the same circumstances that existed in Haiti back in 1986 when Aristide was jointly responsible with Jean-Claude Duvalier for provoking a civil war in Haiti from 1984 through 1986. That Haitian bloodshed gave to Ronald Reagan the juice he needed to recharge the American economy and Reagan became a superstar in the blood of the Haitians, but this time it is different. And lastly, Obama also took steps through the United Nations to ensure that Qaddafi would resign in the face of the opposition against him so he would not interfere with the Haitian bloodshed by showing resistance to the will of Satan, but Qaddafi did just that, he declined to resign and proceeded to crush the opposition. And this was when Obama decided to invade Libya on March 19, 2011, exactly one day before the Haitian presidential runoff election, just as Ronald Reagan had bombed Qaddafi in 1986 to ensure that he would not interfere with the Haitian bloodshed. And ultimately, the Libyan conflict would keep bloodshed from erupting in Haiti and the U.S. through 2011. Those who participated in the Occupy Wall Street movement, the children of Isaac and Jacob were safe as Qaddafi was not killed until October 2011 and by then Hilary, Bill Clinton and Barak Obama had missed their window of opportunity to provoke violence in Haiti and in the U.S. But the resistance was not over because by then, Obama had met with even greater resistance in Syria. The conflict in Syria deteriorated quickly and Bashar Al Assad refused to resign and once again, Obama and Hilary Clinton were faced with a new obstacle in their quest to shed the blood of the Haitian and the black and the white American Hebrews.

The events of 2011 and the fact that Barak Obama totally failed to achieve any significant legislative goal of his evil second term agenda, totally confirm that the theory of "Entanglement of Identical Particles" works, it is voodoo economics, as Reagan called it, it is rooted in the scientific ritual of human sacrifices. This is a law of the universe; this is how the universe works. And with this in mind, Obama and his entourage have no choice, but to risk everything, including war with Russia by bombing and invading Syria in 2014.

Of course, Obama will schedule other events around the date he bombs Syria to hide the Haitian Connection, but I am on to him. The Haitian connection is the only connection that has been consistently linked with every major moment in American history;

the blood of the Haitians must be shed for America to prosper. This statement will be revealed as true when it becomes clear that the American economy will never improve under Obama because Barak Obama will not be allowed under any circumstance to shed the blood of the Haitians, nor the blood of the American Hebrews, there is not going to be another civil war in Haiti or in the United States—Period.

Chapter 27

The Death of Nelson Mandela

Breaking News:

Nelson Mandela, the Black Antichrist Died

On December 5, 2013, the very day Christopher Columbus invaded Haiti 521 years ago in 1492 to shed the blood of the Haitians, the Associated Press (AP) reported that Nelson Mandela, the satanic Christ of the American nation died in South Africa at the age of 95.

Nelson Mandela was a liar and a deceiver; a black Satan who rose to prominence in the natural power and the authority of Mike Tyson to advance the cause of darkness in the world. 1994, the year Mandela became President of South Africa, has been the worst year for black Hebrews around the world. In 1994, Bill Clinton the beast and his wife Lucifer, aka Hilary Clinton invaded Haiti under the guise of returning Jean-Bertrand Aristide to office and they proceed to murder tens of thousands of Haitians. That same year, Bill and Hilary Clinton orchestrated a civil war in Rwanda, which killed millions; it was a shocking carnage, a bloodshed that compares with very few in world history. It was also in 1994 that O.J. Simpson was accused of double murder in Los Angeles and it was also that very same year that Michael Jackson was accused of child molestation; he was arrested and humiliated before his priest, Johnnie Cochran advised him to settle the case for millions of dollars. Johnnie Cochran was the one who successfully defended O.J. Simpson by securing his acquittal in the double murder trial of his ex-wife and her lover.

Clearly, the rise of Nelson Mandela did not help the cause of the American Black Hebrews in America, the people who fought for his release from prison, nor did it help the cause of the Black

Semites in Africa; Mandela, like Barak Obama came to help the cause of the Jews, the cause of darkness.

Mandela appealed to Black South Africans to let go of violent resistance against apartheid and to seek reconciliation. An immediately after his release from prison. He preached reconciliation with no plan to address the cause and the concerns of the blacks. He quickly followed the American model that emerged out of the Civil Rights struggle by integrating a very, very small number of blacks into the South African middle class and he declared a victory for blacks, while the majority of the blacks continue to live in dire poverty in an unjust apartheid system without justice, even until today. In fact, the state of race relations in South Africa today is at its worst and it is just a matter of time before racial tensions erupt to the surface again.

The American Media and the European media have been covering the passing of Nelson Mandela as if they had lost someone precious to them, they are correct. Mandela has served them well; he did not serve the cause of righteousness. The world will be a much better place without such a criminal deceiver because the cause he has championed was the cause of darkness; the cause of homosexuality, the cause of injustice rooted in human sacrifices; that cause is not sustainable and it is coming to an end. The passing of Nelson Mandela moves the world closer to the promise of peace and justice that the Living God, the creator of the universe has made to humanity; the wicked will be punished and Satan will be sequestered for One Thousand years, which would bring an era of One Thousand years of peace in the world. And then peace will reign forever. It is my hope that the likes of Nelson Mandela never reappear on this earth again and that the passing of Nelson Mandela represents the beginning of the lasting peace that God had promised to humanity.

About the Author

Harry Francois is the Faithful Servant of Jesus Christ

Harry Francois is the President of Topaz Enterprises and Publishing LLC.

Mr. Francois' curriculum vitae include the following positions:

Vice-President of Investment—J.P. Turner & Company

Atlanta, GA

Portfolio Manager—Providence Capital

Atlanta, GA

Mr. Francois served on the Board of the American Red Cross as

Vice-President of Financial Advisory Board—1999

President of Financial Advisory Board—2000

Education

Harry Francois; MS, MS, MPA

University of Bridgeport

Harry Francois graduated with a Bachelor of Science in General Studies with a concentration in Social Studies from the University of Bridgeport in Bridgeport, CT

University of New Haven

Harry Francois earned three Masters Degrees and two Graduate Certificates: from the University of New Haven

Master of Science (MS) in business with a concentration in Labor Relations; a Master of Public Administration (MPA); and a Master of Science Degree (MS) in Criminal Justice. He also earned two Graduate Certificates; a Certificate in Criminal Justice Management and a Certificate in Victim Advocacy and Service Management from the University of New Haven in West Haven, CT

Harry Francois has restored almost 6000 years of history by exposing all the lies of Satan.

Harry Francois has authored the following books: "Solomon: The Unholy Messiah", "The True Biblical Promised Land", "Satan", "Obama: A Jewish Antichrist Born in Haiti", "The Haitian Connections to the United States", "ARARAT", "The End of the Bill Clinton's Occupation of Haiti", "A Pictorial Presentation of the Seven Holy Books", "The Corrupt Economic Practices from the Tree of the Knowledge of Good and Evil" and this title, "The First 100 Days".

Hallelujah, the Father, is "Supreme"

Jesus, the Son, is "Great"

And

Harry Francois is

"Doze"

This page intentionally left blank

www.ingramcontent.com/pod-product-compliance
Lightning Source LLC
Chambersburg PA
CBHW060746100426
42813CB00032B/3414/J

* 9 7 8 0 9 9 8 7 6 7 5 0 5 *